IT WORKED FOR US

Best Practices for Ministry With Children and Families

Edited by JUDY COMSTOCK

International Network of

children's
MINISTRY

It Worked For Us
Best Practices for Ministry With Children and Families

ISBN 9780687659920

Table of Contents

A Note From Judy Comstock

This book is practical, relevant, and contains the "stuff" that makes children's and family ministry work. You will use it over and over. It has been exciting for International Network of Children's Ministry (INCM) to partner with Abingdon Press to create this resource made with you in mind. I want to thank Daphna Flegal for inviting me to join her for breakfast the morning after last year's CPC (Children's Pastors' Conference) in San Diego. Our conversation was the catalyst for this project.

Pam Burton worked diligently with me as we determined the topics that needed to be included. Thanks, Pam, for your patience and tenacity.

This book would not exist without the amazing writers who shared their ministry insights without compensation. From the foundation of INCM, children's and family ministry leaders have given from their wealth of experiences for the sheer joy of helping another leader.

Thank you for your contributions. Every dime that INCM receives from the sale of this book will be put into the CPC Scholarship Fund. This fund helps provide training and encouragement for children's and family ministry leaders who might otherwise not be able to attend CPC. I pray that this book will be a blessing to you at every turn.

Judy Comstock, INCM Executive Director

Reproducibles and the CD-ROM

You will find reproducible resource pages throughout *It Worked For Us*. These pages are printed with the articles and also available on the CD-ROM. You have permission to photocopy the pages or download them from the CD-ROM.

Administration

Whatever you do, work at it with all your heart, as though you were working for the Lord and not for people.

Colossians 3:23, GNT

Strategic Plans

by Judy Comstock

Like many of you, I have participated in brainstorming sessions that were promoted as "strategic planning." The time spent brainstorming during these meetings was a healthy way to list our joys, concerns, and dreams. However, these sessions left me asking the question, "Now what?" At the end of the day we had a long list of ideas, but no clearly defined objectives or action steps. In other words, we had ideas but no plan to get us from point A to point B.

During the years I served as Director of Children's Ministry at Church of the Resurrection, our department was expected to develop an annual strategic plan, as were all of the other departments at the church. A business-man from the church taught us how to use an effective planning approach and how to organize our ideas into a workable plan. The resulting document would align children's ministry around common goals that support the church's mission statement. The plan would be used as a guide to accomplish amazing and necessary goals. Each department director was held accountable during a mid-year assessment meeting and a year-end report.

One of the best examples of how this approach worked effectively relates to our move into a new building. The space that would house our church preschool, the nursery, children's ministry classrooms, children's ministry offices, our resource room, and an electronic welcome center was 64,400 square feet. Yes, that area would hold a lot of chairs, tables, bulletin boards, rocking chairs, toys, and teaching supplies. The big move was scheduled during the week preceding Palm Sunday. We had to recruit our own team of volunteers to move the supplies and equipment, to decorate the bulletin boards, and to assemble the nursery equipment. We had plenty of questions. Where would we get all of the boxes?

Who would create the decorating plan? How would our children and Sunday school teachers know how to transition from their classroom into the new sanctuary for the Palm Branch Parade? Due to safety restrictions enforced by the builder and our facilities director, only designated staff members had been allowed into the new structures. How would we reduce the anxiety that our staff, volunteers, the children, and even the ushers had about safely escorting the children from their classrooms into the new sanctuary for the Palm Branch Parade and back to the secure children's ministry area? Our strategic plan would need to have action steps that answered all of these questions and clearly described a successful transition.

Fast forward to Palm Sunday. We were told that this was the smoothest move in our church's fifteen-year, four-building history. I am convinced that the use of our strategic plan was the reason. The positive results are why this approach has been adopted by other churches and by the staff and board of directors at International Network of Children's Ministry. It is my joy to describe how you can develop a strategic plan and use it for your benefit. Using the components of this strategic planning approach will result in measurable goals, shared duties, and reduced distractions.

Schedule Your Initial Meeting

Here is how we have done strategic planning. First, schedule a time and place for your initial planning meeting. Invite key leaders, volunteers, and parents who have a voice in the department or organization. The planning team should involve ten to twenty people. Designate a scribe to ensure that the details and decisions are recorded. You may want to involve your administrative assistant. Allow at least three hours for the meeting. To ensure involvement of your key players, you may need to provide childcare. If the meeting must take place over a lunch or dinner, offer food that requires very little preparation. This might be a good time for pizza to be delivered. In other words, don't let the food distract you or your guests from the focus of the meeting. It is best to have the meeting in a place where the participants are not distracted by phone calls or won't be called out of the meeting for an issue in a nearby office. Even with these guidelines, it will be impossible for the entire plan to be written by the end of your initial meeting. Homework assignments will be necessary for some of the participants in order to get your document ready to use. Another beneficial component is an unbiased meeting facilitator to help you provide an open, honest environment. Some participants may be inhibited if the pastor or the department director guides the session. Make certain that your facilitator clearly understands the process and goal.

The Sandwich Method

After opening with prayer, the expectations for the planning session should be defined. Initially, everyone will participate by painting a word picture of what is working well: people, processes, structure. Write the concepts on large charts on the wall of the room. The facilitator should keep participants off the "problem-solving path" during this time. Acknowledge all of the things that you and others like about your department, as the next portion can be challenging. My mother-in-law described this as the "sandwich method." She said that it is easier to swallow the bad when it is sandwiched between positive reflections. I like her wise perspective and you too will see the blessing of this approach.

After brainstorming the pluses of the department, consider the challenges that block you from reaching the end goal. Don't get distracted by any problem-solving during this time. One facilitator compared effective brainstorming with popping popcorn. There is nothing like the smell of "burnt" ideas, just as we wrinkle our noses at burnt popcorn. Again, record these next ideas on large wall charts.

Identify Major Issues

Now the fun begins! Give each session participant four to six self-adhesive notes.

Instruct them to write their names on each of their note squares. They will use the note squares to "vote" on their top four to six choices of needs. They are not to vote for the same issue more than once. Some of the strategic-planning team members will vote quickly. Others will spend time pondering. Keep an eye on the clock to keep things moving without making participants feel rushed. This is when bowls of snacks and a pitcher of fresh water should be available. Participants will complete their selection or ponder their decisions while waiting on each other.

With the help of the scribe, the facilitator should quickly tally the total votes on each problem area. The goal is to identify only four to six major issues or roadblocks that your department is facing. Getting a buy-in from the strategic planning team is valuable. Some ideas will be so closely aligned that they can be combined. This eliminates redundant ideas. Do not assume that all problems will be addressed. Your goal is to improve or conquer four to six different areas. You may determine some "just do-its." These are plans or ideas for which you have no need to write objectives or programs you will continue doing well.

Write Measurable Objectives

Ask for, or select, a volunteer whose name corresponds with a voting note posted on the list of needs. This process owner will take responsibility for writing a measurable objective or involving a small group committed to the issue. Measurable objectives should include a time dimension or completion date and define a condition or state that describes success. The measurable objective is a snapshot of a desired point in the future.

Example of improperly stated objective:
"Increase participation in Sunday school."

Example of properly stated objective:
"By January 15, 2011 (*time dimension*), 80% of the children affiliated with our church will be participating at least twice a month in our children's programming (*measurable element*) as evidenced by a master attendance roster containing the names of the children on our membership roster (*future condition*)."

Write Strategies

Try to make it this far in your planning day. Hopefully, you will be at a place that the planning team can divide into four to six subgroups. Each subgroup will develop strategies that define how their assigned objective can be accomplished. There will probably be six to ten strategies for each objective. Each strategy should start with an action verb. This is when you consider operational budget, capital expenditures, working capital plans, staffing/organization plans, facilities plans, and compensation or career advancement programs or plans. Strategies may be written to span multiple years.

Example of improperly stated strategy:
"Put together an absentee follow-up plan."

Example of properly stated strategy:
"Select a follow-up plan to be used for absentees (*a specific action*) by September 2010 (*time dimension*)."

Action Steps

Each strategy is generally accomplished through multiple tasks called action steps. This is where you determine the "who," "what," and "when" of your plan. It may sound like a lot of effort, but this thoughtful process works. The action steps are the manageable movements needed to fulfill each objective. There may be, or more likely will be, individuals who are not present but need to be involved. It is acceptable to put their names on the actions steps, but don't forget to invite their participation and define the expectations.

Celebrate the Results

Strategic planning "lays the track" for a systematic process. It identifies what will be done, how it will be done, when it will be accomplished, and who will be involved. The plan is not a neatly organized tool that sits on a shelf in your office or in your computer. Your strategic plan reduces distractions and helps ensure that weak areas are improved, maximizing the use of resources and the effectiveness of various members of the team. The entire process is effective with diligent focus on the calendar, the budget, and the defined steps. Periodic reviews by everyone with responsibilities in the plan should be expected.

Mark the completion dates and indicate the measurable results on each action step. To make sure the process is moving forward, a quarterly update should be scheduled. Celebrate the results after each objective is accomplished or at the end of the timeline. Either way, everyone will know that progress is being made.

I was invited by the pastor of a church in Denver to work with their director of children's ministry to develop a strategic plan. The director and I met and set a date for the planning session. She invited her staff members and key volunteers. It was a great evening as ten of us brainstormed what was going well, listed the areas of concern, and selected the top four areas where specific goals were needed. An objective statement was written for all four of the areas. Each subgroup decided when they would meet to complete their responsibilities. A few weeks after our strategic planning session, I visited the church and was impressed with a unique volunteer recruitment approach. After church I complimented the director of children's ministry about what I observed and experienced in the sanctuary. She applauded the work that had already been accomplished as a result of their strategic plan. I look forward to hearing how strategic planning brings positive results at your church.

The forms and examples we used are included on the following pages and on the CD-ROM included with this book.

Judy Comstock has years of church staff experience, primarily as Director of Children's Ministry. She has a master of arts in Education Leadership and is the author of the Abingdon Press-Church of the Resurrection Ministry Guide Children's Ministry. *After years of serving on the INCM Board of Directors, the Board asked her to become the Executive Director for the ministry.*

Church _____

Children's Ministry
Strategic Plan

1) **By** *March 25, 2010 we will have a plan to increase our attendance at this summer's Vacation Bible School. (sample)*

2) **By**

3) **By**

4) **By**

5) **By**

6) **By**

10 **IT WORKED FOR US**

Church _____

Children's Ministry
Strategic Plan

Primary Objective Number 1:
By March 25, 2010 we will have a plan to increase our attendance at this summer's Vacation Bible School. (sample)

Reference	Strategies — Do What?	By When?
1.1	*Select the VBS curriculum or theme.*	*March 10, 2010*
1.2		
1.3		
1.4		
1.5		
1.6		

Permission granted to copy for local church use.

Church _____

Children's Ministry Strategic Plan

Key Strategy Number 1:
Select the VBS curriculum or theme. (sample)

Action Steps		Responsible	Completion Date	Resource Requirements		Measurable Results
Reference	**Description**			**Other**	**Budget**	
1.1.1	Review 5 published options	Jane Doe	March 1, 2010		$0	VBS curriculum options narrowed
1.1.2						
1.1.3						
1.1.4						

© 2009 Abingdon Press

Church _____

Children's Ministry
Strategic Plan

Key Strategy Number 2: _____

Action Steps		Responsible	Completion Date	Resource Requirements		Measurable Results
Reference	Description			Other	Budget	
1.2.1						
1.2.2						
1.2.3						
1.2.4						

Permission granted to copy for local church use.

Children's Ministry Strategic Plan

Church _____

Key Strategy Number 3: _____

Action Steps		Responsible	Completion Date	Resource Requirements		Measurable Results
Reference	Description			Other	Budget	
1.3.1						
1.3.2						
1.3.3						
1.3.4						

Permission granted to copy for local church use.

Church

Children's Ministry Strategic Plan

Key Strategy Number 4:

Action Steps		Responsible	Completion Date	Resource Requirements		Measurable Results
Reference	Description			Other	Budget	
1.4.1						
1.4.2						
1.4.3						
1.4.4						

Permission granted to copy for local church use.

Children's Ministry
Strategic Plan

Church _____

Key Strategy Number 5:

Action Steps		Responsible	Completion Date	Resource Requirements		Measurable Results
Reference	Description			Other	Budget	
1.5.1						
1.5.2						
1.5.3						
1.5.4						

Permission granted to copy for local church use.

Children's Ministry Strategic Plan

Church _____

Key Strategy Number 6:

Action Steps		Responsible	Completion Date	Resource Requirements		Measurable Results
Reference	Description			Other	Budget	
1.6.1						
1.6.2						
1.6.3						
1.6.4						

Children's Ministry Strategic Plan

Church _____

Primary Objective Number 2:

By

Reference	Strategies — Do What?	By When?
2.1		
2.2		
2.3		
2.4		
2.5		
2.6		

Permission granted to copy for local church use.

Church _____

Children's Ministry
Strategic Plan

Key Strategy Number 1:

Action Steps		Responsible	Completion Date	Resource Requirements		Measurable Results
Reference	Description			Other	Budget	
2.1.1						
2.1.2						
2.1.3						
2.1.4						

Permission granted to copy for local church use.

Children's Ministry Strategic Plan

Church _____

Key Strategy Number 2:

Action Steps		Responsible	Completion Date	Resource Requirements		Measurable Results
Reference	Description			Other	Budget	
2.2.1						
2.2.2						
2.2.3						
2.2.4						

Permission granted to copy for local church use.

Church _____

Children's Ministry Strategic Plan

Key Strategy Number 3:

Action Steps		Responsible	Completion Date	Resource Requirements		Measurable Results
Reference	Description			Other	Budget	
2.3.1						
2.3.2						
2.3.3						
2.3.4						

Permission granted to copy for local church use.

Children's Ministry Strategic Plan

Church _____

Key Strategy Number 4:

Action Steps		Responsible	Completion Date	Resource Requirements		Measurable Results
Reference	Description			Other	Budget	
2.4.1						
2.4.2						
2.4.3						
2.4.4						

Permission granted to copy for local church use.

Church _____

Children's Ministry Strategic Plan

Key Strategy Number 5:

Action Steps		Responsible	Completion Date	Resource Requirements		Measurable Results
Reference	Description			Other	Budget	
2.5.1						
2.5.2						
2.5.3						
2.5.4						

Permission granted to copy for local church use.

Church _____

Children's Ministry
Strategic Plan

Key Strategy Number 6:

Action Steps		Responsible	Completion Date	Resource Requirements		Measurable Results
Reference	**Description**			**Other**	**Budget**	
2.6.1						
2.6.2						
2.6.3						
2.6.4						

Permission granted to copy for local church use.

Church _____

Children's Ministry Strategic Plan

Primary Objective Number 3:
_By_

Reference	Strategies — Do What?	By When?
3.1		
3.2		
3.3		
3.4		
3.5		
3.6		

Permission granted to copy for local church use.

© 2009 Abingdon Press

Church

Children's Ministry Strategic Plan

Key Strategy Number 1: _____

Action Steps		Responsible	Completion Date	Resource Requirements		Measurable Results
Reference	Description			Other	Budget	
3.1.1						
3.1.2						
3.1.3						
3.1.4						

© 2009 Abingdon Press

Church _____

Children's Ministry
Strategic Plan

Key Strategy Number 2: _____

Action Steps		Responsible	Completion Date	Resource Requirements		Measurable Results
Reference	Description			Other	Budget	
3.2.1						
3.2.2						
3.2.3						
3.2.4						

Permission granted to copy for local church use.

Church _____

Children's Ministry
Strategic Plan

Key Strategy Number 3: _____

Action Steps		Responsible	Completion Date	Resource Requirements		Measurable Results
Reference	Description			Other	Budget	
3.3.1						
3.3.2						
3.3.3						
3.3.4						

Permission granted to copy for local church use.

Church _____

Children's Ministry Strategic Plan

Key Strategy Number 4:

Action Steps		Responsible	Completion Date	Resource Requirements		Measurable Results
Reference	Description			Other	Budget	
3.4.1						
3.4.2						
3.4.3						
3.4.4						

Permission granted to copy for local church use.

Church _____

Children's Ministry Strategic Plan

Key Strategy Number 5: _____

Action Steps		Responsible	Completion Date	Resource Requirements		Measurable Results
Reference	**Description**			**Other**	**Budget**	
3.5.1						
3.5.2						
3.5.3						
3.5.4						

Permission granted to copy for local church use.

Church _____

Children's Ministry Strategic Plan

Key Strategy Number 6:

Action Steps		Responsible	Completion Date	Resource Requirements		Measurable Results
Reference	Description			Other	Budget	
3.6.1						
3.6.2						
3.6.3						
3.6.4						

Permission granted to copy for local church use.

Church _____

Children's Ministry Strategic Plan

Primary Objective Number 4:
By

Reference	Strategies — Do What?	By When?
4.1		
4.2		
4.3		
4.4		
4.5		
4.6		

Permission granted to copy for local church use.

Church _____

Children's Ministry
Strategic Plan

Key Strategy Number 1: _____

Action Steps		Responsible	Completion Date	Resource Requirements		Measurable Results
Reference	Description			Other	Budget	
4.1.1						
4.1.2						
4.1.3						
4.1.4						

Permission granted to copy for local church use.

Children's Ministry Strategic Plan

Church _____

Key Strategy Number 2:

Action Steps		Responsible	Completion Date	Resource Requirements		Measurable Results
Reference	Description			Other	Budget	
4.2.1						
4.2.2						
4.2.3						
4.2.4						

Permission granted to copy for local church use.

34 IT WORKED FOR US

Children's Ministry Strategic Plan

Church _____

Key Strategy Number 3:

Action Steps		Responsible	Completion Date	Resource Requirements		Measurable Results
Reference	**Description**			**Other**	**Budget**	
4.3.1						
4.3.2						
4.3.3						
4.3.4						

Permission granted to copy for local church use.

Church _____

Children's Ministry
Strategic Plan

Key Strategy Number 4: _____

Action Steps		Responsible	Completion Date	Resource Requirements		Measurable Results
Reference	Description			Other	Budget	
4.4.1						
4.4.2						
4.4.3						
4.4.4						

Permission granted to copy for local church use.

Children's Ministry Strategic Plan

Church _____

Key Strategy Number 5:

Action Steps		Responsible	Completion Date	Resource Requirements		Measurable Results
Reference	Description			Other	Budget	
4.5.1						
4.5.2						
4.5.3						
4.5.4						

Permission granted to copy for local church use.

Church _____

Children's Ministry Strategic Plan

Key Strategy Number 6: _____

Action Steps		Responsible	Completion Date	Resource Requirements		Measurable Results
Reference	Description			Other	Budget	
4.6.1						
4.6.2						
4.6.3						
4.6.4						

Permission granted to copy for local church use.

Church _____

Children's Ministry Strategic Plan

Primary Objective Number 5:
By

Reference	Strategies — Do What?	By When?
5.1		
5.2		
5.3		
5.4		
5.5		
5.6		

Permission granted to copy for local church use.

Church _____

Children's Ministry Strategic Plan

Key Strategy Number 1:

Action Steps		Responsible	Completion Date	Resource Requirements		Measurable Results
Reference	Description			Other	Budget	
5.1.1						
5.1.2						
5.1.3						
5.1.4						

Permission granted to copy for local church use.

Church _____

Children's Ministry
Strategic Plan

Key Strategy Number 2: _____

Action Steps		Responsible	Completion Date	Resource Requirements		Measurable Results
Reference	Description			Other	Budget	
5.2.1						
5.2.2						
5.2.3						
5.2.4						

Permission granted to copy for local church use.

Children's Ministry Strategic Plan

Church _____

Key Strategy Number 3: _____

Action Steps		Responsible	Completion Date	Resource Requirements		Measurable Results
Reference	Description			Other	Budget	
5.3.1						
5.3.2						
5.3.3						
5.3.4						

Permission granted to copy for local church use.

Church _____

Children's Ministry
Strategic Plan

Key Strategy Number 4:

Action Steps		Responsible	Completion Date	Resource Requirements		Measurable Results
Reference	Description			Other	Budget	
5.4.1						
5.4.2						
5.4.3						
5.4.4						

Permission granted to copy for local church use.

Church _____

Children's Ministry Strategic Plan

Key Strategy Number 5:

Action Steps		Responsible	Completion Date	Resource Requirements		Measurable Results
Reference	Description			Other	Budget	
5.5.1						
5.5.2						
5.5.3						
5.5.4						

Permission granted to copy for local church use.

Church _____

Children's Ministry
Strategic Plan

Key Strategy Number 6: _____

Action Steps		Responsible	Completion Date	Resource Requirements		Measurable Results
Reference	Description			Other	Budget	
5.6.1						
5.6.2						
5.6.3						
5.6.4						

Permission granted to copy for local church use.

© 2009 Abingdon Press

Children's Ministry Strategic Plan

Church _____

Primary Objective Number 6:
By

Reference	Strategies — Do What?	By When?
6.1		
6.2		
6.3		
6.4		
6.5		
6.6		

Permission granted to copy for local church use.

Children's Ministry Strategic Plan

Church_____

Key Strategy Number 1:

Action Steps		Responsible	Completion Date	Resource Requirements		Measurable Results
Reference	Description			Other	Budget	
6.1.1						
6.1.2						
6.1.3						
6.1.4						

Permission granted to copy for local church use.

Church _____

Children's Ministry
Strategic Plan

Key Strategy Number 2: _____

Action Steps		Responsible	Completion Date	Resource Requirements		Measurable Results
Reference	Description			Other	Budget	
6.2.1						
6.2.2						
6.2.3						
6.2.4						

Permission granted to copy for local church use.

Church _____

Children's Ministry
Strategic Plan

Key Strategy Number 3:

Action Steps		Responsible	Completion Date	Resource Requirements		Measurable Results
Reference	Description			Other	Budget	
6.3.1						
6.3.2						
6.3.3						
6.3.4						

Permission granted to copy for local church use.

Church _____

Children's Ministry Strategic Plan

Key Strategy Number 4: _____

Action Steps		Responsible	Completion Date	Resource Requirements		Measurable Results
Reference	Description			Other	Budget	
6.4.1						
6.4.2						
6.4.3						
6.4.4						

Permission granted to copy for local church use.

Church

Children's Ministry Strategic Plan

Key Strategy Number 5:

Action Steps		Responsible	Completion Date	Resource Requirements		Measurable Results
Reference	Description			Other	Budget	
6.5.1						
6.5.2						
6.5.3						
6.5.4						

Permission granted to copy for local church use.

Church _____

Children's Ministry Strategic Plan

Key Strategy Number 6:

Reference	Action Steps Description	Responsible	Completion Date	Resource Requirements Other	Resource Requirements Budget	Measurable Results
6.6.1						
6.6.2						
6.6.3						
6.6.4						

Permission granted to copy for local church use.

How To Publicize Your Events

by Pamela Burton

Imagine this: you've been working many long hours trying to plan your big "Back to School" event. You've got the volunteers, bought the food and drinks, and planned great activities. You're ready to go . . . right?

Not so fast. You missed one very important element: how do you get people to come?

There are the basic, tried-and-true ways to do this. I'm sure many of you have used the standard ways to publicize your event to your congregation. Just to name a few:

- Bulletin announcement.
- Bulletin inserts.
- Pulpit announcement (a very popular one at the church I worked at!).
- Sending announcements with children to take home.
- Posters.
- Video ads before and after services.

Do these sound familiar? The list above includes great (and inexpensive!) ways to promote any event you plan. It taps into a ready-made audience that has already bought into your ministry and will most likely be excited to attend your event. However, what about those people on the fringes: the ones who attend your church but aren't too sure they want to get involved; the ones who only attend church once a month and might miss the announcements during the occasional visit; or the ones who don't attend your church (or any church) at all? How do you reach them with the news of your coming event? Here are some suggestions on how you can make an impact with your promotions.

> Ultimately it's not so much about the event; it is about how to get people involved in a caring and supportive community. Show them that you care and that gives them an incentive to get involved.

Make It Personal

Think back to a time when you were looking for a new church. What made the biggest impact on you in your decision? Was it the amazing decor? The well-designed bulletin? Or was it the people that made you feel welcome and at home? Most likely it was the people that helped you make that decision. It's the same with church events: people are more likely to attend if they feel welcomed and wanted. But how do you do that? Here are a few ways to help give your promotions the personal touch:

1. **A personal, face-to-face invite from you and your staff.** Before you panic, I'm not saying you need to personally go to each person in your church or community and invite them to an event — there just isn't enough time to do that! Instead, greet people as you are walking down the hall/parking lot/etc. and mention you would love to see them at the event. It may seem like these short encounters wouldn't amount to much, but a face-to-face encounter goes a long way. They feel like you cared enough to personally talk to them and that can be a turning point for many.

2. **Make use of your ready-made audience.** Remember the ready-made audience I talked about earlier? *Use them!* They are out there meeting people from all walks of life: people that may need the support of a loving church community but

are not sure how to find it. Ask your ready-made audience (I'll refer to them as RMA's from here on out) to pass out five event-promoting postcards to five of their non-church friends/coworkers/extended family. Creating these postcards can be simple (I'll get into that later) and will include all pertinent information on your event. Even the shyest RMA would be able to do that — it's non-threatening and takes little of their time.

3. **A handwritten note.** Writing a personal note can be time-consuming, but it doesn't have to be utilized all the time. Send someone a short note saying you are praying for them and mention you would love to see them at your next event. Ultimately it's not so much about the event; it is about how to get people involved in a caring and supportive community. Show them that you care and that gives them an incentive to get involved. Most importantly, be sure and pray for them. The note won't mean anything if you don't follow through on your words.

Designing a Postcard

As I mentioned above, postcards are a simple, inexpensive, and non-threatening way to publicize your event. Most churches do not have a communications team, so the creation and design will fall to you or a volunteer. Below are some simple guidelines that will help you create a document that people will actually read!

- Don't try to pack a million graphics on the page — a few well-placed pictures or graphics will make it personal without overwhelming your reader.
- Use fewer words! The majority of your audience does not want to read paragraphs of text. Just give them the basic info.
- Make it easy to read by using headers, bulleted lists, and so forth.
- Make it interesting enough that people

will show their friends. (example: "Pie so good it will melt in your mouth — don't miss the pie social next Sunday!")

- Leave them wanting more. The point is for people to check out your event. So make sure they want more: either they need to know more information or it's so cool they have to check it out.
- Make sure you show your postcard to someone else and get some feedback. Can they understand what you are saying? Is all the pertinent information listed (i.e., place, time, and so forth)? An outside perspective can do wonders.

Viral/Word-of-Mouth Marketing

I'm sure you have all heard about Facebook, Twitter, YouTube, and so on. You may have even heard the phrase "viral marketing." But what do all these mean and how can they get the word out about an event?

You've probably heard the story of Susan Boyle, the singer who wowed the judges and audience on *Britain's Got Talent* television show in 2009. Hours after she performed, the video of her performance was posted on YouTube. People told their friends about it and more people started watching it. I found out about it on Facebook and Twitter, where nearly all my friends were posting links to share this amazing video. I then told everyone at work, as I'm sure many others did. Within days it was the most-watched video on YouTube and a worldwide star was born. That is viral marketing — people retelling a story or event. It's an effective, low-cost way to reach a lot of people very quickly, with little effort.

> Getting people talking is what the church is all about. The Great Commission is based around spreading the word and creating buzz.

Now, how do you use viral marketing to spread the word? Setting up an account and getting friends/followers on a social network or sending an email is easy and free. The hard part is how to craft the message that will grab your friends'/followers' attention, a message that will also be passed on to their friends/followers.

(Remember the RMA's I mentioned above — use them to spread the word with their social networking contacts as well!) Here are a few simple rules to help:

Not sure what social network/media is or how to use it? Check out this website for a good overview — it includes some great videos!

http://www.interactiveinsightsgroup.com/blog1/socialmediabeginnersguide/social-media-tools-101/

> Send someone a short note saying you are praying for them and mention you would love to see them at your next event. Ultimately it's not so much about the event; it is about how to get people involved in a caring and supportive community.

1. Make it emotional

Why was everyone so excited about Susan Boyle? Here was a woman who was laughed at when she first walked onto the stage. Yet when she began to sing, everyone's perception of her changed. She was the underdog who succeeded and most people can relate to that emotion. The more intense someone's response is to your message, the more likely people will be to talk about it. "Picnic Next Sunday" does not elicit an emotional response. Instead say, "Pie so good it will melt in your mouth — don't miss the pie social next Sunday!" One line like that on Facebook or Twitter will get people talking!

2. Provide an essential service

If you want your message to go viral, give people something to say that feels like they're providing a service to the person they're passing it to. "Bible study starts next week" has no urgency and sounds pretty boring. Would you want to tell anyone about this Bible study? It's doubtful. Instead, you could say, "What does God's Word mean for your life today? Find out

Saturday." By passing on this information, people feel like they are providing an important message that could help a friend or acquaintance. This is a message that most would be willing to spread.

3. "Remember this" triggers

Triggers are environmental reminders that cause people to recall your message and nudge them to do something about it. Those yellow Livestrong bracelets? A perfect example. Lance Armstrong uses the bracelets to raise awareness about his organization, and it works! Who hasn't seen one and knew exactly what it meant? It doesn't have to be something big like those yellow bracelets to attract attention — use the same graphic, wording, and so forth to get the point across. The key thing is to make it memorable!

Getting people talking is what the church is all about. The Great Commission is based around spreading the word and creating buzz. While creating buzz with publicity is an important aspect of all your events, ultimately it's about reaching out and connecting to the people who come to your events. And that I leave in the hands of you all who minister each day to the children and families in your church.

Pamela Burton is the Communications Director at INCM. For the past eleven years, she was a Communications Specialist at Colorado Community Church in Denver, CO. Before that, Pam worked at Focus on the Family in the broadcast division and at the United States Olympic Committee media division. On most weekends you can find her hiking, mountain biking, or camping in the beautiful mountains of Colorado.

Getting Inside Your Pastor's Head

by Alan Nelson

I guess I'm a freak of nature. While many ministry people move from working with children and youth to become senior pastors, I'm sort of the opposite. After twenty years of pastoring, seventeen of which I was the lead pastor, I became the executive editor of *Rev!* magazine, which involved even more work with pastors of the senior sort. My passion was leadership development. Having written several books on leadership and church development, I've had the opportunity to teach and train pastors around the country. But after a decade of this, I began to think there must be a better way to grow leaders.

George Barna told me, "Focus on kids." At first, I blew off his friendly advice since I wasn't much of a children's worker. "After all, I'm a leadership development expert," I said to myself. But after some research and God-wrestling, I came to the conclusion that it's true. If you want to raise effective, ethical leaders, you need to get to them while they're moldable. That is why we created *LeadNow*, the only concentrated leadership-training program designed specifically for 10-to-13-year-olds. Not long ago, after three years of prototyping this executive-quality curriculum to identify aptitude and train preteens, I gave up my paycheck and benefits to launch a national nonprofit called *KidLead*. While my former colleagues might suggest I'm devolving, I beg to differ.

Having seen both sides of the age-group fence, I have no doubt there exists a gulf between most senior/lead pastors and children's ministries. Even good pastors providing modest emotional support for children's ministry in their church usually fail to understand how vital it is to the kingdom. While admitting this would be political suicide, we senior pastors treat children's ministry as if it's just one of several subministry equals. But it shouldn't be. Family and children's ministry is the key to our future.

Partial blame certainly lies on the side of the pastor, who is likely consumed with the overarching church infrastructure and a personal bias for leading his fellow adults. Much of this is due to a personal calling, and grown-ups are the ones who give the money to support all the ministries of the church. (I'm using the male pronoun since over 90 percent of lead pastors are men. Adjust if appropriate.) But a savvy children's director can do a lot to advance the cause of kids by getting inside the pastor's head. Here are ten effective ideas to accomplish this.

1. Get to know thy pastor personally. Can you name his pet peeves? What's his personality type? What is he passionate about? Can you quickly name his three biggest strengths and weaknesses? What are his hobbies? Do you know his favorite authors and reading topics? What do you know about his childhood and family of origin? Describe a failure in his past. What's his communication preference (verbal, written, face-to-face, e-mail, formal or informal)? Could you craft your pastor's resume? If you said "no" to more than two of these items, you need to do some homework. If your pastor isn't that open, then do some digging, because the more you know about your pastor personally, the more effective you'll be in building a bridge for your ministry.

> Asking for his advice acknowledges that you're open to coaching and respect his wisdom.

2. Provide unsolicited, updated reports. Your pastor is likely busy and often not apt to ask you for a regular report, so providing a one-page synopsis once or twice a month is key. Include attendance, if it's good. Describe event postmortems and what's ahead. Tell your people connections and any of potential interest to him. Include potential problems, but also how you're addressing them proactively. Convey the attitude of "just keeping you informed, Pastor."

3. Initiate meetings. Don't confuse his being preoccupied with disinterest. Any savvy pastor knows the benefit of a healthy children's ministry, but the bottom line is that most pastors are spinning plates in other areas. Yet don't assume that silence is golden. If a problem arises where you've not paved a way to communicate clearly, you'll hamper your reputation and potentially set back the ministry you love. Get on his calendar at least fifteen minutes bimonthly, whether you're paid or volunteer, in a mega- or micro-church. Make up excuses to meet or provide a verbal update, but one-on-one face time is vital.

4. Come with an agenda in hand. Even congenial senior pastors are thinking to themselves, "Please, don't waste my time." For most of them, task trumps relationships, but realize that you're building a relationship just by getting together to discuss a task, need, agenda item, or vision clarification. If your church does not allow for private male-female time with the senior pastor, don't let that hamper a meeting. Do what it takes to keep protocol, whether it's bringing a team member or whatever.

5. Bring potential solutions when you raise problems. If you only meet when you have a problem, you'll be bad news whenever he sees you coming. This is simple stimulus-response conditioning. We don't enjoy being around people associated with negative info. Show that you've prethought the situation and that he's hired or chosen a leader in children's ministry. Asking for his advice acknowledges that you're open to coaching and respect his wisdom.

> Family and children's ministry is the key to our future.

6. Keep the big picture in mind. One of the biggest frustrations that pastors have with most staff members is the latter's tunnel vision. The pastor, more than anyone else, sees the big view. So be sure to remember the mothership. Know why it is you have the opportunity to do your ministry and from where your budget, salary (small as it may be), facilities, and workers come. In your meetings, note how your ministry fits the overall goals of the church. Avoid the danger of silo thinking, where ministries become islands, drift, and eventually atrophy. Use similar words and phrases when describing your work and plans to the pastor.

7. Educate your leader. Pass along articles, book summaries, and stats on children and families that he can potentially use in sermons. Keep them brief but do this well and consistently. Pharmaceutical reps provide this as a value-added service to doctors. Although their job is to sell drugs, they also highlight research and recent medical studies for busy physicians who may not have time to read up on what's happening in their field. Plus, doing this allows you to set the agenda in the field.

> Don't confuse his being preoccupied with disinterest.

8. Arrange for pastor drop-ins. If the pastor did a great staff devotional or board-training session, ask him if he'd be willing to present it to your teaching staff. Invite the pastor to be a special guest at a children's event or family function. Provide an opportunity for him to be the hero and interact with others in your ministry. If possible, keep it brief and avoid adding extra work. If you have to, come up with reasonable excuses for getting him into your area and to interact with your staff and kids. This also affirms your leadership among your staff by demonstrating your influence on the leader.

9. Vie for "up front" time.

The larger the church becomes, the more difficult it is to get into the worship service announcements, bulletin, and church marketing. Do your best to make your wheel squeak. Do a short video after a VBS or big event. Make your announcements fun and engaging. Ask for the pastor's voice as an advocate. Because of his rapport with "big church" constituents, nothing beats his voice in raising money, workers, and involvement. The church as a whole doesn't know you because either they don't have kids in your program and/or you're sequestered "in the back" during their service.

10. Develop advocates who add ballast to your voice.

Who has the pastor's ear? Who loves what you do, whom you can educate, inform, and inspire and who has influence on the pastor? Who's your ally on the church board? Some churches do this formally, but most do not. Be sure that you're not the sole voice in representing children's ministry to your pastor. Establish reports and face time with others to whom your pastor listens. This is important to do before you need help in selling a big idea or putting out a fire.

The goal is not manipulation, but acceleration. You're the primary lobbyist for children's ministry in your church, so staying close to the "power brokers" is vital. Just because we know the importance of children and preteens doesn't mean everyone else does. You need to be savvy and shrewd in how you gain the influence of others to elevate this value.

The process is called "leading up." Rarely are we ever taught or trained how to influence our superiors. But with intentional, proactive effort, you can elevate the value of children's ministry so that it takes greater priority in your church as a whole. This means bigger budgets, fewer conflicts, greater emphasis, and, who knows, maybe even a healthy raise for you. One of the most important things you can do for your children has little to do with your children, but rather gently herding the shepherd of the flock.

---

*Alan E. Nelson, Ed.D., is a leadership development specialist. After investing more than twenty years as a pastor and in leadership development for adults, he came to the realization that the best hope for the church is to focus on leaders while they're moldable. He is the founder of KidLead (***www.kidlead.com***) and author of KidLead: Growing Great Leaders. Alan lives near Monterey, CA, with his family.*

Used by permission from K Magazine

> Just because we know the importance of children and preteens doesn't mean everyone else does. You need to be savvy and shrewd in how you gain the influence of others to elevate this value.

Children's Ministry Finance 101

by Earl Radford

Let's talk beans, fingers in the pie, cookies in the cookie jar, money—the budget! You may have flipped to this chapter to try to figure out how much money to ask for (which we will outline later on). Or you may be looking for clues regarding what might be missing in your list of accounts. It could be that you are just starting in children's ministry and really don't know where to begin or what goes into a budget.

Some of you may say, "Finance is not my thing." Well, join the crowd. True, it's difficult to develop and balance a budget, especially if you can't balance your own bank statement. But there is hope. You *can* learn to balance the bank statement and balance the budget. If you are in the "clueless" category, connect with a close friend who can get you up to speed. I did that years ago, and I'm grateful to Cami for the hours she spent getting my finances on the computer. Now it's easy and takes about half an hour a month to reconcile my checkbook.

What's a Budget?

Most churches operate on some sort of a budget with the treasurer or bookkeeper keeping track of how much money comes in and what amounts go out. The board, elders, or deacons usually approve the budget and allocate its disbursement. The children's ministry leader would be wise to have someone from the board, elders, or deacons' group serve in children's ministry so that they fully understand the needs of the department. This person can be your ally when it comes time for budget allocations.

From baby wipes to hand sanitizers, from donuts to dodgeballs, from curriculum to crayons—these are the items that should be included in your budget. Make a list of categories where all your money will be spent. At the same time, make another list of things you'd like to have someday. Call it your "wish list."

Here is a sample alphabetical list of categories:

1. Classroom Supplies (Consumables)
- **Nursery:** disposable diapers, baby wipes, fish crackers, hand sanitizers, name tags, stickie labels (e.g., allergies, special feeding instructions, "I've been changed" labels), "Welcome to our Nursery" gift bags.
- **Preschool:** See the above list, then add…markers, sanitizer for tabletops, paper towels, bathroom supplies, more fish crackers, small paper cups, all kinds of tape, glue sticks, craft and art supplies, age-appropriate scissors.
- **Elementary:** Review the above lists for ideas. Then add pencils, paper, paints, scissors, snacks, rewards, paper or plastic tablecloths, tape, name tags.
- **Tweens:** juice, donuts, markers, class Bibles, awards, props for skits, room décor.

2. Copier/Printing
- Parent connection, information brochures, written activities

3. Curriculum
- Age-level lessons, visual aids

4. Curriculum Supplies
- Objects needed for object lessons or games as noted in the curriculum, e.g., "5 marbles for each student."

5. Electronic Check-in/Check-out System and Pagers for Nursery

6. Furniture
- Items such as age-appropriate tables and chairs, equipment (e.g. playground), carpeting (every ten years), maintenance (e.g., wall paint every five years, fiber or wood chips for outdoor playground)

7. General Resource Room Supplies
- Shared supplies A to Z, includes crackers, die-cut machine, music DVD's, egg cartons, fabric, felts, laminator, laminator film, markers, paint, picture books, ribbon, rolls of colored bulletin board paper, blocks, yarn, and so forth.

8. Guest Speakers, Performers, Musicals

9. Paper
- Copier, poster board, construction paper

10. Special BIG Events
- Easter, Independance Day, back to school, Thanksgiving, Christmas, New Year's.

11. Summer Camp and Specialty Camps
- These may be fee-based activities, e.g., Remote Control Airplane Flying Camp, Computer Camp, Cooking Camp, Art Camp, Music Camp, Basketball Camp.

You will want to have one category in the budget rather than a separate line item for each camp. It is important to have a budget for these to ensure proper accounting of funds, as well a way to know how you will cover expenses before the registrations are received.

12. Vacation Bible School (or insert your own special name for this event).
- You will also calculate the cost of Day Camp or a Week of Outreach here.

13. Volunteers
- Recruitment, screening, appreciation, training, cool, trendy staff-identification clothing, team-building events (go-cart racing, bowling), Children's Pastor Conference registrations (**www.incm.org**).

Who Owns Your Budget?

God owns the budget and we are the stewards of the tithes and offerings given by the people in the church. Your line-by-line accountability, and the accountability of staff members or a key volunteer who is treated as a staff member, includes the authority and responsibility for managing specific lines of the budget. For example, the nursery director "owns" the nursery budget.

Different Budget Approaches

1. No Money, but a Dream Budget

Some churches do not designate money for specific departments. They desire to someday have curriculum and furnished classrooms, but right now they depend on contributions from volunteers to meet the needs of the program. This was the case in the first church where I served. The pastor rented a grange hall in the little town of Woodinville. Seriously, we were excited when we upgraded the two 25-watt light bulbs to 100 watts each in our basement classroom. In this church, we saw marriages reunited, parents come to the Lord, and children excited to be in church. Money cannot buy enthusiasm or passionate teachers.

2. No Budget

A church that has no budget often has a checkbook. Items are purchased as needed and funds are available.

3. Unknown Budget

An unknown budget simply means that there has been a budget established, but either no one who works with the children knows how much has been allocated for that area or the person who knows won't tell you. If you ask the right question to the right person you may score. It's like a game of dodgeball. The budget is a moving target. On some things you get funding…you score. On other requests, you miss and don't understand why. I was in a church that had this philosophy. For example, we needed a projector bulb for our children's worship projector. (These are *not* cheap.) However, we were told it wasn't in the budget. With this management style, the children's ministry staff never knows what is available. Usually only one person knows.

4. A Tight and Underfunded Budget

This is when you have more mouths to feed than you have food on the table. Can you offer quality children's ministry with two fish crackers and half a cup of water per child? It's possible—when Jesus performed the feeding of the 5,000 they had plenty left over. But before you cry, "Unfair," take a deep breath. When you have done all that you can do, trust God. I'm not kidding. Ask friends to cut out diaper coupons for the nursery. They will get the hint that things are tight. Negotiate the purchase of juice and crackers from a wholesale grocer. In the Northwest, our best prices for large quantities of diapers, wipes, and crackers are at Costco. Free delivery is included on orders over $200. I understand that other ministries use Sam's Club. The organizations called Gleaners can also provide help.

You may think that a lot of money is needed for prizes to give the kids. Often the meaning has more value than cost of the items. My son cherishes a reward he earned at church when he was in sixth grade. It is an old painted bowling pin with encouraging words on it.

5. Carte Blanche Budget
Wouldn't it be wonderful to have an unlimited budget? There would be no accountability and funds would be available to spend on whatever you wanted, whenever you wanted it. If you find this blessed and enriched church, please let me know.

6. Spend It or Lose It Budget
This style uses the expenses from the previous year as a reference for the upcoming year. It often results in year-end spending frenzy and stockpiling resources. I believe that it is wiser for a church to carefully consider future budget development based on the church's annual strategy, not merely on how much money was spent. For example, when a church has established a growth goal, then the budget should reflect a comparable increase.

Mid-course Corrections
Once a budget is established it is up to the "steward" to closely monitor income and expense. Regularly, weekly, or at least monthly, the status of the budget should be reviewed. How many cookies are left? What supplies are needed? An effective budget process will ask directors of programs or departments for their input. The directors are held accountable for each line in the budget where their initials are listed. Their input is considered as monthly adjustments to the outlook of the budget are made.

At my church, we base our VBS budget on 125 children. Our early registration deadline indicated that 75 children would be involved.

The children's ministry team members came together and prayed over the lack of response. At this point we adjusted the budget outlook to reflect the real picture. We adjusted our outlook to 100 children. That means that everything was reduced by twenty per cent (tee shirts, crafts, curriculum, and so forth).

Vision Alignment
The church's strategic plan is the heart of what you will do. Hudson Taylor said, "God's work, done in God's way, will never lack God's support." It is important for the children's ministry to have the same vision as the rest of the church. This is called vision alignment.

For example, one year the church's goal or "vision" was to attract fifty new families to the church and have 50 percent of those involved in some aspect of church programming. It was important for the children's department to embrace the same goal. Therefore, the children's ministry budget and plans needed to reflect an emphasis on attracting and retaining new families. This is called budget alignment. Other existing programs may need to sacrifice part of their budget in order to reach this "all-church goal." (See "Strategic Plans," pages 7-52). Specific lines in your budget should be connected to specific action steps in your strategic plan. This ensures that you will have the funds when needed.

Asking for Money
Asking funds for something the church does not currently value can be frustrating. To make your need known, prepare an introductory letter containing two or three brief paragraphs stating how much money you need and how the funds will be used. Attach a second page titled "Proposal for XYZ." Include a detailed description and cost in bullet-point format with photographs (find them on the Internet if necessary). The cost of items listed in your budget should reflect discounted prices. Include examples such as this in your letter: "We could spend $5,000 on our curriculum, but if it is purchased from one of the providers who exhibit at CPC, our cost is reduced to only $3,500." Think strategically regarding who will receive your introductory budget letter and when the presentation will be made.

Averages

As a general rule, thriving children's ministry budgets will average between $2 to $3 per child for each worship service and each program. For example, if 100 children attend classes Sunday morning, about $300 per Sunday should be allocated. This expense will be divided into the appropriate categories throughout the year in your budget. Other churches may be able to budget only $1 per child per service or program. This gives you a way to plan for the year.

Donations

Make known your children's ministry department needs through the weekly church bulletin or website. Then list projected donations in a separate area of the budget. For example, you may ask your congregation to donate candy worth $1,000 for your Harvest Party. If more than $1,000 worth of candy will be needed, then list the balance in your budget. If you receive a windfall and more candy than expected is received, do not spend the budgeted money without permission. Report to the congregation how their giving exceeded your expectations.

Budget Presentation

When you submit a budget, use color pictures, quality paper, and calculations that have been double-checked by a second set of eyes. Care for your presentation adds professionalism and value. Include hotlinks to websites and names of catalog resource providers. This shows you have done your homework and helps validate your request. Be prepared for dialogue and anticipate questions and objections. In other words, *do your homework*. Cast the vision for what can happen through the budget. Paint a picture of the need and the results that will follow—especially if you are requesting something like a big-screen television.

Share Expenses

Some purchases can be shared with another department or church. A Spring Mother/Daughter Tea could be combined with the Women's Ministry so decorations and speaker expenses are shared. To finance an inflatable, purchase it with monies from the youth or outreach department. Calculate carefully. Some rentals may be equal to the cost of a purchase. INCM purchased inflatable giant slides, climbing walls, and obstacle courses. After being used at conferences, they were sold to churches at a bargain price. This approach was a financial benefit for everyone involved.

Find another church in town that plans to use the same Vacation Bible School theme or curriculum as you will use. Share the supplies, unless a site license or publisher restricts unauthorized reproduction. Curriculum purchased and downloaded from a website is not free to share with all your friends at the local network meeting. They will have to purchase their own. However, the props, resources, costumes, stage sets, and art supplies can be shared.

Find Out What's Free

Many curriculum publishers offer a free trial quarter of curriculum. By taking advantage of these free "kick the tire" offers you will have curriculum for Sunday night or weekday activities for a portion of your year. When I attend the Children's Pastor Conference, I bring along an extra suitcase to fill with books, free curriculum, gifts, gizmos, gadgets, and give-away items offered in the general sessions, breakout sessions, and from the resource center. Outdated curriculum, last year's VBS craft supplies, or back issues of magazines are often available for the asking.

Good Advice

Finally, here's some advice from someone who has been doing ministry for a long time: "Spend only what you have." Just like Jesus took the loaves and fishes and multiplied them, I believe God will bless your efforts.

The worksheets are on the following pages and on the CD-ROM included with this book. A sample budget is also included on the CD-ROM.

Earl Radford is the Associate Children's Pastor at Overlake and enjoys challenging young people to serve the Lord as well as motivating parents and volunteers to have an impact on the lives of children. He is a graduate of Berean University in Missouri and has had the privilege of serving in some of the largest churches on the West Coast. In addition, Earl has helped build a sports and recreation ministry called T.E.A.M. that reaches over 1,000 children and has been published in local/national magazines for children and parents.

Page #

Account #:

Expense Description / Area	2008 - 2009 Budget	2008 - 2009 Actual	2009 - 2010 Request	Rationale
Total or Sub Total				

Account #:		2008 - 2009 Budget	2008 - 2009 Actual	2009 - 2010 Request	Rationale				Page #
Revenue Description / Area									
Total or Sub Total									

Early Childhood

Jesus said, "Let the little children come to me, and do not stop them; for it is to such as these that the kingdom of heaven belongs."

Matthew 19:14

Children's Ministry Begins at Conception: Birthing a Cradle-Care Ministry

by Amy Fenton Lee

It's no secret that well-done children's programming grows a church. But the spiritual awareness often arises in a family's life during a child's gestation, well before the age of participation in VBS, music camps, or a children's Christmas pageant. Expectant couples regularly begin thinking about their faith and deeper matters affecting the views they will instill in their offspring. Inevitably at least one spouse feels a pull to have some tie to "religion." At the same time, the pregnancy and new family addition may be the catalyst for increasing life complications. The transition from newlywed couple to family status is an opportunity for added marital strife, financial pressures, and boundary struggles with the extended family. Many churches have the relational and learning environments to support and mature the wandering expectant couple. The dilemma becomes attracting the couple or keeping them engaged in the church through the demanding, sleepless first year of their children's lives.

Several churches are reinventing the idea of Cradle Care to draw in and cement such an expectant couple. In 2000, Dawn Burgess assumed the role of Dawson Memorial Baptist Church's preschool minister. She took a minimally effective "Cradle Club" program and rebirthed it as a serious outreach ministry for the church. Over the coming years, Cradle Care would grow to be an integral part of Dawson's strategy for life-on-life relational impact and a key tool in marketing the church to unchurched families. Expectant parents are now invited or drawn to the church and the ministry because of the way Dawson celebrates a newborn. However, the real goal of Cradle Care is to create the avenue to connect young couples (or even single mothers) to a longer-term source for spiritual development. Gary Fenton, the senior pastor of Dawson, shares that the Cradle Care ministry has generated incredible growth in so many ways for this church. "We can easily trace a large number of now involved church families to a Cradle Care beginning at Dawson," he says. "But what is most satisfying is watching those one-time care recipients develop into servant leaders in our family of faith and, more importantly, inside their own homes." Dawson's ministry team tells about some essential ingredients to an effective Cradle Care Ministry: celebration, honor, equipping, and relationship cultivation.

Celebration

Cradle Care givers place a cradle-shaped yard sign in front of a family's home upon the infant's arrival. The eye-catching sign prominently displays, "Dawson Cradle Care" and reveals the sex of the new baby to neighbors and others passing by. The Dawson ministry team laughs as they tell stories of families going to incredible lengths in pursuit of the popular Dawson Cradle Care yard sign. The church also brings attention to pregnancies and new births on a large, attractively designed bulletin board displayed in a prominent area of the church campus. Expectant families' names, due months, and ensuing birth dates are featured on the board, which has become a favorite gathering spot for church members of all ages.

Honor

The birth of a new child is worthy of commemoration. Many families come from backgrounds where a child's baptism or dedication before the church is a sacred occasion or even sacrament. Regardless of the nuances of various Protestant theologies for infant baptism and christening, the birth is significant in the life of a family and a church. Even today's generation appreciates the importance of ceremony when used sparingly and for the right events. Dawson's pastor leads the church in a time of corporate prayer and dedication for each new infant and his or her family during a worship service. Only one family dedication is done in a single worship service. In the past twelve months, Dawson has led more than seventy individual baby dedications. The church's personal and heart-felt recognition time has become a church and community trademark.

Equipping

The Cradle Care ministry caregivers are hand picked, established, and outreach-oriented women who are young mothers themselves. These already active and involved church members are committed to regular prayer for their care recipients and prepared to assist in times of crises. Caregivers are coached to handle and support families through high-risk pregnancies, stillbirths, and a myriad of other problems which can arise during this time of change. Caregivers also understand that their primary role is to help the young mother find and acclimate to a longer-term church ministry environment such as a Bible-study small group, Sunday morning stage-of-life class, or "Moms-n-More." Caregivers commit to attend monthly meetings and contribute to the planning and preparation of all ministry activities.

Relationship Cultivation

Numerous opportunities for relationship development are created through ministry events, contacts, and sign or gift deliveries. Even the pastor's wife meets and prays privately with the new family just prior to their participation in the worship dedication. Burgess explains that every "touchpoint" is important for both helping the family feel connected to the church and for the preschool staff or caregivers to discover any underlying ministry needs.

> The real goal of Cradle Care is to create the avenue to connect young couples (or even single mothers) to a longer-term source for spiritual development.

Cradle Care's central event is a semi-annual church-sponsored dinner. Expectant or new parents are hosted by their caregivers. Their table "teams" take part in interactive trivia and ice-breaker games. Small but helpful prizes (such as a package of baby spoons) encourage conversation in what is a fun approach to educate participants on nursery policy or comical topics such as daddy awareness. Various married couples from the church who are one step ahead in their parenting and spiritual journey are the featured speakers. These young but further-along parents speak of truths they have learned in their parenting experience while weaving in the importance of raising children with a Christ-centered focus. The event is designed to be an intimate gathering where parents can build friendships with the other families who will have children in the same age group. Equally important is the goal of helping first-time parents become comfortable with the nursery care their child will soon receive. The dinner concludes with a tour of the childcare facilities. During this time, the preschool minister reassures the sometimes nervous parents of their child's safety in the nursery.

Amy Fenton Lee is an active volunteer in the Moms-n-More and preschool ministries of Perimeter Church in Duluth, Georgia. Amy's father is the senior pastor of Dawson Memorial Baptist Church in Birmingham, Alabama. Amy enjoys writing to equip ministers and lay leaders for ministry-minded relationships. She receives email at **amyflee@bellsouth.net.**

Caregiver information sheet

Parent Name(s): _____

Address: _____

_____

Phone Number: _____

E-mail: _____

Month Due: _____

SS Class:_____ Service:_____

Older brothers or sisters: _____

_____

Caregiver Record

- ❑ Initial contact
- ❑ Delivered expectant parents' book
- ❑ Mail a prayer card
- ❑ Checked on mom close to due date
- ❑ Reported info of birth to church
- ❑ Baby's full name (with spelling)
- ❑ Hospital
- ❑ Date born: _____
- ❑ Delivered yard sign # _____
- ❑ Delivered Basket
- ❑ Returned yard sign
- ❑ Assisted with dedication

Office use:
Turned in by _____

Starbucks for Preschoolers

By Dienna Goscha

As a children's pastor, I realized that I was becoming insulated from the community. All of my work was taking place within the church. How was I to be the salt of the earth and light to the world if I lived in a cocoon built inside the walls of the church? How could I be Jesus to my community so that relationships could be built and sustained? The answers to my questions came inside a coffee shop surrounded by preschoolers and their moms.

Each Thursday morning at ten o'clock, do not look for me lurking around my church office. Instead, you can find me drinking a medium one-shot, skim mocha while reading about hungry caterpillars, lonely fireflies, and mad llamas. You will find new little friends of mine named Alex and Daniel and Olivia sitting around me with their moms hovering not too far away. You will probably feel the sense of community and energy that fills the coffee shop for half an hour. And you will find lots of smiling people as they witness the enthralled looks on each child's face.

Storytime consists of more than just reading a few random stories to whatever children happen to show up. Instead, it is an intentional time of character-building activities. Each storytime contains two classic read-aloud books based on a theme such as "I can help my family" or "I can share with my friends." Finger plays, puppets, and child-friendly props are also integrated into the sessions. God moments naturally happen as a child will mention that he or she belongs to God or that Christmas is Jesus' birthday. While the goal is not a spiritual lesson, the character-building books naturally lead to short conversations that plant seeds with the children and their families. Each session, the children walk away with a fun activity page and a tangible object such as floppy dog ears or a candy cane. Parents walk away with a much needed break and a take-home page with a list of books read and suggestions for extension activities to do at home.

> **S**torytime consists of more than just reading a few random stories to whatever children happen to show up.

> **G**od moments naturally happen as a child will mention that he or she belongs to God or that Christmas is Jesus' birthday.

To start a storytime, first pray about the location. Look for a coffee shop that is child friendly. Talk to management, pointing out the advantages a storytime would bring to their shop. Advertise in the paper, on community bulletin boards, and with mom's groups. Create a mobile story area by using a rolling cart for supplies and blankets for children to sit on. Carefully choose books that have large, colorful pictures. Rhyming books are especially popular and keep children's attention. Use simple, short books that tell stories that have unspoken morals or lessons.

The desired outcome of the coffee shop storytime has been to build relationships that would lead to real conversations about life. I know which child's mom is struggling with having to go back to work to make ends meet. I know which child's grandma loves to come after storytime for a cup of coffee and to hear her grandson tell her about a dirty dog named Harry or a boy that remembered to say thank you. I know which child's mom quit teaching to stay home with her kids and is exhausted. I know that these moms cannot help but feel loved by the church as they know that someone is dedicating a portion of time to provide a valuable experience for their children and a much-needed break for them.

The outcome that I was not expecting was how surprised by joy I would be each Thursday. I love the excitement, the wide-eyed wonder, and even the spills of hot chocolate and other unscripted interruptions. Imagine ministering outside the walls of your church, planting seeds of God's love and anticipating how the Lord will make those seeds grow. Imagine breaking out of your usual routine, going outside the church walls and being Jesus to your community. Take a step out of your comfort zone and head to your local coffee shop with an armful of books and a heart full of God's love.

> The outcome that I was not expecting was how surprised by joy I would be each Thursday. I love the excitement, the wide-eyed wonder, and even the spills of hot chocolate and other unscripted interruptions. Imagine ministering outside the walls of your church, planting seeds of God's love and anticipating how the Lord will make those seeds grow. Imagine breaking out of your usual routine, going outside the church walls and being Jesus to your community.

Dienna Goscha, cofounder and author of River's Edge Curriculum, serves as Family and Children Pastor at Real Life Church in Elk River, Minnesota. Dienna has a passion for creating an environment where children can connect with Christ in fun and relevant ways. She is also the author of "Coffeeshop Storytime" (found at www.riversec.com), a curriculum to be used with preschoolers in a storytime setting. Dienna can be contacted at **dienna.goscha@gmail.com**.

> I know that these moms cannot help but feel loved by the church as they know that someone is dedicating a portion of time to provide a valuable experience for their children and a much-needed break for them.

Coffee Shop Storytime

Week 1

Belonging

Theme Story
The Very Lonely Firefly, by Eric Carle

Secondary Story:
The Foot Book, by Dr. Suess

Supplies:
- Books (listed above)
- Firefly stick puppets
- Four light sources (tiny flashlight, large flashlight, lamp, light stick, stuffed animal's eyes)
- Activity take-home papers
- Parent take-home papers

Creating a Learning Environment for Babies, 1's & 2's

by Ann Edwards

Have you ever seen a baby almost leap from a mother's arms into the arms of a caring teacher? How does that happen? What elements are needed for this to occur?

Social/Emotional Influence in the Environment

First, we must understand what babies, 1's, and 2's need in order to learn. The first thing they need are caregivers who are a nurturing, caring, and comforting force in their lives. Without this kind of loving care, the children may not have the wiring needed to form strong relationships.

Babies, 1's, and 2's who come to church each Sunday need consistent teachers they can know and trust. Trust is an important element in any relationship in life. Trusting relationships are built over time and out of trusting experiences children will hopefully learn to trust God.

Emotional Checklist

- ❑ Are teachers ready when the first child arrives?
- ❑ Are young preschoolers reassured when they are anxious and do not want to be separated from Mom or Dad?
- ❑ Do teachers interact with each child using the Bible, biblical teaching pictures, blocks, books, manipulative toys, and nature items?
- ❑ Do teachers encourage language skills by talking about what they are doing and using simple Bible verses and songs?

Physical Environment

Young preschoolers need an environment where they can feel comfortable. They need opportunities to explore and investigate their physical environment. The children need opportunities to move and manipulate the teaching resources and equipment around them. Provide space where preschoolers can move easily without hazards (like tables and chairs that do not meet their physical development).

Babies will need cribs to rest in, mats for teachers to sit beside them while they play with specific resources, and rocking chairs where teachers can feed, cuddle, and comfort them.

Ones are developing skills needed for the rest of life. They are on-the-move and need plenty of space. Being mobile for the first time is like opening a present at every new experience. Provide blocks (cardboard), a doll crib, a child-sized rocker, and a non-breakable mirror attached to the wall. The children will begin to engage in pretend play (playing out actions they have seen others do). What a great opportunity to say as the child plays with the doll: "Jesus was once a baby just like you. Jesus loves you."

Twos need a little more equipment to create Bible-learning centers such as a child-sized stove and sink, a small table with child-sized chairs, a doll crib, a child-sized rocker, cardboard blocks, an art easel/table, and a place to experience nature items (nonpoisonous and safe). As the child grows, so will his or her play needs. Teachers need to be prepared with activities that stimulate a child's understanding of God, Jesus, Bible, church, family, community, world, self, and creation. Activities in each learning center serve as a vehicle to teach the Bible and encourage understanding of the biblical content of the teaching session. Provide for success and satisfaction in each activity. This will encourage the child's ability to try something new.

Physical Environment Checklist

❑ Are the Bible-learning centers set up for use as soon as the first child arrives?

❑ Are distractions removed that hinder teaching the biblical content?

❑ Do teachers use Bible verses as children work in the Bible-learning centers?

❑ Are security procedures used by parents and teachers?

❑ Are all materials safe for all children?

Mental Environment

All preschoolers are multisensory learners. Babies use their senses to understand the world around them. Teachers must utilize the child's senses to help the learning process begin.

Place a blanket on the floor with the Bible or a Bible teaching picture underneath. When the child reaches for the blanket and lifts it up, he or she is surprised to find a Bible. This is one way we might encourage learning mentally.

In understanding a one-year-olds' need to investigate a non-poisonous flower or reach for a large picture of a flower, we can say: "God made the flower for you. God loves you." These kinds of firsthand experiences help the child make "life applications" about God and apply a Bible truth … God loves them.

Through activities and adult interaction in the session, a relationship is built between the teacher and the child. The child will begin to expect to have "fun" at church because their learning needs, as well as physical and emotional needs, are being met. It is through this consistency that child begins the journey to know God, Jesus, the Bible, and the church.

Mental Environment Checklist

❑ Are babies, 1's and 2's encouraged to try new things?

❑ Do activities stimulate several senses?

❑ Are Bible truths relayed in ways the children can understand?

❑ Is variety in activities used from Sunday-to-Sunday?

Spiritual Environment

God created children with the capacity to learn about Him. If you believe this statement it will guide you to help the child learn in ways God intended for them to learn.

Babies, 1's, & 2's learn through:

- *Repetition.* Provide a Bible each Sunday so that the child can learn it is a special book that tells us about God and Jesus.
- *Senses.* Provide opportunities for children to explore through touch, sight, hearing, smell, and taste (based on age).
- *Relationships.* Be consistent in attendance.
- *Curiosity.* Use books, pictures, nature items (safe and nonpoisonous), blocks, puzzles, and toys to stimulate interest.
- *Play.* Interact and encourage two-way communication and parallel play.
- *Imitation.* Encourage language development and interaction.
- *Hands-on experiences.* Allow the children to use their skills and curiosity to touch and play with new and familiar things.
- *Satisfaction.* "Plan" successful experiences. Know what each child is capable of learning and doing.

Spiritual Environment Checklist

❑ Do you have more than one Bible in the classroom?

❑ Do teachers use prayer thoughts and Bible phrases and verses?

❑ Do teachers use songs, including the name of the child in the song?

❑ Do teachers use Bible conversation as they make life applications to the biblical content?

Teaching babies, 1's, and 2's is truly a gift. The investment we make in their lives now will pay off when we see them walk through the church doors with expectancy and joy. A child this age may not remember what you said about God but you have started the child on his or her own journey, and perhaps this same young child encouraged you along your own spiritual journey. Have fun and join God in what He is doing in the life of the child!

Ann is a Childhood Ministry Specialist with LifeWay Christian Resources in Nashville, Tennessee. She holds a Bachelor of Arts Degree from Judson College in Marion, Alabama, and a Masters in Religious Education from New Orleans Baptist Theological Seminary.

Over-the-Top Preschool Bible Stories and Worship

by Karen Apple

Years ago, I learned that 75% of moral values are learned by age five. This statistic confirmed my resolve to make preschool ministry a top priority. No longer would I call preschoolers "toddlers" or consider their department part of the "nursery." Three- to five-year-olds are ready to learn. They're ready for *meaningful, memorable, and life-changing* Bible lessons and worship. It may seem simplistic; but it all happens through sensory stimulation, action, relevant stories, and meaningful relationships.

A perfect example of this readiness to learn is a boy and his dad. Have you ever seen a preschooler and his father with the identical stance? It's not just genetics; it's imitation born out of observation, love, and respect. It's relationship.

I can't think of a better place for children and families to build relationships and internalize life-changing stories than at church. A moral value is re-inforced each time a child experiences a volunteer's loving encouragement because he or she shared. And the Bible is the best source of stories about God's values!

Moral values seems to be the current catch phrase; but in our effort to teach values, we need to *make the main thing the main thing!* The source of our values is *God,* and a relationship with the Lord is our goal—not the details of the story, the character in the story, or even the moral value itself. We all have the same goal, so let's make it over the top for our kids!

I've observed lots of churches in action, and we all tend to do the same things. Planned worship time usually includes the same elements for each of us. But while many churches plan well, others actually go over the top. What is the difference between the planning-well church and the over-the-top church?

Key 1: Make it *meaningful.*

The content of our material becomes *meaningful* to youngsters when the focus is on God's character and work. We love others not because someone stood with a wagging finger telling us to be good, love others, and be kind. We love God and others "because he first loved us." (1 John 4:19). A preschooler isn't sophisticated enough to ask, "What would Jesus do?" She would begin to resemble Jesus because of her blossoming understanding of God and her observation of leaders who are Christlike.

1. Build relationships.

As a worship leader, when you greet children and parents in the hall as they enter the department, you have an edge when you sit down with them for worship time. Your loving spirit and delight to be in their presence will engage kids and keep them tuned in. Strange as it may seem, if you know what's fun and funny to kids, they'll want a relationship with you. Why? Because "you know me, you like me, and you care enough to engage me on my terms."

Relationships are forged on the floor. It's true. Small-group leaders who sit on the same level with kids provide loving care, a shoulder to lean on, quiet direction, and a model for involvement during large group time.

Key 2: Make it *memorable.*

Adapt to the way preschoolers learn. Leaders who succeed at teaching provide Bible stories, prayertime, music, activities, and loving attention that children remember.

1. Use short bites.

Give them something to talk about on the way home! Because they have short attention spans, you must break your Bible lesson into short bites interrupted by action, music, and "The Point" review. It doesn't mean they need a three-minute Bible story. Repeat the main point and Bible verse throughout the lesson so that it's clear and unforgettable. Whenever the main point fits into the story, say it while the kids mime the motions; then continue the lesson without a break.

Example: The lesson is Noah. The Point: You can say, "God keeps His promises" while you and the children make a rainbow motion over your heads. Now re-emphasize The Point with each animal that enters the ark. You do have stuffed animals of every kind in the world, don't you?

2. Build anticipation and expectation.

Keep three-, four- and five-year-olds tuned in and focused. Let them sit at their special spots on the rainbow carpet or carpet squares, all while waiting for the theme song to begin. Their expectation of great things can be a joy! That theme song should remain the same all year. The song alone draws them in and gives a sense of belonging and anticipation. Think about it—if you tuned in to your favorite TV program and the opening song changed each week, you wouldn't settle in to watch immediately. You'd check the channel or the program title.

The order of service should also remain the same. Avoid the urge to mix things up. Kids want to know what to expect. Routine, anticipation, and an engaging leader provide the incentive for the kids to be seated, involved, and attentive without lots of direction. Parents tell me, "It's like magic! Will it work at home?"

3. Use key phrases.

Key phrases, cues, and motions are a hit with preschoolers and keeps them moving. Kids learn what to do when they hear, "Sit down, sit down, everybody sit down. Sit down, sit down, sit with me." Or their attention is grabbed and kept with the words, "I wonder who is coming to visit us today. Will the visitor come to the door in the barn, or will he come through the hall door?"

Briefly interview the person who walks through the door, sing a related song with motions, and say, "That reminds me of something in the Bible." When you say this phrase consistently each week, the kids will shout out, "Bible!" without prompting. They know what comes next, and they're prepared to listen. Next, you can hold up your Bible, splash a picture of the Bible on the screen, or hold up a Bible poster. "The Bible isn't everything God knows. It's everything He wants us to know from His written Word." Point to the passage in your Bible with a huge arm movement, and start the lesson with no dead air.

4. Surprise the senses.

Engaging the senses will make the lesson memorable, and every preschooler will chatter about it on the ride home. Have a guest fireman or a dog puppet dressed up like a doctor to remind kids how God cares for us. Pipe in calls and cries of animals as you describe them loping, hopping, and charging into the ark. Have fans running and equip leaders with spray bottles to mist the children as you describe the rain falling and the waters rising from the deep. Adults may not understand the wonder of it, but kids *love* it! Try waving forest-scented deodorizers to indicate that the land was finally dry.

5. Tell the story.

You can tell a story in some amazing ways! I love to become the character and tell the story from the Bible character's point of view.

> A moral value is reinforced each time a child experiences a volunteer's loving encouragement because he or she shared. And the Bible is the best source of stories about God's values!

Preschoolers love to see live action, so tell the story while actors mime the action. Your actors can speak their own lines if the dialogue is simple and the meaning is clear.

> O ver-the-top music means "I can sing it, I like it, it's fun, and I can move." Think outside the adult box.

6. Include multimedia.

Vary your media, and get tech savvy. Use presentation software, props, costumes, puppets, DVDs, CDs, digital audio players, cameras, lights, and people. I visited one church recently that used every visual and audio media known to humankind in one lesson. The stimulation overload scrambled my brain and wiped the message out of my head. Used wisely, however, technology can help engage the learners and re-inforce the message. A great example is the use of audio amplification for puppets. The point of the skit may be lost if the puppets aren't heard.

Some examples:
- Kids love to see familiar faces on the screen. Develop a multimedia presentation by using the faces of your kids; or project a skit filmed with parents, teachers, and siblings.
- Singing into a microphone will bring out the "ham" in every child. Record the children singing with individual voices highlighted. The next time you sing the song, play the recording and the kids will tune in like never before. Compile a series of these songs with kids' voices, and send them home with them. *(Remember to consider copyright laws. Don't use background music from a CD.)*
- We all know music "repeats and repeats in your head," so it provides the perfect vehicle to make the message stick. Preschoolers love music almost as much as

stories, but there are a few guidelines to remember. Over-the-top music means "I can sing it, I like it, it's fun, and I can move." Think outside the adult box. Vary the volume, tempo, and feel of the music. Introduce a calypso or country theme. Get the interactive instruments and streamers out of mothballs, and get jammin'. Preschoolers lift joyful, loving worship to God each time they clap, twirl, and hop to a praise song.
- Music is the perfect way to introduce each segment of large-group time. Slow and contemplative music will cue children to sit quietly and prepare for prayertime. The most effective leaders use rote prayers sparingly. They use poetry to quiet the heart but speak to God as a loving and present Father who cares and listens. It seems that the act of prayer demonstrates most effectively our relationship to God. The "You Are Here With Me" song on the *Touch the Sky* CD from Willow Creek Association (ISBN 633277000628) is a wonderful song to prepare kids for prayer.

7. Pray.

Prayer is an effective way to make the day's message personal. Be a leader like Jesus. Demonstrate how to pray. Later the children can participate with echo prayers, prayer songs, and personal prayers in small groups.

8. Sparkle up offering and outreach.

One children's pastor visits during the preschool large group for offering time. While the background music plays and the offering is taken, he walks around to each child, looks them in the eye, and asks about something in their life. It's meaningful, personal, and very moving.

We all know kids bring their money because they're "supposed to," but they wonder why. They're curious about where the money goes. Give them concrete examples of the process. Bring in a "money-counter person" that carries re-sealable zipper bags. Show how the offering is used by displaying a huge stack of books, crayons, pencils, toys, and Bibles bought with it. You can also post pictures of the missionaries you support.

> We want children to do more than copy Bible words. We want them to know that God made them, God loves them, and Jesus wants to be their forever friend.

Outreach events also help each child think outside his or her own box. An overseas offering project helps kids think globally. Every Sunday, show a multimedia presentation of chickens and goats. I collect these pictures online. Tell the children that their offering will buy animals for children who need help feeding their families. The children will be amazed and excited to hear the number of chickens and goats their offerings provide.

Another suggestion is to help a local charity by displaying a Christmas tree where the children can hang hats, mittens, and scarves. The kids see the progress of this giving and know they're helping kids in their own community. On a cold day in January, remind them about the children who are warm today because they were kind and generous with their giving.

Key 3: Make it *life changing.*
We want children to do more than copy Bible words. We want them to know that God made them, God loves them, and Jesus wants to be their forever friend. The result of internalizing and understanding these truths is immeasurable. Preschoolers may not be able to verbalize their understanding, but they will respond in ever-increasing love, trust, and joyful obedience to Jesus.

Lives change as a result of a relationship with God. Therefore we must make the main thing the main thing. God wants an intimate relationship with *me?* Yes, *you!* It's a wonderful concept, but kids need more than words. Three- to five-year-olds need people to demonstrate the concepts and relevant stories to make the ideas "kid size."

I observed an amazing presentation of the Christmas story in the preschool department of one church. At the conclusion of the lesson, the leader said, "Now I want you to remember: Wise men still seek Him." I wanted to shout, "What's wrong with this picture?!" Just a few additional sentences could make this conclusion personal and wrap up what was an amazing presentation. Make it personal by saying, "When I point to you kids, I want you to say your name out loud just one time. Then I'll keep talking. Remember, say it just one time. God loves _____ so much that He sent His one and only Son.'"

A "kid like me" is one of the best teaching tools. Applaud good behavior in the classroom, and include application stories and skits about kids who demonstrate the point of your Bible lesson. Sometimes when nothing else penetrates, the good and bad choices of a puppet drive home the point like nothing else.

Children will understand God loves them when they experience the consistent, ongoing care of adults and teens. Consistent personnel cannot be overstated. When I was a child, Mrs. Kapell was my favorite large-group leader. She never failed me. She was there every week. She greeted me every time I saw her, even when I aged out of her department. This faithful servant of God used every tool available to help us understand God's unconditional love. She inspired me to seek Jesus, to live for him, and to serve him. I am a Christ follower because of her words and her life.

Preschoolers *will* follow. They *will* learn. They *will* change.

Give every lesson a little extra thought and lots of prayer; and take it over the top, because preschoolers have incredible potential to learn.

And never underestimate the power of God to take it over the top through you and your volunteers.

_____

Karen Apple has developed an innovative church children's ministry, which included an over-the-top weekday preschool and a classroom and counseling program for children whose parents are divorced or separated. She writes and consults for publishers and churches.

Elementary

Even children show what they are by what they do....

(Proverbs 20:11*a*, Good News Translation)

Children's Church . . . It's the "Main Service!"

by Rev. Eric N. Hamp

One of the most powerful things going on Sunday morning is that boys and girls are praising God. . . . The Bible says in Psalm 8:2 (NIV), "From the lips of children and infants you have ordained praise because of your enemies, to silence the foe and the avenger."

I'll help you map out a service to children that lets you systematically make a lasting impression on their worship experience. Conducting a children's church service is like riding a roller coaster. I lived near one of the world's largest amusement parks, with the most roller coasters of any park. Both offer a series of ups and downs.

We live in a society that is so technologically advanced that children have access to amazement at their fingertips. We have to be very creative, since we are competing somewhat with what they watch on television and the computer. We want to accomplish a few standard things in a worship experience with children. We need innovative ways to do that.

Here is an outline of an effective children's church service and a few ideas that may help. This is by no means an exhaustive list or formula that must be followed, just a children's pastor sharing his heart. Let's go to church!

Opening/Introduction
The most important part of anything is the beginning. First impressions are everything. I like to start each service like a huge production. I do this whether I am in front of 10 children or 1,000. My mentor told me that ministering to children is like putting your big toe into a electrical socket: You need to be "on" from start to finish.

Start with a video clip, an upbeat song, or a funny character that makes an exciting entrance. Video countdowns are a great way to let everyone know that the service is getting ready to start. This creates a definite beginning and ending. During this introduction time, I tell the children that I am looking for children who are doing a certain action (for example: participating, singing loudly, praying with power, or sitting still and listening intently.) If they are "found," they will be rewarded. I set the stage for the entire service with this introduction. If you don't give clear expectations at the beginning, there will be nothing to strive for.

You may choose to introduce a Quiet Seat Prize (QSP) that your volunteers give out to those who are participating.

Action Songs
Children do not have the same attention span as adults. I like to do "action songs," praise songs that have motions or make you want to get out of your seat and move to the beat. We may even have a conga line. The actions are not only an expression of praise; They also help to expend extra energy. Whether you are using a live band or canned music, you must use it to your advantage. During the song, hit pause or abruptly stop the music and yell, "Freeze!" Then look around the room to see who is frozen and doing the correct motion for that place in the song.

This is a great time to find participants for a competitive game that you will do later in the service. Let everyone know at the beginning of the song: "I am looking for 5 boys and 5 girls doing 5 things at once—singing, clapping, dancing, smiling, and praising the Lord—to play the next game." If you are the one leading the song, try to find others to pick the children so that you don't forget to pick them.

Game Time
Zechariah 8:5 (NIV) says, "The city streets will be filled with boys and girls playing there." God doesn't seem to mind the fact that kids like to play. Even heaven will have kids playing in the streets.

Competition is a reality of life. It is important for kids to learn how to win and lose. They will experience plenty of winning and losing as they grow up.

You don't need to reinvent the wheel every week. *The Price Is Right* game show has been on the air for almost 40 years, with only 102 games ever played on the show.

Use games in your service, but don't let games be the main focus. Several types of games can be used in a service: ice breakers, crowd control games, memory verses, reviews, team competitions, or individual races.

Your game can go along with the main theme or exist purely for entertainment. I often use the game as an incentive for good behavior. I may repeat the game two to three times in a service to include more children. Depending on the length of your service, you may need to keep a game in your "back pocket" for later.

Sermon Jazzers

At the beginning of the service, reinforce the main theme of the lesson for the day. I look for something to jazz up my sermon or lesson. This may be an illustration to introduce the subject in a way that the children won't quickly forget.

You may choose to have some adults or older children act out a skit, put on a puppet show, sing a song, or have a simple interaction with a costumed character. You may choose to use a clip from a movie or music video. An object lesson can drive the point home. The "jazzer" is not the full lesson, just a teaser to the main teaching.

Offering

Offering time is a golden opportunity to teach children about the importance of giving and to show them some biblical examples of giving. Teach principles of sowing and reaping and the importance of giving with a cheerful heart. Allow 5–10 minutes to teach and explain why and how we give. That time may be followed by a creative way of bringing the offering to the container.

Creative Offerings

- *The world's longest offering:* Lay the money side by side and get a tape measure to see which team has the longest line-up.
- *The world's tallest offering:* Stack the money.
- *The world's fastest/slowest offering:* See which teams are the fastest or slowest at taking up an offering.
- *Shoot a basket offering:* During basketball season, have the children shoot the offering into a basket.

Have a child lead the end of each time of giving with a prayer of thanksgiving to God for providing the funds and with a blessing of the gifts and the givers. We quote Luke 6:38 as a confession of our giving.

Memory Verse Teaching

Look for creative ways to teach the children to memorize or learn the daily key Scripture verse. We want the children to go home with an answer to their parents' age-old question: "What did you learn today?" Instead of the famous answer: "I don't know," wouldn't it be great to have the children quoting Scriptures to Mom and Dad as the children leave your classroom? Psalm 119:11 (NIV) says, "I have hidden your word in my heart that I might not sin against you." I would much rather a student leave knowing the word of God than remembering the game we played.

This is not the time to teach what the verse is saying or how to apply it. Instead, it is a time for the children to learn the verse and commit the words, in whole or in part, to memory. You may use some sort of game; put the verse to music, such as a rap or chant; use the call and response technique; use rebuses or other puzzles; make use of chalkboards or dry-erase boards. Other good ideas include the following:

- Project the verse on a screen and take away a word or section as the verse is recited.
- Place the words from the verse in separate envelope taped under chairs. Then have the children remove the words and work together to put the words in order.
- Have the children race against the clock to see who can unscramble the word fastest.

Give an award to any child who memorizes the verse within a set length of time.

Worship Song

When it is time to worship, we should help the children focus on God. Worship songs are vertical. These songs should be directed to God, with words about who God is and what God means to us. These songs are generally slower and not for moving around to. Instead, the children are to be reflective and to prepare their hearts to receive the Word. Use sign language to get great participation during a worship song. I usually plan one or two songs and repeat the songs that the children respond to.

It is our job as a worship leader to be like an old-time usher at the movie theater. We guide the children to a place in God's presence. Don't think that children are too young to genuinely experience God. Sometimes children are more open to God's leading than adults are.

The Sermon or Teaching

Most pastors would say that the sermon is the most important part of the worship experience. However, I think of the whole service as a sermon. The teaching should include the following:

- *Hook*—This is an illustration or attention grabber to introduce the topic or lesson. This might be a funny story, a movie clip, a question with an audience response, a catchy title.

- *Book*—This is the Scripture portion or Bible story that you use. This might be presented by dramatically acting out a story, having a puppet/character read the Scripture, reading from a different version of the Bible. Using a Power Point presentation or some other visual device for the Scripture is always a plus.

- *Look*—This answers the question, How does this apply to my life today? The children must know what the story or message has to do with their everyday life. The things that children deal with on a daily basis, things that adults may think are trivial, are the reality of who they are. Use object lessons, visuals, illusions or things to bring it home.

- *Took*—This is what the children take away from your teaching and then put into practice in their lives after they hear the message. It may be an assignment to carry out during the week or a commitment to the Lord.

The message portion should not be longer than 20–30 minutes and should be presented in a manner that doesn't lose the children's attention. The children's participation in the lesson will help make the message stick.

Preaching/teaching doesn't have to be in the traditional lecture setting. Be creative in your delivery.

I've always liked the following maxim attributed to St. Francis of Assisi: "Preach the gospel. And if necessary, use words."

Ministry/Altar Time

After the Word of God is taught, have a time of reflection and consecration to the Lord. I believe that children can make commitments to God at an early age. (I was 12 when God called me into ministry.) You may choose to have the children write a note to God, draw a picture for the Lord, repeat a prayer, or just spend quiet time.

Closing/Review

The last part of the service should be a recap of the day and should drive home the main point. You should start and finish with a bang. Do another game, song, or high-energy activity to end the service. Use this time as well to make announcements of upcoming events and to hand out take-home pages or other things that reinforce the lesson.

Ideas of ways to do children's church are as vast as the sand on the beach, but the main elements are the same. I believe that children are not the church of tomorrow but the church of *today.* So let's do our part in shaping the leaders of the next great move of God!

Eric Hamp is the Director of Children's Ministries at Word of Life Christian Center in Denver, Colorado, and the Global Focus Director of the International Network of Children's Ministry. Eric travels extensively as the founder and president of Hamp International Ministries, conducting Kid's Crusades and Leadership Training. He has more than 20 years experience in ministering to children and has led a weekly inner-city ministry to 700–800 children. He is married to his best friend, April.

Bible Exploration Club

by Nick Ransom

It's a Friday afternoon in late February, usually a quiet night at our church, as we make one final push toward our big weekend programming. However, this Friday night is a little different. In just a few moments, hundreds of excited third graders will be entering the children's wing, ready for a night of fun. And guess what is in their hand … their brand-new Bibles!

In just a few moments, hundreds of excited third graders will be entering the children's wing, ready for a night of fun. And guess what is in their hand … their brand-new Bibles!

Each fall, this picture becomes a reality, as every third grader in our church receives a brand-new Bible. This presentation is followed a few months later by an event that allows them to have fun as they learn about the Bible and how to use it. Many churches give Bibles away during the third grade year, Those in churches that have built this as a fun and meaningful tradition know the benefits of it.

First, the number of third graders and their families who come out for this Bible presentation ceremony is quite remarkable, at least in every ceremony I have been part of (seven so far). Even families who are rarely seen at church will come out for this event so that their third graders can receive new Bibles and learn how to use them.

Second, there is a benefit in the excitement the kids have after receiving their new Bibles and in the desire they have to use them right away. In the following weeks at Sunday school, there is never a problem getting third graders to bring their Bibles to church and to be ready to use them. However, as with most gifts, the momentum fades and it becomes a challenge again to get the kids to bring their Bibles and to use them. Some of the third graders' families begin to slip back into the not-so-regular attendee group. Another shot of excitement must be injected into your new Bible owners. This is

where a Bible exploration event comes in. Just when you think that the excitement has fizzled, you bring on your Bible exploration event. When done well, the excitement returns to life and momentum is recovered. So let's jump into the Bible exploration event, and see what components are needed to make it a success.

Here are a few helpful keys to having a successful Bible exploration event:

1. **Plan well.** I have found that a Bible exploration event is most effective a few months after the Bible presentation event. For example, present Bibles in October. Then in early February, bring your kids back together for a great event. At the time of the Bible presentation, be sure to include a dated registration form with each Bible so that families can save the date. Then during the intervening months, wherever third graders are gathered, advertise the Bible exploration event to the kids.

2. **Food is a crowd pleaser.** Include pizza and other snacks as part of your event. Let the kids have some fun.

3. **Have plenty of help.** A good ratio for a successful event is 1 adult to every 7 or 8 kids. This ensures that, when it comes time to use the Bible and look up verses,

someone is on hand to help any child who is not sure how to use his or her Bible.

4. **Take it home!** Always include an activity, a Bible search, or something else that the kids must do at home and bring with them to the next weekend's children's program. Give the children an incentive, such as a candy bar or small, cool toy for bringing in the completed activity. This also gives your not-so-regular attendees another reason to come back on a Sunday.

Now let's talk details of how Bible exploration night might look. The details below assume that you, the coordinator or leader of the event, have 35 kids and 6 adult volunteers. However, you can tweak this format to work with smaller and larger groups.

5:30 PM–5:50 PM—Registration and Pizza Party: Divide the kids into groups of 6 or 7 and have each group sit with an adult volunteer at a table, preferably a round one. While everyone eats pizza, the adult volunteer plays a few casual, get-to-know-you games with the group. If you have access to a projector and/or big-screen TV, you can use some great PowerPoint games that require no additional adults—just you and the kids having fun interacting with the screen.

5:50 PM–6:45 PM—Large Group Time: This is the time when you and the adult volunteers have a few minutes to give the kids an overview of the Bible. Begin with the basics. Have the kids answer questions such as the following: What is the Bible? Where did the Bible come from? How do we use the Bible? How is the Bible organized? Talk to the kids about how to look up information, where to find the table of contents, and how knowing such information is helpful in finding verses. Show kids the chapter and verse

numbers, and let the kids see how well organized the Bible is.

Next, give the kids a chance to practice looking up a few verses. I find it fun to give them the longest verse in the Bible (Esther 8:9), the shortest verse in the Bible (John 11:35), and other verses that have fun facts attached to them.

Following this, take the kids on a very quick walk through the Bible. Talk about some of the amazing Old Testament stories. (*Use a video clip from* **Prince of Egypt** *to show an amazing story from Moses' life*.) Talk about the unique things you can find in Psalms and Proverbs. Play a game where a saying is shown on a screen, and the kids have to guess whether it's in the Bible or just a wise saying. Talk about how the prophets predicted the coming of the Messiah. Then move to the New Testament. Talk about the birth and life of Jesus Christ and how the Gospel is Good News. (*Use a video clip from* **The Gospel of John.**)

The purpose of this large-group time is to get the kids comfortable with their Bibles and to get them excited about the great stuff they can now read for themselves.

Note: This large group time is most effective if, every 3–5 minutes, you change the way you teach. Talk for 3 minutes, have the kids work together on a task for 3–5 minutes, play a game for 5 minutes, and show a video clip that is about 3 minutes long. You get the picture. Fifty-five minutes can seem like a long time and *will be* a long time if you don't keep the pace moving. I have found that when following this format the 55 minutes fly by and I want more time to talk with the kids. Always, always, always end while the kids still want more. Don't drag it out.

6:45 PM–8:00 PM—Small Group Activities: These can be done in the same room or if you have another room (s) those will work too. Here are some ideas for small group activities:

> The purpose of this large-group time is to get the kids comfortable with their Bibles and to get them excited about the great stuff they can now read for themselves.

1. Play "Who Wants to Be an Israelite?" similar to the TV game show *Who Wants to Be a Millionaire*, except that kids answer Bible trivia questions and try to earn shekels, instead of dollars.

2. Make Bible covers by decorating pre-made canvas covers or posterboard that is custom cut and covered with self-adhesive vinyl to protect their Bibles.

3. Play a game called "Seek and Find." If you have a large group or only a short amount of time, have the kids play in teams. Have a tub of 12 or more similar items for each team or individual if not playing in teams. The items are related to the verses that the kids will look up. For example, Psalm 119:105 says, "Your word is a lamp to my feet and a light to my path." The individual or team who finds and reads this verse will go to the tub and retrieve a flashlight, which represents light. Be careful not to have any other items that might fool the kids. For instance, in the case of Psalm 119:105, don't have any items that might relate to feet or a path.

    Give everyone the same 12 Bible references to look up. Display the list on a markerboard, on slips of paper, or however you choose. The object is to find a verse, read it, and retrieve from the tub a related item. The first team or individual to retrieve all 12 items wins a small prize.

8:00 PM–8:15 PM—Break Time: This allows kids to finish any of their crafts/projects, if needed.

However you decide to explore the Bible with the kids in your ministry, make it exciting and meaningful. Most importantly, make it your own.

8:15 PM–8:30 PM—A Meaningful Ending: So far the night has been all fun, but now it is time to bring all the kids together for one final meaningful moment. Now is the time to challenge the kids to read their Bibles and let the Bible influence the way they live. The Bible is God's Word to us. We have found real meaning in ending the night with Communion or a candlelight ceremony encouraging the kids to be lights in the world.

Be sure to invite your pastor and the kids' families to be part of the closing. We've found that inviting the parents to return about 20 minutes or so before the closing works well. The families respond positively to being a part of this special time. Sometimes the parents tell us that they still have their third grade Bible, and they explain how important that Bible is to them. Plan carefully and don't allow this time to drag on, or the moment will be lost. Whatever you decide to include in the closing, make it meaningful for the kids.

However you decide to explore the Bible with the kids in your ministry, make it exciting and meaningful. Most importantly, make it your own. You know your kids; you know what they need.

I hope that these ideas are a springboard to help reach the goal of bringing the kids in our ministry to a deeper relationship with Jesus Christ.

Each year, I enjoy seeing the pride the third graders get in receiving their new Bibles, the excitement they have in getting to use them, and the encouragement I receive from watching the kids participate in these moments. I know that you will enjoy these moments just as much as the kids enjoy participating.

Nick Ransom is the Director of Children's Ministries at the United Methodist Church of the Resurrection, in Kansas City. He has been on staff at the church for four years and has been involved in children's ministry for more than seven years. He has been married for almost seven years and has two-year-old triplet sons.

Christianity in Public Schools: Our Only Hope

by Finn Laursen

As the battle for the minds of our children continues, our schools have become a major battleground. Some in the Christian community are even calling for a mass exodus from our "government schools."

Is there any hope for reform of the nation's public schools?

Is abandoning our public schools the only hope for our youth?

Whereas home schooling and private Christian schools are alternatives to public school education for many, for many others these alternatives are not practical or possible. So abandoning public schools cannot be the only hope.

There is hope for reform and restoration within our public schools. "For God all things are possible" (Matthew 19:26). That hope is not based on any state or national reform movement. It is not based on "No Child Left Behind."

The hope of our public schools is in Jesus Christ and in professional educators who follow Christ and model him in the workplace.

Our founding fathers had great foresight when they penned the Constitution. They realized that building a country could not happen without the help of the Lord; and in the First Amendment, they made sure that the government would not establish a religion nor prohibit the expression of religion.

At the Constitutional Convention, Benjamin Franklin set the tone for the writing. He realized that they had been meeting to draft a guiding document for a new nation and had neglected to seek The Creator. After the following speech, overflowing with Biblical allusions, all future sessions were commenced with prayer:

"I have lived, Sir, a long time, and the longer I live, the more convincing proofs I see of this truth—that God governs in the affairs of men. And if a sparrow cannot fall to the ground without His notice, is it probable that an empire can rise without His aid? We have been assured, Sir, in the sacred writings, that 'except the Lord build the House, they labor in vain that build it.' I firmly believe this; and I also believe that without His concurring aid we shall succeed in this political building no better than the Builders of Babel."
—Benjamin Franklin

As these early founders penned the Constitution, they assured that future government agencies, like schools, would not control religion or silence the convictions of a religious people.

The First Amendment— United States Constitution

"Congress shall make no law respecting an establishment of religion or prohibiting the free exercise thereof....abridging the freedom of speech,... or the right of the people peaceably to assemble, and to petition the government for a redress of grievances."

Establishment Clause, Free Exercise Clause

How would the First Amendment affect an elementary public school teacher?

The courts have equated teachers as arms of the government, since they are supported by federal public dollars. Thus, a public school teacher may not establish his or her religion in that classroom. In other words, a Christian educator may not use his or her public position to force his or her beliefs on students.

However, the school may not use its power to ban the free exercise of religion in the school. If a teacher of faith believes that his or her expression of religion includes communicating with God, schools may not prohibit such expression.

Teachers may engage in personal prayer. In fact, every superintendent in the nation must annually sign an assurance document that he or she has no policies that inhibit constitutionally protected prayer.

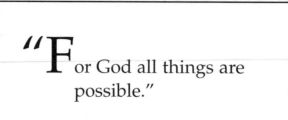

"For God all things are possible."

Teachers may attend student- or staff-initiated prayer groups, Bible studies, or worship activities. If these meetings are held during the workday, the teachers should not lead them, but they are free to fully participate before and after the workday.

All elementary curriculums include some reference to religion, and teachers are free to teach about religion and to even go beyond the basic required curriculum.

Since they are public employees, they cannot lead religion devotionally, but they may clearly teach about it.

If teachers are questioned by students about their faith, they may certainly answer honestly. The courts have clearly communicated that teachers do not lose their freedom of speech rights when entering the public school classroom.

Freedoms for Educators
- Personal prayer
- Attendance at student/staff activities, including prayer, Bible study, and worship
- Lead after-school religious clubs
- Personal expression
- Religion in curriculum

Christian Educators Association International (CEAI) exists to help Christian educators understand and carry out their mission.

Founded in 1953, CEAI is a professional association for Christian educators in both public and private schools, with most of its members serving in public schools. Its focus is to encourage, equip, and empower Christian educators to make a positive impact in the schools where they serve.

CEAI provides resources such as magazines, newsletters, daily devotionals, and many other printed and digital resources from a Christian worldview. The association also provides professional liability insurance and legal support.

Student Freedoms
- Prayer
- Bible
- Distribution of material
- Discussion/school assignment
- Access to space and media
- Religious garb
- Release time
- Objectionable lesson or activity release

Our public school elementary students have total freedom of religious expression in school, since they are not government employees. Students may lead prayer, read aloud or distribute Bibles or other religious material, openly discuss their faith publically or through assignments, be given the same access to facilities as others get for non-religious activities.

In other words, school employees must be "blind to religion." They may not treat religious expression differently from non-religious expression.

Precisely because there are so many negative influences bombarding public school students today, CEAI considers our public schools a mission field ripe for harvest. Through public schools, we have access to many who will never enter our churches.

Like no other time in history our children are continually inundated with negative information. Media saturation has reached a level that our children, starting in elementary school, experience greater influence from outside the home than from within. They are exposed to a sexualization in our culture that has expanded to all areas and ages. Hard-core pornography is just a point and click away, with many of our children unintentionally being exposed to unimaginable perversions.

According to Barna Research, only four to six percent of school-age children self-identify as Christian. Christian educators interacting with young people daily can have a life-changing effect on those not having a personal relationship with our Lord and, at the same time, can be a powerful role model for Christian students on campus.

CEAI's position is "God's Love and Truth transforming our schools."

Their Mission

- Encourage, equip and empower educators according to biblical principles
- Proclaim God's Word as the source of wisdom and knowledge
- Portray teaching as a God-given calling and ministry
- Promote educational excellence as an expression of Christian commitment
- Preserve our Judeo-Christian heritage and values through education
- Promote the legal rights of Christians in public schools
- Provide a forum on educational issues with a Christian world view
- Partner with churches, para-church organizations, educational institutions, and parents
- Provide resources and benefits for educators, including professional liability insurance

The Core Values

- Love
- Biblical knowledge
- Respect
- Integrity
- Prayer
- Patience
- Self-control
- Worship
- Truth
- Unity
- Forgiveness
- Faith
- Servanthood
- Joy
- Professional excellence

For in-depth information about Christian Educators Association International, visit *www.ceai.org.*

Since 2003, Finn Laursen has served as Executive Director of Christian Educators Association International. He came to the position after a 32-year career in Ohio public school education, during which time he served as teacher, counselor, assistant principal, principal, and superintendent

Religion in Public School's Seminar

INCM is partnering with CEAI to bring **The Religion in Public School's Seminar.** *The seminar will include much of what was discussed in this article. It's a chance to learn how a church might positively impact their local public school. For more information, contact Finn Laursen at 888-798-1124, 440-250-9566, or finn@ceai.org.*

Notes

Family Ministry

Hear, O Israel: The LORD is our God, the LORD alone. You shall love the LORD your God with all your heart, and with all your soul, and with all your might. Keep these words that I am commanding you today in your heart. Recite them to your children and talk about them when you are at home and when you are away, when you lie down and when you rise.

(Deuteronomy 6:4-7)

How to Conduct a Wildly Successful Family Event

by Roger Fields

Since 1996, Kidz Blitz has conducted hundreds of family events in every denomination across America. Here are the secrets we have learned.

Why Do It?

Like anything else you do, you need a reason why you would want to conduct a family event. The last thing you need is more responsibility for no good reason. Unless you have a clear objective, don't do it. But, there are some good reasons for hosting a family event. Here are the best ones.

First, an event structured for both parents and kids generates a shared family experience. In other words, everybody enjoys doing an event together. That's rare in our society and even rarer in church. Kids do most activities by themselves or with other kids: school, sports, play, computer, and so forth. It is not typical for parents and kids to engage in an activity together. The days of family farm work are gone. However, kids need to feel they are woven into a family. This is vital as they grow older and need adult input into life's decisions. Shared activities help weave families together.

Second, family events can be effective outreach tools. Since there are few events in the community that engage parents and kids together, non-churched and church-attending families will often consider attending a creative event in a church that appeals to them. Think about this, polls have shown that ninety percent of the parents in America say they believe they are responsible for the spiritual upbringing of their kids. Even non-churched parents have a felt need when it comes to impacting their kids spiritually. If the church offers an event that looks enjoyable and it helps parents connect with their kids, it will resonate with most families in your community. Don't be afraid to make the event evangelistic. Non-churched families are not offended as long as the invitation to accept the Lord is not pushy or manipulative.

Third, family events are the perfect way to get fringe people in your church involved. No volunteer position is safer than the one that will expire when the job is over. Mr. Johnson is not about to get involved in children's ministry, because he knows he might get trapped into volunteering indefinitely. But, a family event is different. He knows his kids will probably want to attend anyway, so it is a small, safe step for him to jump in and help. What he doesn't know is that he might actually enjoy working with people from the church. This temp. job might be the perfect doorway into serving in the church on a regular basis. For this reason, family events almost always produce new church volunteers.

Secrets

Here are a few secrets that will help you promote your event without spending a lot of money.

1. **Choose your words carefully.** "Shared family experience" is often better received than "family event." To many people, "family event" does not mean the entire family will enjoy it. It means the event is appropriate for kids. It might be considered a "family event" just because there is no profanity, violence, or sexual material. Here are some phrases that work well.
    a. "An exciting event for parents and kids"
    b. "A super-cool event parents and kids will both enjoy"
    c. "A red hot, fun event for mom, dad, and the kids"

2.   **Charge for tickets.** Always. Never conduct a family event in the U.S. for free. Americans assume "free" means "worthless." If you want to make the event an outreach event for non-churched families, then *never* do it for free. Non-churched families do not understand a free event. They think there is a catch somewhere. (Who knows, you might try to sell them a time-share.) They would rather shell out the money than risk being tricked into something that was promoted as "free." I get a lot of resistance when I teach this in seminars, but this truth is a universal perception in America, even in low-income areas.

3.   **Setting a door price and a lower advance price will help you predict the size of your event.** If the price at the door is the same as the advance price, you will have no idea how many people are coming to your event. If there is no incentive for them to buy tickets early, they won't. If you decide to offer free tickets, you cannot rely on ticket distribution to indicate the size of the crowd. People will take free tickets in case they decide to come later. If there is no outlay upfront, there is no commitment to attend. If you give out free tickets, give out twice as many as the capacity of your auditorium. I have found that half the people who take free tickets will not come. The exception to this rule is some Christmas programs that have a capacity crowd each year and divide the crowd over several nights using free tickets.

4.   **Motivate people to invite other people.** People draw people. If the kids and parents of your church are enthused enough to invite other families to your event, it will be well attended. With the exception of a celebrity they already follow, people do not attend anything unfamiliar. Few people will attend your family event because they saw a poster, heard it on the radio, or saw it on T.V. Americans are advertisement resistant. Unless someone they trust encourages them to attend a particular event, they probably won't come. Here are a few of the most effective—and inexpensive—ways to encourage your church to invite people:

a. Show the kids an exciting promotional video so they will want their friends to experience the event.
b. Give away guest passes to paying families that can be used only for families outside of the church. They, in turn, will give them to their friends. This is different than a free ticket. A "guest pass" is a ticket worth the face value; therefore, it is viewed as more valuable than a free ticket. Give kids guest passes. Something they can hold in their hands reminds them to invite other kids.
c. Reward kids who bring three friends. It's better to give away several small prizes as opposed to one large prize. A large prize will motivate; but when you give it away, you will have made one person happy and disappointed all the rest.
d. Put up cool posters around the church.

5.   **Enlist a large core of workers.** Your event workers will not only help you run the event, but will generate promotional momentum. They will talk to others about their responsibilities and start a buzz. Once you get a buzz going, you are more then halfway to a well-attended event.

6.   **Choose an event that appeals to all ages.** Most concerts and speakers appeal to only a specific age demographic. Events that prompt participation across age lines are the best family events. Fall festivals work well. An exciting field trip (ball game, zoo, and so forth) provides an activity that families can do together. *Kidz Blitz Live* (my personal favorite) is the premier, Christian, family event in America. Choose an event that has the potential to create a buzz.

The more you conduct family events, the better you will get. From each experience you will learn something new. Build on what you learn, and soon you will be conducting events that connect parents with their kids, reach out to new families, and involve new workers. That's what I would call "wildly successful."

---

*Roger Fields is the president of Kidz Blitz Ministries and the creator of Kidz Blitz Live, America's premier Christian event for the whole family. Roger has conducted hundreds of events coast to coast in every major denomination. Since 1996, Kidz Blitz Live has reached more than 800,000 children and families with the Word of God, and more than 30,000 made first-time confessions of faith in Christ. Today, three event directors conduct these high-octane, family events nationwide and in Canada. Roger hangs out at **KidzBlitz.com**.*

Children's Ministry That Empowers Parents to Impact Their Homes and Communities

by Kirk Weaver

Now Hiring! *Children's Ministry Director. Responsible for developing a state-of-the-art children's ministry facility. Abundant resources for purchasing curriculum and training Sunday school teachers.*

Too good to be true? Yes…but perhaps not for the reasons you think.

There is an alignment problem within children's ministry. We spend more money today than ever before in the history of the church to reach children for Christ. At the same time, we are losing more children than ever before.

To help us understand the alignment problem and the change that needs to take place, let's look at the change that occurred in mission work beginning in the 1930's. In both missionology of the 1930's and children's ministry today, there is an alignment problem between what the church is doing and God's plan for the church.

In September 1935, more than 70 years ago, Melvin and Lois Hodges were called to be missionaries in Nicaragua, Central America. They traveled by plane, donkey, and on foot to share the Gospel with entire communities that had never heard about Jesus.

There were two widely accepted strategies for missionaries to use when delivering the good news. First, go to the targeted area and build a compound where the missionaries and mission workers would live apart from the nationals. After the compound was finished, build a church.

Second, the missionary was "the professional" who would lead the church. Preaching, teaching, administration and implementation of the sacraments would all be done by the missionary. If another church was needed in a nearby village, then another missionary would be called and the process repeated. Before long, Reverend Hodges, began to notice a disconnect between the strategy for planted mission churches and the way Paul developed new churches in the New Testament.

The Apostle Paul's strategy for building churches was to travel from city to city, live with the residents, and raise up indigenous leadership to run the local church. Church leaders lived and worked in the communities where they served.

Imagine going to a mission class in seminary today that said: "When you go to the mission field, the first thing you do is build a compound and then you, as the missionary, do all the work of the church." That way of thinking would be seen as absurd! Today, we understand the value of living and working with those God has called us to serve. We understand the value of raising up indigenous leadership to lead the church.

In children's ministry today there are parallels between the "professional" leader and "compound" mentality. The children's minister and Sunday school volunteer have become the "professionals." The church building has become the compound.

Here is a simple test for churches and families to see if they have adapted the professional-compound mentality.

1. In the church, what percentage of the resources allocated to children's ministry (staff time, finances, special events) is spent on *doing* spiritual training for the family, and how much is spent on *equipping* families to provide their own spiritual training?

2. In the church, what percentage of the spiritual training takes place in the church building or in a church-sponsored location?

3. If a family missed church on Sunday morning, what percentage of the intentional spiritual training would be lost that week in the lives of children?

4. If a family does not go to the church building or a church-sponsored event, what percentage of the intentional spiritual training would be lost in the lives of their children?

Let's be honest. In the majority of Christian families, the Sunday school teacher has become the professional. That's why we hear silly stories of parents saying to teachers, "How come you aren't doing more Scripture memorization with my son?" Or, "How come you don't do more in-depth training with my daughter?" As if the teacher is responsible for the child's spiritual training!

Let's be honest. In the majority of Christian homes, little, if any, intentional spiritual training is taking place. The church building has become the compound.

In the same way we look back on missions in the 1930's and say, "Remember when missionology was built around compounds and professional clergy doing all the leading? Wasn't that bizarre?" I look forward to the day when we can look back and say, "Can you remember when we thought all spiritual training had to take place in the church and we needed professional church staff to lead the training? Wasn't that strange?"

So, how did missionology change and what can children's ministry today learn from those changes? Melvin Hodges wrote about his experiences of change in a book titled *The Indigenous Church*. Reverend Hodges was not the only one talking about indigenous principles. God was raising up multiple leaders who had the same passion for change.

The Indigenous Church concept is built around three biblical principles taken from the example of the Apostle Paul. A church needs to be:

1. **Self-governing.** Don't do anything for the nationals that they can do themselves.

2. **Self-propagating.** Train and equip nationals to build and expand their own church.

3. **Self-supporting.** Do not rely on outside sources. Encourage the community to build at their own standard of living and ability to provide.

What Melvin Hodges called The Indigenous Church in his work with missionaries, I would call The Indigenous Family when working with children's ministers. The Bible is filled with Scriptures directing parents to teach their children. Proverbs is a letter from a father to a son…a parent to a child.

Deuteronomy 6:6-7 teaches: "These commandments that I give you today are to be upon your hearts. Impress them on your children. Talk about them when you sit at home and when you walk along the road, when you lie down and when you get up" (NIV).

Psalm 78:5-6 teaches: "{God} commanded our forefathers to teach their children {the law}, so the next generation would know them, even the

The Apostle Paul's strategy for building churches was to travel from city to city, live with the residents, and raise up indigenous leadership to run the local church. Church leaders lived and worked in the communities where they served.

children yet to be born, and they in turn would tell their children" (NIV).

John 14:26 teaches: "But the Counselor, the Holy Spirit, whom the Father will send in my name, will teach you all things and will remind you of everything I have said to you" (NIV).

Three points about God's plan for passing the faith:

1. The Holy Spirit is the ultimate teacher.

2. Family, more than the church, is God's primary vehicle for spiritual training.

3. Spiritual training takes place 168 hours a week, not just one or two hours on Sunday morning.

Reverend Hodges' book is subtitled *A Complete Handbook on How to Grow Young Churches*. How about *An Indigenous Family Ministry Handbook for Growing Young Christian Families*? Follow the same three principles:

1. **Self-governing.** Children's ministry is not what you do at church or in the Sunday school classroom, it is what you do to equip and support parents to teach in their own homes. When evaluating programs and their impact on families, consider asking the following questions (adapted from Ben Freudenberg's *The Family-Friendly Church*):

- Is the program/activity structured to include all family members? All the time? Sometimes?

- Does the program/activity support families as the primary spiritual trainers, or does it put the church in the position of primary spiritual trainer?

- Does the activity train and equip families to advance the faith in their homes and neighborhoods?

- Is this activity one of the exceptions when family members will learn best by being separated?

- What is the desired outcome for families who participate in this activity, and is it measurable?

2. **Self-propagating.** The most effective tool that I have used in equipping families to provide home-based spiritual training is Family Time Training, **www.famtime.com**. Parents are encouraged to use fun object lessons and activities specifically designed to teach character qualities, values, and beliefs.

When neighbors see you using sidewalk chalk to draw a big fish on the driveway or watch you march around the house with a box—ark of the covenant—on two broom handles…they start to notice and ask questions. In fourteen years of doing Family Time at home, every child in a two-block radius attended at least one Family Time. Two girls on our street do not go to church—except when we invite them—but have attended more than forty Family Times in our home.

Families who do spiritual training in the home can become the "church" to other families in their neighborhood.

3. **Self-supporting.** When spiritual training is done in the home, the family can modify the lesson to match the resources they have. When leading Family Time in India, we used lessons that required dirt, air, water, and paper.

When doing lessons in the United States, we may include DVD players, arts and craft supplies, and so forth.

The transition in missionology helps us see our current misalignment. The Indigenous Church helps us set a new target, the Indigenous Family. So what are the first steps we can take toward reaching the new target?

First, keep it simple! Baby steps. Do not try to change everything overnight. Be careful about trying to make changes outside your scope of influence. Do you have the support of the entire church staff? More change is possible! Do you have control over one classroom? Then that is your scope for implementing change. Home-based spiritual training does not replace church-based spiritual training! I want my family to have both.

Spiritual training takes place 168 hours a week, not just one or two hours on Sunday morning.

It is the Spirit that moves the truth from the mind to the heart. Parents and children's ministers alike must constantly pray for God's Spirit to be the ultimate teacher and spiritual trainer.

In 1937, there were 3 missionary compounds in Nicaragua. After implementing Indigenous Church principles, there were 9 local pastors in 1941. By 1953, 400 churches. Today, there are more than 4,000!

Second, begin to train and equip families to assume their role as the primary spiritual trainers in the lives of children. You get what you measure, so measure how many families have been educated, equipped, and are doing home-based spiritual training.

Third, start with one class. Don't just send home a piece of paper that says "read this" or "color this." Send home a fun activity! In a resealable plastic bag, provide the activity with the simple materials they need. Include a form so families can report back on their participation. Measure how many families are actually doing the weekly lesson at home. Set a reasonable goal of ten families and each year expand the number. Finally, recognize the families who are doing regular home-based spiritual training. Consider a Family of Faith recognition for those families who do at least thirteen lessons in their home over a twenty-six week period.

These are the simple first steps. Families who experience the fun and value of spiritual training in the home are more receptive to additional resources.

- Age-appropriate Bible reading
- Letter writing from parents to children on core values
- Rite of Passage retreats
- Family mission trips

Most importantly, recognize that Family Time is just a tool. Be honest, Sunday school is just a tool too. In both cases, we are seeking to expose our children to the truth of the gospel. Sunday school and Family Time get information into children's minds.

Pouring money into the one or two hours that families use the church building, curriculum, and staff may attract more kids and keep parents happy, but research shows it is a poor way to build a lasting faith. Pouring resources into families is not just effective, it's God's plan for passing on the faith. Imagine the families in your children's ministry program trained, equipped, and released to be the church at home, on their blocks, and in their neighborhoods! A children's ministry that impacts thousands instead of tens.

Kirk Weaver and his wife, Kelly, have been doing Family Time activities with their children, Madison and McKinley, since 1994. In 1999, Kirk founded a new ministry called Family Time Training. The ministry has averaged more than 80 trainings each year to 8,000+ family members. Kirk has written eight books containing Family Time object lessons, including: Wiggles, Giggles, & Popcorn; Seeing Is Believing; Tried & True; Bible Stories for Preschoolers (*Old Testament & New Testament*). *He is a graduate of Wheaton College in Wheaton, Illinois, and has a Masters Degree from the University of Missouri, Columbia, Missouri. Kirk lives in Littleton, Colorado, and devotes his time to the greater challenge of raising his children in the faith.*

Family Ministry

by Jim Weidmann

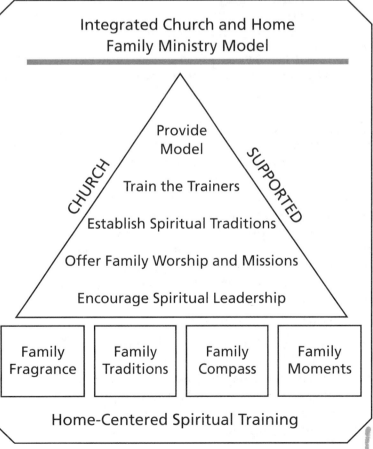

"Do not expect the Church or School to resurrect what the Family has put to death!" - Chuck Swindoll

Families must provide a spiritual foundation for the church to build upon. However, the irony is that the families must be taught, through family ministry, how to build their foundation. Only ten percent of parents talk to their children about spiritual truths at home.

Each church is different and called to a community to meet the various needs of its members, whether they are spiritual, relational, or physical. Every staff has their ideas of what is required to meet their calling. Although there are associations of churches trying to leverage what is working in one church, the application of family ministry looks different in each unique setting. Therefore, a common solution does not exist across the spectrum of church ministries. What does exist, to help each church drive their vision, programs, and participation, is a common architecture of effective family ministry elements. These elements represent categories of church programming. Each element will take on a different application to meet the unique needs of a congregation.

The architecture provides the framework for an individual church's integrated strategy. Integration must be addressed at three levels:

1. Integration with the church's overall vision
2. Integration with the overall program offerings of a church
3. Integration with the home and family efforts to pass the faith to their children

(Willow Creek's Reveal survey showed that faith formation in the home is vital to fulfilling the overall church strategy.)

The Architecture

Drawing on the experience from numerous churches that have experienced a positive impact in engaging their families in the spiritual training of their children, the architecture brings together five areas that are mutually exclusive and collectively exhaustive in representing their offerings. The key understanding is that these areas are viewed from the perspective of impacting the home through education, support, engagement, or encouragement.

The Architectural Model

Integrated Church and Home
Family Ministry Model

CHURCH — SUPPORTED

- Provide Model
- Train the Trainers
- Establish Spiritual Traditions
- Offer Family Worship and Missions
- Encourage Spiritual Leadership

| Family Fragrance | Family Traditions | Family Compass | Family Moments |

Home-Centered Spiritual Training

The Church's Role

The foundational biblical understanding, found in Deuteronomy 6:4-7, is that the parents, not the church, are responsible for the spiritual training of children. God created the family, not the church, as the primary "institution" to pass the faith to the next generation. However, the church must have a plan, based on the architecture, to support the family in their efforts by:

1. Providing a Model
Objective: *Give parents a plan that they can follow.*

In a survey conducted with more than 600 parents, the number one reason parents do not engage in the spiritual training of their children is that they do not have a plan or model to follow. They do not know what spiritual leadership looks like in the home. It all starts by defining what a heritage looks like—begin with the goal in mind. Heritage Builders identifies a heritage as consisting of three components.

- **Spiritual Legacy:** The process whereby parents model and reinforce the unseen realities of the spiritual life.

- **Emotional Legacy:** An enduring sense of security and stability nurtured in an environment of safety and love.

- **Social Legacy:** Giving children the insights skills necessary to cultivate healthy and stable relationships.

The husband comes to the marriage with his legacy elements and the wife with hers—good or bad. They make an intentional decision on what to keep and what *not* to pass on. Then, by focusing on the "tools" for passing on a legacy— the environment of the home *(Family Fragrance)*, the spiritual milestones established *(Family Traditions)*, the ongoing emphasis on biblical truth *(Family Compass)*, and the creation of teachable opportunities *(Family Moments)*—a family can be successful in passing their faith on to their children.

- **The key to the plan is Execution.** The church must provide families with a plan identifying what they want them to do to engage on the spiritual formation process at home. There are two components: strategic (traditions/milestones) and tactical (daily and weekly activities). Strategic traditions/milestones are determined by events, such as Easter, Christmas, Family Mission trip, and so forth, or by age-appropriate markers such as the Purity Ring or Rite of Passage. The tactical elements are created through decisions on prayer time, family nights, or weekly table discussions on spiritual issues. The parents must be encouraged to set aside time at the beginning of each year to set clear goals and objectives for their families and plan accordingly.

- **The Senior Pastor must teach "Family" from the pulpit and assign a champion.** Just as the families must have a plan, the church must identify, communicate, and support their plan for their family ministry. The senior pastor is like a CEO and must balance many areas of responsibility; therefore, a Champion for Family Ministry must be identified who can execute the plans at the church level.

2. Training the Trainers (Parents) Through Education, Equipping, Encouragement
Objective: *Position parents as children's pastors.*

We live in a culture that is spiritually illiterate. *Parents are not confident in their understanding of biblical principles* (Barna). The concept here is to train the trainers by educating parents on spiritual impact opportunities, teaching and equipping them with the "curriculum" they need to teach their children, and encouraging them by celebrating their achievements in the church.

- **Parents must be brought to a level of confidence in their faith.** If the parents are to be the Children's Pastors, then they should be offered classes that lay a solid foundation in their understanding of their faith and how to teach it to children.

- **Parents must be taught how to lead their children to Christ.** It is one of the greatest privileges a parent has and, due to lack of understanding and confidence, they give it to the "children's/youth" pastors.

- **Small Groups provide intergenerational opportunity for leadership training and education.** *Focus on the Family* found the number one source of parenting advice is other parents. Therefore, by creating small groups, with a mentor couple, parents can discuss relevant, age-appropriate topics such as tattoos, schooling options, and so forth under the guidance of mentors.

- **Church can provide special "Catalytic" equipping classes.** These can be incorporated into the church calendar and address parenting issues, such as discipline, or spiritual milestones, such as purity or life stage issues.

- **Church can provide a library of resources.** Parenting books—classic works such as *Dare to Discipline*—can be made available and a book of the month highlighted in the bulletin to inform parents.

- **Church Governance** can practice the biblical concept that until they (parents) lead at home they do not lead in church. Do not pull parents out of home leadership too early. Let them lead their families.

3. **Establishing Spiritual Traditions**
   Objective: *Create opportunities for parents to train and celebrate spiritual milestones on child's maturation journey.*

As churches have moved away from denominational affiliations, they have left traditions behind. Traditions were critical in the Old Testament to help carry the understanding of our faith from generation to generation. Today, they can provide the strategic plan for the spiritual training of children and engage parents in the process, if used to drive and encourage the spiritual growth process. By establishing traditions that require the parents to "teach" their children and reinforcing through existing youth and adult programming, a church can be successful in transferring the spiritual leadership role to the home.

Pastor Ryan Rush of Bannockburn Church uses the preceding diagram to help illustrate the power to impact and engage families with spiritual milestones. He defines the elements as the following:

Spiritual Breakthroughs occur when three key components come together: discovery of a spiritual truth, a milestone event, and a celebration. Ceremony establishes value!

- **Milestones and events** mark a key change in the seasons of life or let it happen more spontaneously and bring about key decisions in the life of a believer.

- **Spiritual Training** leads to spiritual discovery from God's Word.

- **Ceremonies** are symbols, statements in which fellow believers are invited into the process to drive home the discovery and create a sense of "value" in the mind of the celebrant.

- **Church can use key events to create opportunities for spiritual training**, just as a church uses marriage as a requirement for pre-marital classes, so it can use baby dedication to teach a spiritual parenting plan to equip parents to become intentional. Or, it can use baptism to teach parents the apologetics of the faith, or it can use the transition into college to teach a joint parent-teen Christian Worldview class.

- **Church can use Family "crisis points" to cultivate relationship opportunities, turning them into spiritual breakthroughs**. The top family-related points include marriage, birth of child, transition to an empty nest.

- **Integrate church strategy with home to equip and engage parents.** The goal is always to look at the impact in the home, not the program offerings. So, whatever is offered at church, it must be done with an understanding of a desired impact in the home.

- **Family Spiritual Milestones can become the backbone of church traditions.** If the desire of the Spiritual Milestones is to move a child through the maturation steps, then the church should teach, equip, and celebrate in the church the "catalytic" events so as to motivate parents to engage.

4. Offering Family Worship and Missions
Objective: *Provide real-life faith experience for lasting impact.*

Passion is caught more than taught. Children need to see and experience with their parents true worship and true faith being lived out through mission work. The Church needs to provide those opportunities that bring families together for life-changing impact.

- **Create family ministry programming**, such as family VBS, or family projects, such as "Trunk or Treat" for Halloween.

- **Develop a monthly worship service** to bring "big people to little people church" where both can worship together. One approach is to shut down all activities one week for family worship service so as not to conflict with current offerings. It also gives teachers a break.

- **Provide take-home/bring-back exercises**, such as Awana® uses during the week, but for Sunday school programs.

- **Offer service projects or mission trips for families.** You reach the next generation of parents through experience, compassion, community and story—all of which can be incorporated into a project or a trip.

5. Encouraging Spiritual Leadership
Objective: *Parents lead children through spiritual maturation process, growing personal relationships.*

The goal of any family ministry should be to firmly establish the parents in their God-given roles of being spiritual leaders of their children. The church can create opportunities that provide experiential learning and modeling examples.

- **Place fathers as the spiritual leaders in their homes** by having fathers serve Communion to their families, hold family worship services, or call fathers forward after the services for a three-minute object lesson to be used in the car on the way home to reinforce the message. All place the fathers as the spiritual leaders within their homes.

- **Teach the men how to use God's Word in their spiritual leadership role.** Just as a pastor learns the study methods in seminary, so a father should be equipped to pastor his family. He needs to know about concordances, translations, and research methods.

- **Equip the men with the apologetics of faith and Christian World View.** Dad needs to know how to present and defend the faith against the secular views.

- **Model the plan.** If encouraging Family Night, use object lessons in sermons; if encouraging spiritual milestones, the pastor should take his or her own children through.

Through effective church programming, leveraging the elements of the architecture, a church can enable their families to build a solid foundation of faith that will transcend generations to come! For more information on how to use this architecture, go to **www.HeritageBuilders.com.**

Jim Weidmann is the Executive Director of Heritage Builders and has served as the Sr. VP/COO of Promise Keepers, Vice Chairman of the National Day of Prayer Taskforce, and a cabinet member of Focus on the Family. With his wife of twenty-four years, he has published more than seventeen books on spiritual leadership within the home, including the Family Night Tool Chest *series and* Spiritual Milestones. *Jim is also the voice of the Family Night Guy radio feature heard on more than 2,600 stations nationwide.*

Yours, Mine, and Ours...
a Role for the Church

by Judy Comstock

The Cleavers (Ward and June) and the Nelsons (Ozzie and Harriet) were a weekly part of television entertainment a few decades ago. These two families are sometimes used as examples of how family members related to each other in the 1950's and how families are significantly different today. One of the most noticeable changes in the demographics of families in our churches and communities is the increase in blended families. A blended family is created when a child is brought into a home where one or both of the marriage partners are not the biological parents. Not all blended families are the result of divorce and remarriage. The death of one of the spouses may have preceded the second marriage. It is estimated that at least one-third of all children in the U.S. will be part of a stepfamily before they reach age eighteen.

Newlyweds, without children, use their early marriage years to build on their relationship. Newlyweds with children don't have that luxury. The issues they must immediately face may include stepchildren, ex-partners, child-custody schedules, a child of their own, and the challenge of acclimating to different parenting styles. There is usually more than enough blame to go around in blended families. Guilt from the dissolution of a previous marriage can encroach on positive conversations and actions toward the children from those marriages. There may be jealous reactions when a step-sibling is in the home every other weekend and two weeks in the summer. It is not unusual for children to sense a parent's fear that the children will tear the family apart.

Integrating families is a challenge. More than sixty percent of all second marriages with children will end in divorce. This tragedy only deepens the wounds for the children. It is difficult to blend a family. So, what can church

> It is estimated that at least one-third of all children in the U.S. will be part of a stepfamily before they reach age eighteen.

leaders do to minister to this growing segment of today's family population?

A few years ago, Pastor Laurie Barnes started a Sunday school class in response to the needs of four couples. These couples represented several family configurations:

1. a widow with two children had married a man who had never been married;

2. a man with three children from a previous marriage had married a woman who also had been married before, but had no children;

3. both husband and wife had been married before and had children from the previous marriages;

4. a man with children from a previous marriage had married a woman who had not been married before.

While the dynamics of the four couples differed, they had enough in common to realize that at least one hour together each week at church was important. The class grew to ten couples. Their mutual focus resulted in empathy for each other, meaningful prayer time, and insights that strengthened their families.

Thankfully, children's ministry leaders are recognizing the value of partnering with parents. We can facilitate opportunities for these struggling families to blend and grow stronger.

Here are some suggestions for leaders who want to make a difference:

- Read books and seek insight from a counselor or therapist to increase your understanding of the dynamics of these families.

- Pray that God will give you compelling compassion and a desire to respond with plans that meet some of the needs.

- Eliminate judgment in your response as you reach out and minister to blended families. Strive to reflect the love of Christ. I believe that the children will read your intentions, perhaps more insightfully than any other member of the family.

- Host a think tank for blended families at your church to discover what the needs are and to determine what your church can do for and with these family members. You will want to customize the program and strategies at your church. That's why taking time for the think tank is vital.

- Enlist members of blended families to start a Bible study or Sunday school class.

- Plan opportunities for the families to play together at a retreat or fun events (monthly, quarterly, or annually). Stimulate the development of new family traditions and rituals.

- Create a newsletter or website where pertinent information and updates can be posted. Make family enrichment magazines available, such as *HomeLife* and *ParentLife* from LifeWay.

- Offer conflict resolution and discipline classes.

- Work with a counselor who has a support group in the community or may be willing to host a support group at your church. If your church is smaller, partner with one to two other churches in your area to host a support group and the presence of a qualified facilitator.

- When mailing or e-mailing notices of upcoming activities, include all parents, unless asked to do otherwise.

- Train your volunteers. Insecure children can learn to trust and bond with people who treat them with consistent respect and attention. Children of all ages respond to praise and encouragement.

- Kids often feel unimportant or invisible when decisions are made in a blended family. Recognize their role and value in the programs at the church. Children like to feel appreciated and able to contribute.

- Evaluate your program schedule and rules to see if adjustments need to be made so that children in all families can routinely be involved in meaningful church programming.

John and Jane Smith are among the growing numbers of American blended families. Their experiences have been the catalyst for helping church leaders understand the value of facilitating programs that welcome, instead of block, participation by members of every family. Here are some of the experiences their family had that created challenges for being fully involved at church:

> Kids often feel unimportant or invisible when decisions are made in a blended family. Recognize their role and value in the programs at the church. Children like to feel appreciated and able to contribute.

The Brady Bunch may have been a funny television show, but we must remember that their lines were scripted. Most blended families don't acclimate as easily or quickly as these six children and their parents did.

1. Two of their children could see their natural dad only on the first, third, and fifth weekends, since he lived in another town seventy miles away. Church activities on Sunday night created the dilemma that required choosing between missing the church activity and missing their dad on the alternate weekends when they were scheduled to be with him.

2. The rule that allowed only two absences in the children's choir made it impossible for their kids to participate and created a negative impact on helping them feel that they were part of the church family.

3. They determined that Wednesday night programming was reserved for the in-town parents.

4. At their church, no classes, fellowship, or care groups were offered to address non-traditional family issues.

5. Camps and summer events were offered the first six weeks of summer, when their children—and most of the other children in blended families—had summer visitation. This automatically excluded them from the church's camps and early summer activities.

6. There was no divorce recovery program at their church to help children deal with their pain, anger, upset, and abandonment issues. They were expected to "handle it."

Thankfully, several churches are incorporating classes and changes that are impacting blended families in a positive way, such as:

- Southeast Christian Church in Louisville, Kentucky, provides classes such as "Lifeline of Hope for Blended Families," an ongoing support group that families can join at any time.

- Richland Hills Church of Christ in Richland Hills, Texas, has a "Blended 101" class and periodically offers "Blended Families Events."

- Southeast Christian Church in Parker, Colorado, schedules "DivorceCare4Kids" for children ages 5 to 12 whose parents are going through the DivorceCare class.

- Calvary Church in Souderton, Pennsylvania, includes Hope Ministries for blended families in their community.

- Church of the Resurrection in Leawood, Kansas, offers family counseling.

The Brady Bunch may have been a funny television show, but we must remember that their lines were scripted. Most blended families don't acclimate as easily or quickly as these six children and their parents did. Some families can go through the blending process in as little as four years. Many families take about seven years for trust and the dance of family relationships to be choreographed.

Eliminate judgment in your response as you reach out and minister to blended families. Strive to reflect the love of Christ.

You and I can help improve the playing field by creating an environment that welcomes each family into our churches. By providing programs that address the struggles these families face, we validate the love of Christ for each child. We can change the perception and make decisions that help ensure inclusion and recognition. Healing can take place for these children and their parents.

Helpful Resources

Curriculum

- *Confident Kids* is a Christian Support Group Program that offers help for hurting kids and struggling parents. The curriculum includes "All My Feelings Are OK," in which children and parents learn how to name their feelings and express them in healthy and appropriate ways. They learn how to practice a variety of family living skills in "There Are No Perfect Families." Children and parents learn to deal with the significant changes in their lives by grieving the losses in "Nothing Stays the Same Forever."

- *Celebration Station Kit* from Group Publishing offers a 52-week program that mirrors the Celebrate Recovery teaching schedule. While the adults explore topics that bring healing and wholeness, their kids are discovering the same truths in age-appropriate ways.

- *Hope No Matter What* by Kim Hill is an interactive 31-day devotional that will help parents guide their children through the fallout of divorce. This book allows readers to process their feelings, express their fears, and focus on God's faithfulness in spite of their sadness and disappointment. It opens the door to meaningful conversations that calm fears and dispel emotional confusion. This Gospel Light resource includes song lyrics, a devotion, Scripture, and a daily prayer with a directed activity for parent-child interaction.

Books for Your Library

- *Does Your Church Connect With Blended Families?*, by Shane Stutzman

- *Can Step-families Be Done Right?*, by Joann and Seth Webster

- *Living in a Step-Family Without Getting Stepped On*, by Kevin Leman

---

Judy Comstock has years of church staff experience, primarily as Director of Children's Ministry. She has a master of arts in Education Leadership and is the author of The Children's Ministry Guidebook, *published by Abingdon Press. After years of serving on the INCM Board of Directors, the Board asked her to become the Executive Director for the ministry.*

> By providing programs that address the struggles these families face, we validate the love of Christ for each child. We can change the perception and make decisions that help ensure inclusion and recognition. Healing can take place for these children and their parents.

Global

Children, you show love for others by truly helping them, and not merely by talking about it.

1 John 3:18, CEV

Think Globally, Act Locally…

by Pam Burton

Have you heard the phrase "Think Globally, Act Locally?" You may think that we are talking about environmental issues. Instead, I would like to propose that we use this for community and global outreach (mission) opportunities for your children's and family ministry.

- How are you involving your kids and families in meaningful mission projects?

- How are you teaching children to be caring and compassionate?

- Do you support a missionary with Sunday school offerings?

- Are local service projects included in your plans?

- Are you reaching another country with the gospel?

I talked to children's and family leaders throughout the country to find out what they are doing. Some churches offer a different project each month of the year. Take a look at their responses!

We organized a **Family Mission Trip** in which the kids are the missionaries and the parents/guardians are there to support and guide them along the way. Learn about **Family Mission Trips** at the website: **www.namb.com** Go to POPULAR LINKS. Search for Mission Education; then search for Families.
Our goal for **Family Mission Trip** is to help parents lead by example as kids learn how to do missions.

Chad Smith, Director of Preschool
Hermitage Baptist Church in Hermitage, TN

Don't let anyone look down on you because you are young, but set an example for the believers in speech, in life, in love, in faith, and in purity.
1 Timothy 4:12 (NIV)

This Scripture is the basis for our **Kids In Motion** program. The program was designed to encourage our children to learn four key concepts (serve, pray, love, and teach) by putting compassion into action. Through this program, we have connected with children around the world. Some of the projects include: Fleece blankets for Ecuador (people from other states heard about this and contributed); Salvation bracelets for Kwambekenya Africa; Christmas angels for Kwambekenya Africa; God's Eyes (Crosses for Kenya); Welcome Baby Kits for Hope Center (local mission); Bookmarks for Cobb County Older Adult Enrichment Program; Christmas Cards for Cobb County Older Adult Enrichment Program; Letters for children in India; Sandwiches packed and bags decorated; and Greeting Cards for Soldiers.

A six-week **World Missions Study** with our elementary children on Wednesday nights ended with a churchwide **Global Mission's Impact Dinner**. Adults attended because of the interest their children had expressed. God blessed us with a pastor from Africa, and a missionary from Romania shared stories with our children.

We take photographs (with parental permission) of the children making the mission projects and send them to the children receiving the items. We have been sent photographs of the children receiving the items. The photos illustrate the exchange of joy. The children see that there is no physical boundary, language barrier, or living condition that can separate them from the body of Christ all over God's world!

Think Globally, Act Locally...

We support these three organizations with the projects we make:

410 Bridge — Their vision is to provide the people of American churches, communities, and families a bridge to a nation in need. It is a way to answer the call to serve, to give and to make a difference in God's kingdom. **www.410bridge.org**

Servants in Faith and Technology (SIFAT) — This is a Christian, nonprofit organization that provides training in self-help programs for a needy world. **www.sifat.org**

International Leadership Institute (ILI) — accelerates the spread of the Gospel around the world by training and mobilizing leaders of leaders to reach their nations with the Gospel of Jesus Christ. **www.iliteam.org**

Dianne Hylton, Director of Children's Education
Susan Preece, Children's Ministry & Web Ministry
Sherri Juliani, Elementary Coordinator
Mt. Bethel UMC in Marietta, GA

I have been part of a **Samaritan's Purse Operation Shoebox** mission project. **(www.samaritan.org)** Our mission committee adopted this in the early fall as a churchwide project. **Samaritan's Purse** catalog of gifts kids can give includes: blanket $6.00, sports gear $8.00, Jesus loves me lamb $4.00, Bible lessons for children $10.00, and a week's worth of milk $4.00.

During Vacation Bible School we held a school supply drive. Rather than collecting money (offering) during our VBS, we asked kids and parents to bring school supplies that we could donate to the **"Stuff the Bus" School Supply Drive** in our city. We donated the supplies to the elementary school that served our area.

During the Awana year, we encourage the children to donate to a missionary whom we select at the beginning of the year. The missionary for the year changes from year to year, which allows church members to nominate a missionary. We focused primarily on three mission projects:

1. Food Bank. The church is in a small town. All of the children in our church attend the same two schools. We have 2 to 3 food drives and donate the food to a local mission agency in the community during the holidays. I wrote a study on the Ten Commandments. The study included weekly family activities. When discussing the commandment "You shall not steal," our family activity was to do the opposite of stealing — to give. We asked the children to bring food items to donate to the food bank.

2. Sock Drive. During Christmas, we display a giant stocking and fill it with socks. We donated the socks to the county women and children's shelter.

3. Rice Bowls. I heard about Rice Bowls at the CPC '09. When we studied the Commandment "You shall not murder," we practiced the opposite. Rather than take a life, we gave so that others can live. The children continued to bring *rice bowls* well after the project ended. This ministry provides food for the body and spirit of orphans in the name of Christ throughout the world. You collect money in specially designed *rice bowls*. The money is used to purchase food for orphans. **www.ricebowls.org/**

Margaret Carey, Children's Minister
Caddo Mills, TX

Our church has been sending families to the **Pine Ridge Indian Reservation** for thirteen years. Our family has made this South Dakota trip a priority for our summer vacation. The primary focus of this trip is to connect with the people who live on the Reservation and try to build relationships, as well as share Christ with them. This annual one-week trip takes place in the summer during the school summer break. Our team offers a bicycle ministry to the children, a basketball camp, and VBS. It is a busy week! Planning this trip is a lot of work, but the rewards are many. It's an inexpensive way to reach out to a community in need and get the entire family involved.

Jill Umemura
Colorado Community Church in Aurora, CO

Here are ideas that Johanna Townsend, **For Kids Only, Inc.** suggested:

www.worldrelief.org
Select from a *Catalog of Hope* and purchase a brood of chickens for $35.00, water for $40.00, and seeds and a hoe for $24.00.

www.worldconcern.org
Their *Global Gift Guide*™ includes: a year of learning for $50.00, break the silence for hearing-impaired children for $60.00, and provide a teacher's salary for one month for $150.00.

www.serrv.org
This nonprofit organization is striving to eradicate poverty by providing opportunities and support to artisans and farmers worldwide.

www.worldvision.org
A gift catalog can be used to select life-changing gifts, such as 2 chickens for $25.00, hope for sexually exploited girls for $35.00, share of a deep well for $100.00, and backpack and school supplies for $35.00.

www.mcc.org
School kits are given to refugee children. Donate money, fill a bag; or you can even sew the bag yourself and fill it.

www.freewheelchairmission.org
Donations help provide wheelchairs for the impoverished disabled in developing nations. One wheelchair costs $59.20.

www.heifer.org
You can help children and families around the world receive training and animal gifts that allows them to become self-reliant. The animals that are provided include, flock of chickens for $20.00, trio of rabbits for $60.00, honeybees for $30.00, and trees for $60.00.

www.simpleliving.org
This ministry helps families of faith think of alternatives to excessive consumerism and will help you create meaningful celebrations.

Still need more ideas? These are from CPC:

Compassion International
Sponsor a child through **Compassion International**. When you sponsor a child, you are linked with one particular child who will know who his or her sponsor is, write to you, and treasure the thought that you care. You can sponsor a child with one of your Sunday school classes or your entire children's ministry. **www.compassion.com**

Hoops of Hope
Hoops of Hope is the world's largest free-throw marathon. Similar to a walk-a-thon, participants raise awareness and funds for children who have been orphaned by HIV / AIDS by shooting free throws. One hundred per cent of all funds raised through our free-throw marathons go directly to care for orphan children in highly affected areas. **Hoops for Hope** was founded five years ago by Austin Gutwein, who was nine years old at the time! **www.hoopsofhope.org**

Group Workcamps
Group Workcamps strives to grow the faith of young people through unforgettable Christian service opportunities. Many needy individuals and communities benefit from the projects, but the focus is always on the students. **Group Workcamps** are located throughout the United States. You can take a group of young people ages twelve and above to serve during the week-long camp. **www.groupworkcamps.com**

Joni and Friends
Joni and Friends is dedicated to extending the love and message of Christ to people who are affected by disability. The extension of love is to the disabled person, a family member, or a friend of the disabled individual. The objective is to meet the physical, emotional, and spiritual needs of this group of people in practical ways. **Wheels for the World** is **Joni and Friends'** flagship wheelchair outreach program. On the **Joni and Friends** website you can discover how to donate a wheelchair, crutches, canes, walkers or other rehabilitation equipment through a volunteer organization called **Chair Corps.** **www.joniandfriends.org**

iGive.com

Do the kids in your ministry like to shop or search on the internet? Get them to shop for a purpose! **iGive.com** is a free and simple way for you and the children in your ministry to support mission causes. How? You select your favorite cause, or add a new one. Then, register with **iGive.com** and shop at brand name online stores through the **iGive Mall**. A portion of each purchase is donated to your cause. **Handi Vangelism Ministries International**, as resource provider for Children's Pastors' Conference, uses iGive for their ministry. **www.igive.com | www.hvmi.org**

Kids With Purpose

This is an action-based outreach program that engages children in acts of Christian service in their local community. It is a program that allows you to actively involve children in community service. The aim is to make outreach and service to others an everyday and lifelong activity. **Kids With Purpose** has done the leg work for you by developing quality program materials that you can implement at your location. **www.kidswithpurpose.org**

Mission Possible Kids

Kids want to change the world. This non-profit organization empowers children to change the world by helping others. **Mission Possible Kids** has them collecting goods for food banks, cooking meals for homeless shelters, making gifts for hospitalized children, raising money to end world hunger, and so much more. Each MPKids agent can touch as many as one hundred lives in one school year. They offer detailed mission plans, which you can use as is, adapt or use as a guide to create your own. **www.mpkids.org**

Helpful books on this topic include:

Teaching Kids to Care and Share, by Jolene L. Roehlkepartain.

Beyond Leaf Raking: Learning to Serve/Serving to Learn, by Peter L. Benson and Eugene C. Roehlkepartain.

160 Ways to Help the World: Community Service Projects for Young People, by Linda Leeb Duper.

Teaching Your Kids to Care: How to Discover and Develop the Spirit of Charity in Your Children, by Deborah Spaide.

Just Family Nights, Susan Vogt, Editor.

Trevor's Place: The Story of the Boy Who Brings Hope to the Homeless, by Frank and Janet Ferrell.

All Kids Are Our Kids: What Communities Must Do to Raise Caring and Responsible Children and Adolescents, by Peter L. Benson.

A Kids' Guide to Hunger & Homelessness: How to Take Action!, by Cathryn Berger Kaye, M.A.

Pam is the Communications Director at INCM. For the past 11 years, she was a Communications Specialist at Colorado Community Church in Denver, CO. Before that, Pam worked at Focus on the Family in the broadcast division and at the United States Olympic Committee media division. On most weekends you can find her hiking, mountain biking, or camping in the beautiful mountains of Colorado.

Hung Used to Go to Bed Hungry

by Jodi L. Cataldo

Are the children of your local church aware that they live in a global village? Children's Pastors and Christian Educators have the awesome opportunity of connecting children in mission by providing mission awareness activities. This can range from finding ways to capture life in another area of the world through stories, videos, food tastings, dramas, songs, and even games from that particular culture, to actually having the children participate in "works of mercy."

Materials, such as **The United Methodist Children's Fund for Christian Mission** packet provides leaders with materials that can be used to educate children through stories, background information, and mission awareness activities. This particular tool includes a focus on four different mission projects every year, two international and two national. The packet gives ways children can learn, interact, and experience mission in a different context, even in an intergenerational setting.

The following two stories are but brief examples of what is possible when children partner with children in God's mission to the world. When children learn at a young age what it means to participate in mission, they are able to look beyond themselves and not only see a world as God intends it, but pursue such a world—a world where all people can know and experience God's love, peace, and justice for all.

Hung's Story

Hung used to go to bed hungry. He didn't have much—a grass mat for a bed and just one set of clothing. Hung is eleven years old and lives on the outskirts of Vientiane, Laos. Hung's life changed when missionaries came to his village and taught the people how to grow rice and mushrooms, which would then be sold to provide income for his family, his church, and his community. Through donations, the missionaries are able to provide seeds for these families to begin their own rice and mushroom projects. Families are finding new ways to become self-sustaining which brings them one step further from a life of poverty.

Hung also began to attend school for the very first time in his life. Before classes started, he went to visit the school where he touched a school desk in wonder and practiced holding a pencil in his hand. He was very nervous about going to school but also so excited to have the chance to learn. Through the **United Methodist Children's Fund for Christian Mission**—children in mission together with other children—a Sunday school class learned about Hung and were led to reflect on all they have access to and to compare that with what was denied Hung in his young life. The children were able to "interact" with Hung, learn about his life, and to celebrate the joy of Hung finally being able to go to school.

Children can be empowered to learn through a variety of activities:

- Plant a community garden and have the children act as caretakers of the garden. When it is time to harvest, share the produce with the local community cupboard or food kitchen. Plan a time when the children can actually be a part of the distribution or serving of food.

- Place a display board with an empty field on one side and mushrooms on the other. Give the children the opportunity to "buy" mushrooms for a dollar that can then be placed in the empty field. When the established time for "buying" mushrooms is completed, announce at church as to how many mushrooms the children were able to grow in Laos.

- Fill a "virtual backpack." Have the children "purchase" all the items (these can be pictures of items glued onto tagboard) necessary for a child in Laos to go to school; and as they "purchase" them, move the items "into" the "virtual backpack."

- Invite members of the Laotian community in your area to come share their culture, food, music, and games with the children of your church. Eating "sticky" rice on a mat on the floor can be a wonderful sharing experience in itself.

Tameca's Story

"Dream Chasing" is now a big part of Tameca''s life. Tameca is in the eighth grade and dreams for a better life apart from the inner city poverty she experiences in Milwaukee, Wisconsin. Because of this burning desire within her, she was chosen to be a part of the "Dream Chasing" program at Solomon Community Temple UMC. Over the next two years, she will learn new computer skills, learn how to research college possibilities, explore career options, and discover how she can fulfill her dreams. Tameca uses her babysitting money to be able to take part in "Dream Chasing." When the program is completed, she will have the opportunity to visit different colleges to help her as she steps out and begins pursuing those dreams.

The neighborhood in which Tameca lives is highly transient. Many children are raised by their grandparents or foster families because of issues within the immediate family such as drug usage, mental instability, or other social issues.

The United Methodist Children's Fund for Christian Mission provides concrete ways in which children can be in mission with other children through such programs as "Dream Chasing," as well as other community programs that help Tameca and other children realize their dreams. Some examples include:

- Look through newspapers for stories that involve children. Make a collage of these stories and pictures and talk about different experiences children might have. Pray specifically for these children.

- Collect food items that could be used in the ministry of your church.

- Talk about dreams and have the children create symbols for their own personal dreams. Have them take their symbols home and use them, not only to help guide them to their own dream, but to remember to pray for the dreams of another child.

The United Methodist Children's Fund packets are available online at **www.gbod.org/children** or by contacting Global Ministries at 212-870-3615.

Jodi L. Cataldo, is Executive Secretary for Emerging Churches' Resources at the General Board of Global Ministries and is responsible for facilitating the development of contextual Christian education materials in new churches throughout the world. Ms. Cataldo is the Global Ministries staff person who works together with the General Board of Discipleship in the coordination of projects for The United Methodist Children's Fund for Christian Mission. (Stories adapted from the 2009 Children's Fund for Christian Mission packet.)

> When children learn at a young age what it means to participate in mission, they are able to look beyond themselves and not only see a world as God intends it, but pursue such a world—a world where all people can know and experience God's love, peace, and justice for all.

Models

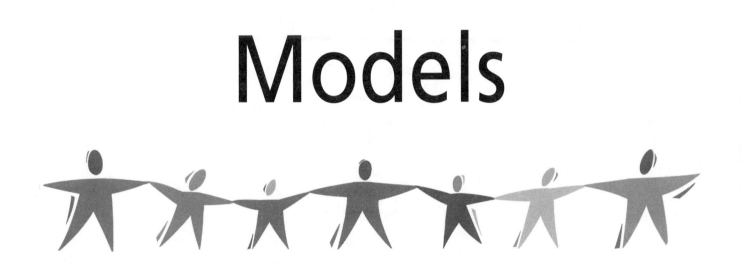

Make me to know your ways, O Lord; teach me your paths.

Psalm 25:4

The Workshop Rotation Model and How to Get Started

by Pamela Riedy and Mary Jane Huber

The **Workshop Rotation Model (WRM)** is an innovative approach to Sunday school programs for all ages. It incorporates solid faith formation practices with multiple intelligence theory in such a way that the programs are not only transformed but transformative.

Imagine that it is Sunday morning and the focus for the month is the Lord's Prayer. The first-graders are in the *Moved by the Spirit* workshop experiencing how our physical attitudes become part of our prayer life. The second-graders are in the *Bedouin Encampment* creating a sacred space for prayer and meditation. The third-graders are in *Bible Improv* creating contemporary skits to answer the question: "What is God's will?" The fourth-graders are in *Eat Your Way Through the Bible* learning about the food pyramid and how God provides our daily bread. The fifth-graders are in *Puppetry*, creating puppet shows that resolve temptation issues. The sixth-graders are in the *Video Live* making a film of a dialogue between God and a prayer group. Notice how the children have the opportunity to experience the story in several settings. In this exciting model, the seeds of faith are planted for a lifelong journey of faith.

In this model, children move from one workshop to another over several weeks, learning about one Bible or faith story. Teachers stay in one workshop, teaching the same lesson to a different group each week. The **WRM** is educationally founded on the concept of multiple intelligences. Howard Gardner's work revealed that people have eight different intelligences, some stronger than others. They include: verbal-linguistic, mathematical-logical, spatial, musical-rhythmic, kinesthetic, interpersonal, intrapersonal, and naturalist.

A WRM program appeals to all of the intelligences, opening many doors for a lesson to enter the hearts of the participants. To teach through only one intelligence, i.e., verbal-linguistic (the use of words), limits the education of those who learn primarily through movement or visuals or music or nature. God gave everyone gifts to use so that humankind could become the body of Christ, the incarnate presence of God on earth.

The WRM is talent-based. The opportunity to teach is for a limited time and is focused on one workshop. Invitations to teach are made by approaching people based on their talents, hobbies, or spiritual gifts and matching them to a specific workshop. For example, the activity in a Christmas storytelling workshop is to make drip candles; ponder who in the congregation makes candles and invite him or her to teach. In the cooking workshop for *Noah*, the class makes gingerbread arks; who in the congregation makes gingerbread houses? The science workshop for the *Garden of Eden* gets into organic gardening; who is an organic gardener?

Shepherds are an integral part of a WRM program. They provide continuity and establish relationships as they stay with one group over time. They know the participants by name, know which workshop to attend, and provide classroom assistance. At the end of each workshop, they weave together the information the class is learning from workshop to workshop. Shepherds can perform administrative tasks, such as taking attendance and communicating with families, but the relational aspect of the shepherds cannot be underestimated.

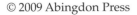

Rooms can be transformed into learning environments that reinforce the stories of faith. No longer are the rooms generic with a single picture of Jesus on the wall. They become *Mary and Martha's Bed and Breakfast*, an art studio, a movie theater, or a television station. The very spaces speak of the stories of faith, strengthening the power of the lessons. A word of caution: Fantastic rooms do not make a fantastic program. Transformative, inspiring, and engaging lessons are the key to a successful program when measured by the opportunity to change the hearts of the participants.

How to Get Started: It's a Team Effort

Step One: Hold an Initial Gathering
Invite a small group of people who are visionaries, parents, veteran Sunday school teachers, a minister, and other interested volunteers.

❑ Present the basic concept of the **Workshop Rotation Model**.

❑ Create a planning committee. This must be a program that has congregational support; otherwise it will become a one-person show, which innately denies the program of a wide range of talent.

❑ Brainstorm about the people in the congregation who can assist in transitioning to the model.

Step Two: Vision-Casting
The Planning Committee sets the vision for the program, determines its scope, and extends an invitation to the congregation to get involved.

❑ Create a mission statement about the purpose of the program.

❑ Determine the scope of your program
  - How many workshops will you need?
  - What age groups will participate?
  - How many classes for each age group already exist?
  - Are there enough children for each age group to have its own class or will some groups be merged?

> **G**od gave everyone gifts to use so that humankind could become the body of Christ, the incarnate presence of God on earth.

  - How many weeks will the average rotation run?
  - In a small church, could this function as a one-room Sunday school?

❑ What rooms will you use?
  - Are you going to decorate any classrooms or hallways?
  - Do you want permanent spaces where you always run the same workshops, perhaps art, cooking, storytelling, and drama?
  - Do you want flexible spaces where drama, puppetry, and make-your-own video share a room; geography and missions outreach share a room; art and science share a room; movement and music share a room? This facilitates more creativity in terms of using the talents of the congregation.
  - Is there going to be a theme for the entire program? (Alamo Heights United Methodist Church is built on a quarry. They fashioned their Christian Education wing to look like stone and named it *God's Quarry: Where Kids R.O.C.K. (Rely on Christian Knowledge).*
  - Estimate the work to be done, labor, cost, and timetable.

Step Three: Marketing the Program to the Congregation
❑ Who needs to get on board?
  - Board of Trustees or Executive Council
  - Children's Board
  - Ministers
  - Small group ministries
  - Women's and men's groups

☐ How, when, and where can a presentation be made to the whole congregation?
- Explain the Workshop Rotation Model.
- Offer a walk-through of one unit where participants can get a five-minute experience in four workshops focused on one story.

☐ Build teams
- Space design
- Curriculum
- Workshop coordinators
- Teachers and shepherds

Step Four: Create Ownership With Teamwork

The Planning Committee communicates its vision to each team. Now the teams get to work. The role of Christian Education director should be a cheerleader, delegating the details of the program to teams. Empower, encourage, and provide resources and give credit to those who make it work.

☐ Space Design Team
- Who will act as the general contractor overseeing the project as a whole?
- Identify the projects, who can do them and a timetable
  + Muralists
  + Scavengers of props
  + Donors of goods
  + Sewers of biblical costumes
  + Collectors of art supplies
- Are there small groups, families, couples, talented teens, Eagle Scouts who would adopt a room and transform it into something that would capture the

imagination of the children in the workshop?

☐ Curriculum Design Team
- Decide whether to purchase curriculum or write your own. There are several companies, both denominational and ecumenical, that offer a solid scope and sequence and a diverse choice of lessons at a reasonable price.
- If you choose to write your own, who will do that?
  Director of Christian Education: Is writing within the current job description?
  Writing Team: Are there enough dedicated and qualified people to write a full year of curriculum with the lead time that is needed for the teachers?
  Clergy: Will they provide oversight for biblical integrity?

☐ Coordination Team
It is very important that a team run the program rather than just one person.
- Option A: One coordinator per workshop
  Invite the teachers for the rotation.
  Communicate with the shepherds.
  Get the supplies.
  Prepare the room.
- Option B: Task coordinators
  One person invites all teachers.
  One person gets all supplies.
  One person coordinates the shepherds.

Step Five: Invitation to Get Involved

Let go of "recruitment" and start extending "invitations." Harness the talents within the congregation to pass the faith on to the next generation. Every conversation becomes an invitation.

> Transformative, inspiring, and engaging lessons are the key to a successful program when measured by the opportunity to change the hearts of the participants.

In 1997, Pam Riedy and Mary Jane Huber started Cornerstones Publishing, the premier publisher of Workshop Rotation Model *curriculum. Pam has a Masters degree in Education. Mary Jane has a Bachelor's degree in Christian Education and is currently in seminary. They both have over twenty-five years of experience in Christian Education and are nationally known speakers about the Workshop Rotation Model. Visit them at* **www.cstones.com**.

Rotation Samples

#1: Storytelling	**#4: Kinesthetics or Kitchen**
#2: Drama, Video, Puppetry	**#5: Geography or Faith Today**
#3: Art	**#6: Special Talent**

3 Classes

	Workshop 1	Workshop 2	Workshop 3	Workshop 4
Week 1	1st/2nd	3rd/4th	5th/6th	xxx
Week 2	xxx	1st/2nd	3rd/4th	5th/6th
Week 3	5th/6th	xxx	1st/2nd	3rd/4th
Week 4	3rd/4th	5th/6th	xxx	1st/2nd

Teachers only teach 3 of the 4 weeks; all students participate in all workshops
(full experience even for small church).

4 Classes

	Workshop 1	Workshop 2	Workshop 3	Workshop 4
Week 1	1st	2nd	3rd/4th	5th/6th
Week 2	2nd	3rd/4th	5th/6th	1st
Week 3	3rd/4th	5th/6th	1st	2nd
Week 4	5th/6th	1st	2nd	3rd/4th

All teachers and all students participate in all workshops.

6 Classes

	Wkshop 1	Wkshop 2	Wkshop 3	Wkshop 4	Wkshop 5	Wkshop 6
Week 1	3rd	4th	5th	6th	1st	2nd
Week 2	6th	1st	2nd	3rd	4th	5th
Week 3	5th	6th	1st	2nd	3rd	4th
Week 4	4th	5th	6th	1st	2nd	3rd

Some grades will miss some workshops. The younger grades can be placed in the workshops for early readers; the older grades can be placed in more challenging workshops.

What I've Learned About Rotational Learning

by Daphna Flegal

In 1990, Rev. Neil MacQueen and Melissa Armstrong-Hansche, staff members at the Barrington Presbyterian Church in Barrington, Illinois, created what became known as the Workshop Rotation Model for Sunday school. Other Christian educators in the area soon became involved in using and further developing the model. In a rotational learning setting, the same Bible story or theme is taught for several weeks. Each week learners rotate to a different station. The story or theme remains the same, but the children encounter it in different ways in each station. The model soon spread beyond the Chicago area to churches across the country.

We have much to learn from one another, and we can offer valuable support to each other. Check with your denominational office to learn who else in your area is using rotational learning. Check also to learn if a rotational network group exists nearby. Interestingly, even churches with varying theologies can help one another with aspects of this model. For example, the content of your stations may be very different, but how to invite volunteers or how to decorate a room may be areas where you can have fruitful conversation with one another. Here are some things I have learned from churches across the United States that will help you move to rotational learning, if that is the direction you are going.

Size Doesn't Matter

Rotational Learning has been used successfully in churches of varying sizes. Some churches have the space and resources for elaborate setup, while others share space or have limited options for decorating. For example, one church created a theater for the Video Station. This church has theater seats, movie posters on the walls, and a theater-style popcorn machine. Another church created a living-room environment, with a TV and DVD player, couches and comfortable chairs, an end table, and a lamp.

A Rose By Any Other Name...

Many churches rename their Sunday school programs and then name their stations to fit the theme. Always look at your church's mission statement before choosing a name. For example, if your mission statement is to help persons be faithful disciples throughout their lifetime, you might use the name "Journey of Faith." The stations could include Expression of Faith (Art), Windows to Faith (Computer), Faith in Action (Storytelling), and Faith Theater (Movies).

Show Me the Money

How does the cost of rotational learning compare with using traditional curriculum? Curriculum costs will often be less, but you will need a variety of resources and supplies for each unit, such as groceries or computer software. Many churches have found that their spending is about the same with rotational learning as it was with other types of curriculum.

Look at alternative ways to provide equipment and supplies. Publish a "Wish List" in the bulletin or newsletter and post it on a large display board. Ask the congregation to bring things from their attics, their garages, and their homes.

You Need a License?

Most movies are licensed for home use. If you plan to show movies, you will need an umbrella license for your church. For a fee each year, this license gives you permission to legally show the videos produced by the cooperating distributors in your setting. For more information or to request a licensing application, contact:

Motion Picture Licensing Corporation
5455 Centinela Avenue
Los Angeles, CA 90066-6970
800-462-8855
www.mplc.com

Inviting Staff

Rotational learning will change the way you invite people to teach. The nature of the stations will increase the number of potential teachers. For example, if you plan to build an ark (What's a cubit?), you may be looking for a carpenter. As you approach people, many may not be willing to commit to teaching for a whole year, but they may be willing to spend several weeks in Sunday school teaching in an area where their gifts lie.

Staffing Tips

- Staffing is an ongoing process with rotational learning. When your staff is in place for one rotation, it is time to invite leaders for the next one! Some people may teach for several rotations during the year; others will not.

- Because children will rotate to a new station each week, they will not have the opportunity to develop a relationship with one teacher over the course of the year. Since such relationships are important, you will want to use "shepherds." It is the shepherd who knows the children by name and has the most opportunities to talk with the children, to hear their questions, and to know what is going on in their lives.

- Provide job descriptions for teachers and for shepherds to help them know exactly what they are to do. (See pages 123–124.)

- As you start using rotational learning, be sensitive to those who have faithfully taught in the past, and find ways to honor their contributions.

It Takes Two

Your staff needs two kinds of training. First, both teachers and shepherds need opportunities to become comfortable with rotational learning and Multiple Intelligences Theory.

Second, leaders need opportunities to become familiar with the Bible story or theme of each unit and with the activities they will be leading to help children explore that Scripture. Some churches have found that with rotational learning, it is helpful to have a workshop a week or two before the beginning of each new unit. One church invites teachers to meet the day a new unit begins. While the children view a movie for the unit with the shepherds, the teachers meet in another area. The other stations used in that unit begin the next week. Other churches send a Bible study for the unit to teachers by e-mail.

Go to the Blue Door

In the rotational learning model, children will rotate to a new station each week, rather than going to the same room every Sunday. If you have a large group opening, you will end the time by sending children to the appropriate places. If you do not have a large group time, you will need a mechanism for getting the children to their stations. Here are some ideas that have worked for other churches.

- Paint the doorway to each classroom a different color. In the entryway, set up a large chart with large squares the color of each doorway. Attach a piece of hook-and-loop tape to the middle of each square. Prepare small squares with the name or grade level of each class (K, 1, 2, 3, 4, 5, 6 or Younger Children and Older Children and so forth). Attach the other side of the hook-and-loop tape to the back of each of these squares. Each week put the grade-level square on the colored square that indicates the station where that grade will be meeting.

- Have flags or signs for each group of children. The shepherd can meet them at the sign and accompany them to class.

Look Backward to Move Forward

Take the time to evaluate after each unit. Use the evaluation form on page 125 to guide your staff or committee through an evaluation process.

adapted from *PowerXpress!® Director's Manual* © 2002, 2006, 2009 Abingdon Press

Daphna Flegal is the Lead Editor for the Children's Department at The United Methodist Publishing House. Daphna led the development team for PowerXpress!®, a curriculum designed for rotational learning.
www.PowerXpress.com

Job Description— Shepherd

Your role as a shepherd is to build relationships with the children in the class to which you are assigned and to nurture each child so she or he will experience the love of Christ through you. You will also assist teachers in the classroom.

To fulfill your responsibilities, you will

- Participate in the staff meeting before the unit begins.

- Be present for each learning session.

- Before the children arrive, become familiar with the Bible story and objectives.

- Introduce yourself to the teacher with whom you will be working. Ask about specific ways you can help with any of the activities.

- Greet the children as they arrive. Meet their parents, if possible. Make sure you know where to reach a parent in case of an emergency. Learn about any special needs, including information about allergies.

- Focus on the children. Learn their names; get acquainted with them.

- Help the children in your group get to know one another and work together.

- Be in conversation with children in order to build relationships with them and to provide consistency from session to session.

- Assist the teacher with activities as needed.

- Watch for visitors. Help them meet the other children and get involved in the activities.

- Watch for children who need assistance.

- Watch for children who are off-track. Help them focus.

- Attend training meetings as requested.

- Arrange for a substitute anytime you cannot be present.

- Pray for the children who will be in your care.

PowerXpress!® *Director's Manual:* Inviting Staff
Permission granted to photocopy for local church use. © 2002, 2006, 2009 Abingdon Press.

Job Description— Teacher

Your role as a teacher in a rotational learning unit is to plan and implement weekly lessons that will provide each child with an opportunity to learn and grow in faith and to nurture each child so that she or he will experience the love of Christ through you.

To fulfill your responsibilities, you will

- Participate in the staff meeting before the unit begins.

- Read and study the Bible story or theme that will be the focus of the unit you are teaching.

- Prepare by reading the introductory materials for the unit.

- Read the plan for your station or workshop. Select the options that you will use for each group of children you will teach.

- Notify the shepherds of any specific activities with which you will want them to be prepared to assist you.

- Recruit additional adult help if you choose options that will require more adult supervision than you and the shepherd can handle alone.

- Verify that the required supplies and resources will be available.

- Prepare any samples or room decorations that will be needed in your station.

- Attend training sessions as requested.

- Pray for the children who will be in your care.

- Teach your station or workshop each week, making age-appropriate adjustments.

Evaluation

Look Backward to Move Forward
Answer the following questions with your staff or committee.

Look Backward
1. What was the goal of this program?

2. What is exciting and going well?

3. What are any concerns about students?

4. What are any concerns about staff?

5. What was a particularly good experience?

6. What became a challenge?

Move Forward
1. What is our goal for the next program?

2. What do we want to continue?

3. What are some recommendations for change?

4. What will we do to address concerns about students?

5. What will we do to address concerns about staff?

6. What is one area that needs improvement?

Mixed-Age Matters

by Patty Smith

As Sunday school teachers, children's ministers, and pastors, our goal is to follow Jesus' command to "Let the children come." How we do that is once again the topic du jour. In some churches, the mixed-age-level versus age-graded classroom debate is the focus of much discussion. For nearly 150 years, the majority of the secular teaching world has embraced the use of age-graded classrooms. Today, cutting-edge schools are now evaluating the possibility and promise of mixed-age grouping. Could mixed-age groupings be best for the kids in our ministries?

Mixed-age-level Sunday school settings group children of different ages and abilities in the same class or small group. There are advantages and disadvantages to this approach.

Advantages

The advantages are numerous and benefit both the teacher and the learner. Using mixed-age groups helps us foster friendships between older and younger children. These friendships nurture positive social skills such as cooperation, collaboration, and sharing.

Mixed-age groups also provide opportunities for older kids to develop essential leadership skills as they help younger children perform various tasks. As younger children look to their older friends for ideas, inspiration, and encouragement, they receive the guidance they desperately need.

This interdependence reduces the need for competition within the group and increases the opportunity for more peer-to-peer learning. In fact, studies show that children remember up to eighty percent of what they teach each other.

Incorporating mixed-age groups into our churches allows kids to be role models for each other. Younger kids who have been nurtured by older children will imitate the behaviors demonstrated by their older friends. This principle, sometimes referred to as "haloing up," affirms the developmental stages of all kids by leveling the inequities of chronological age. Kids are each allowed to progress at their own pace and are valued for areas where they excel rather than struggle.

Mixed-age groups introduce children to a broad spectrum of ideas, talents, interests, and personalities. As each child shares his or her unique thoughts and perspective, all members of the group experience points of view other than their own. This fosters a community and culture of inclusiveness that helps kids value others.

Finally, teachers benefit from mixed-age groups as they partner with older kids to enhance the learning environment. Older kids can guide younger children through activities and transitions. They can also assist the teacher to field questions. Mixed-age groupings allow teachers to incorporate more complex creative learning experiences such as drama and music into the curriculum. For example, dramatic play showcases the acquired talents of older kids, while still allowing younger children to participate, even if as "trees." Everyone in the group has an inherent place and purpose.

> **M**ixed-age groups also provide opportunities for older kids to develop essential leadership skills as they help younger children perform various tasks.

Disadvantages

Although the advantages of mixed-age classrooms and groups are numerous, some disadvantages exist that might deter their usage in the church setting.

First, segregated classrooms are the norm. Children spend most of their early childhood education, elementary education, and upper education in same-age groupings. Kids are accustomed to this structure and expect it. Providing kids with a new learning environment with mixed ages requires new instruction and changing old behaviors and expectations.

Furthermore, mixed-age groups often create an imbalance of responsibilities and participation for the children involved. In some cases, older children dominate the group, preventing younger children from being fully engaged. In other situations, the opposite occurs. Younger children become overly dependent on their older peers and assume a passive, helpless role. A properly trained teacher can easily avoid both situations.

In addition, mixed-age classrooms require more in-class review of the subject matter. Teachers need to wrap up the concepts explored in the small groups and clarify questions and comments shared. Although this time can seem redundant for older children, it is critical for younger learners.

Finally, using mixed-age groups entails more work for the teacher or leader. Most often, more advanced preparation is needed for class time. Teachers need to select curriculum that considers the skill sets of all learners—one that challenges older kids and doesn't overwhelm younger participants. Teachers must also monitor the length of each activity more closely since kids of different ages have varying attention spans. Teachers need to shepherd each group carefully in order to define direction, offer insight, or redirect any misbehavior.

> In fact, multi-age grouping is ideal to help kids experience the true meaning of Christian community, discipleship, and servanthood.

Careful examination of both the advantages and disadvantages of mixed-age groupings in the church setting reveals that the advantages certainly outweigh the challenges. In fact, multi-age grouping is ideal to help kids experience the true meaning of Christian community, discipleship, and servanthood. As teachers guide, nurture, and share God's Word with children in this structure, they model the very spirit of an Acts 2:42 church, where people of all ages gathered together to learn and grow in God's Word.

"Let the Children Come"

We must remember to "Let the children come." When Jesus proclaimed those powerful words, he didn't invite the children to form age-level groups as they walked toward him. Doing so would have been awkward and unnatural. He said, "Come." Older siblings probably gathered younger ones and older kids helped younger children as they ran toward him. It was an inclusive, communal, and encouraging moment—much like the atmosphere in a multi-age class.

Eliminate Hurdles

Eliminating the hurdles to using mixed-age settings is possible. Strategies to eliminate these hurdles are simple, clear, and easy to implement. First, cast the vision for mixed-age levels with your church leaders, parents, and kids. Tout the benefits. Get support and endorsement from the key stakeholders in your church and ministry.

Next, train your leaders and volunteers. Teaching multi-age groups will be new to some of your teachers. The more equipped they are, the more kids will learn and enjoy themselves. Simulate the use of multi-age groups in your training session. Divide participants into groups of six. If possible, vary the age of leaders in each group. Doing so allows leaders to experience the power of multi-age groups firsthand.

Include the use of kids' roles in your training session. Assign each member of a small group a specific task such as supplies manager, thank-you person, prayer pal, guide, reader, and so forth. Defining roles allows each member to be actively involved in the group. Roles also build self-esteem since everyone has something valuable to contribute.

Be sure to equip leaders with current age-level characteristics for all the ages of learners in their groups. This information is vital to the success of a multi-age setting. With this information, teachers can create experiences that will be meaningful, memorable, and age-appropriate for their children.

Finally, give leaders tools for mixed-age classroom success. Teach them how to ask good open-ended questions that apply to all ages and redirect negative behaviors. Often, good questions initiate powerful discussions that reveal amazing insights offered by both younger and older children. Negative behaviors are just as powerful. They can disrupt an entire lesson, diminish the cooperation among peers, and frustrate any teacher. Equipping teachers with good questions and tools for classroom management is a must.

After training your leaders, beta test mixed-age levels. Conduct an experiment at your church using a test group. Use curriculum that is designed for multi-age groups. Gather feedback from leaders after each session. Then, share your success stories and the stories of other churches.

> '**I** wish you were my brother. You help me all the time and never make fun of me.'

Don't be surprised if you hear a story similar to one shared by a crew leader during a recent VBS field test with mixed-age groups. With tears in her eyes she said, "I know people question the use of mixed-age groups. But today, I saw firsthand the amazing things that can happen when they're used. The oldest and youngest boys have become friends. The older boy helps the younger one with crafts and games. He eagerly awaits the arrival of his young buddy every morning. The younger boy looks to his older friend for guidance, friendship, and encouragement. In fact, I overheard the younger boy say to his friend, 'I wish you were my brother. You help me all the time and never make fun of me.' The older boy smiled proudly and extended his hand. As the younger friend grabbed it, I hugged them both."

This kind of interaction could be taking place at your church starting next Sunday. Children helping children, leaders encouraging children, and parents hurrying to get their kids to church.

Maybe it will resemble that day long ago when parents rushed to bring their kids to Jesus. It can happen—and you're the key!

Patty Smith is currently the Director of Children and Family Ministries in the Tennessee Conference of The United Methodist Church where she engages, encourages, equips, and empowers children's ministry leaders and volunteers in over 1000 churches. Before joining the Conference Staff, she was the Senior Product Developer for Children and Youth Ministries at Group Publishing in Loveland, Colorado. While at Group, she developed numerous resources including books, music videos, and Bible studies. Before joining the Group family, she served as the Minister to Children and Families at Christ Church United Methodist in Fort Lauderdale, Florida. Patty is an avid runner, ardent reader, and an awful cook!
psmith@tnumc.org
www.tnumc.org

Using Media With Children

by Daphna Flegal

Today's children are surrounded by multimedia output. They are the first generation to grow up completely digital. They have never known a world without cell phones and the Internet. In 1999, the Kaiser Family Foundation Study, "Kids and Media," found that the average American child grows up in a home with three TVs, two VCRs, three tape players, three radios, two CD players, one video game system, and one computer. The survey also found that one of ten children had Internet access in their own bedrooms.

In 2005, the Kaiser Family Foundation conducted a new research study, "Children's Media Use." The study found that 8- to 18-year-olds spent an average of six-and-a-half hours a day, seven days a week with media. What is interesting is that when compared to the study five years ago, the time children spent watching TV and reading is the same. What is different is that the time spent playing video games doubled and the time spent on computers more than doubled. The number of children with Internet access in their bedrooms doubled to one in five. This new research shows that as media has been introduced to children's lives, they haven't cut back on old media, they have just added the new.

Whatever our feelings about children and media, it is obvious that media is an important part of our children's world. More and more resources include electronic media as part of the package. The aim of these resources is to use media as a tool to engage our children and enhance their faith experiences. As leaders, we need to be sure that our use of this media is more than sitting the children in front of a TV screen for twenty minutes or playing the latest CD as the children make the day's craft project. Active viewing is the key. Active viewing integrates the media directly into the "lesson" and intentionally involves children in participating with the media.

Active viewing means media becomes more than a spectator sport.

Active Viewing

1. Set clear expectations.
Let the children know what you expect before using the media. You might have the children look for how a character handles a difficult situation. Or you might have the children count how many times they hear a particular word or see an object.

2. Ask questions before, during, and after using media.
Use questions for discovery and understanding. The questions "Who?" "What?" "When?" and "Where?" test the children's knowledge of facts. Who climbed the tree to see Jesus? What did Jesus do when he saw Zacchaeus? Where did Jesus tell Zacchaeus he was going? These questions have right answers. The answers can be found by the children themselves. You do not need to be the answer person, but rather the person who helps the children discover the answer in the story or other resource.

The questions "Why?" "Which?" explore the meanings and feelings of the activity or story. Why do you think Zacchaeus wanted to see Jesus? Why do you think Jesus wanted to go to Zacchaeus's home? Why were the people surprised when Jesus went with Zacchaeus? These questions have neither right nor wrong answers.

The question "How?" encourages the children to connect the activity or story to their own lives. How did meeting Jesus change Zacchaeus? How does knowing Jesus change your life? How did Zacchaeus show that he wanted to be a follower of Jesus? How do you show that you want to be a follower of Jesus? Again, these questions have neither right nor wrong answers.

Active viewing integrates the media directly into the "lesson" and intentionally involves children in participating with the media.

3. Talk with the children about what they have just heard, seen, or read.

Talk about the feelings evoked by the media. "How did you feel when the White Witch cut Aslan's mane?" Talk about the characters. "How did Lucy feel when her brother and sister did not believe her about Narnia?"

4. Add movement to enhance the children's experience of Christian music.

Encourage the children to imitate the movements of the performers on a DVD, or let the children make up their own movements. Recruit a music team of children to choose music and learn the movements. Let this team lead the other children as they sing and dance.

5. Help the children relate to the story by retelling the story themselves.

They can write and illustrate, make PowerPoint® presentations, use puppetry and drama, and film their own movies. Show videos that show Christians living out the story. Film your children as they live out the story with their own examples of service and mission.

6. Have the children operate the media themselves.

They probably know how to do it better than you do anyway! Create a technical team that handles any setup and take down. This is a great way to involve children who would rather be behind the scenes than on the stage.

Practical Points

Preview and Practice

When you are choosing any kind of media for use with your children's program, always preview the program. Check the fright factor for younger children and, of course, the appropriateness of the content. Always practice with the equipment. If you are using a technical team, meet with them to practice.

Pause

Use the pause button if you are watching a video. Stop and discuss what is happening. Let the children predict what they think will happen next. Discuss the consequences for each prediction.

Play It Again

Show the video, listen to the music, or retell the story more than once. Encourage the children to look for different items. Repeat just a small portion of the program and focus on its point.

Participate

If you want the children to dance, sing, or shout out responses, be sure to participate yourself. Standing in the back, drinking coffee, and talking with a co-leader tells children that what's happening is not important enough for you to give it your attention, so why should they?

Pursue

Choose follow-up activities that connect to hands-on or real-world experiences. It might be an art experience, research assignment, or service project. These kinds of connections help the children learn and remember.

Ponder

Debrief with the children. Give the children time to reflect on the experience as individuals and as a group. This might include writing or drawing in a journal, discussion, quiet reflection, prayer, a graffiti wall, or working together to make a worship banner.

Remember, media is only a tool. When it helps accomplish your purpose, it is a tool worth using.

Daphna Flegal is the Lead Editor for the Children's Department of The United Methodist Publishing House. She was instrumental in the development of Live B.I.G., *a curriculum which integrates media into the teaching-learning plan. For more information on* Live B.I.G., *visit* **www.iLiveBIG.com**.

Living Large While Connecting Small— Building a Large Group/ Small Group Program

by Lisa Hiteshaw

All children's ministry leaders want to offer an amazing experience for the kids in their program. We want sound biblical teaching, teachers who engage and connect with the kids, and a consistent message.

How many times have you prepared a lesson only to walk around and hear Sunday school teachers teaching something that does not sound anything like you had prepared? How many times have you heard a volunteer say, "I don't want to lead the class, I just want to help"? Plus, we do not always know the level of biblical knowledge or the depth of faith of our volunteers.

With the Large Group/Small Group model, you have much more control over what the kids are learning and experiencing. It is a "best of both worlds" approach that allows for consistent teaching and relationship building.

We are currently using the Large Group/Small Group model at our church, which is a large church where we serve roughly 750 elementary kids each Sunday. I have also used this model in a much smaller church setting and have found that it works well no matter what your church size. The common element with the Large Group/Small Group model across any size church is the ability to expose kids to the same theme or message through a variety of different teaching modes. What they learn in large group is then reinforced and supported during their small group time.

In a traditional Sunday school setting, most Sunday school teachers are asked to "do it all" when it comes to the lessons. They have to prepare the lesson, be a storyteller, pray, gather and/or purchase craft supplies, run music, serve snacks, and discipline kids. Is it any wonder that we have such a difficult time finding enough people, let alone the right people, to be in the classrooms?

In the Large Group/Small Group model, these tasks are broken up in such a way that there is a place for everyone, depending on their own God-given gifts and talents.

Large Group

Large group is where the main teaching happens. Large group should be just that— **large!** It is a place where kids can come together to not just hear God's Word, but to understand how they can then go out and live out these lessons in their own lives.

Create a Team

The large group time requires a handful of volunteers to run. By creating a large group team, you can have a consistent message week after week.

Praise and Worship

During large group, kids start off with praise and worship. Many kids may not get the chance to be in "big church" and experience this time of connecting with God through music, so this is an important part of the large group experience.

Praise and worship can be done by using a live band or a praise-and-worship DVD or CD. We have found that there are both adults and youth in the church with great talent, so check around and see if someone in your church would be willing to play some live music for your kids. Don't have a band? Don't panic; there are some great worship DVDs and CDs out there as well. You can also mix it up some and have someone come and play live for the kids on occasion, even if it is just one person on an acoustic guitar.

Having motions to go along with your songs makes for an even better interactive praise and worship experience. You can come up with your own motions or ask some of the youth in your church to come and lead the kids through motions. There are also many DVDs out there that not only have great music, but will have video that teach motions to the songs.

Biblical Teaching

Next up during large group time is the biblical teaching moment. Kids don't just hear the Bible story, but rather experience it in many different ways. For example, the lesson can be introduced with a skit, a movie clip, or an object lesson. The idea is to mix it up. Kids enjoy a mix of live action drama, multimedia, and thought-provoking object lessons. This would then be followed by teaching. You want to make the Bible story relevant to the lives of these kids and to make the Bible story come to life. We want to drive home the point of the lesson and help the kids understand the "what does this have to do with me?".

The lesson is best taught by someone with knowledge of both the Bible and kids. This is the beauty of the Large Group/Small Group model. We can have control over the message by teaching it ourselves or by a trusted volunteer who possesses the gifts and talents needed to reach our kids.

Games

Large group games are another great way to reinforce the lesson point. Incorporate games where either a few select kids are called up front to participate or run a game where the entire group can participate.

Review games, such as "Four Corners," are always fun and help the kids remember the lesson points. In "Four Corners," kids hear a multiple-choice question, and each answer is given a color. Each corner of the room is also assigned a color. Kids then choose their answer and run to the corresponding color. Kids who did not choose correctly sit out while the others move on to the next question. Play until you have a winner or winners are out of questions.

Scripture Memorization

Don't forget to include Scripture memorization in your large group time. Adding motions to your Bible verse makes it not only fun, but helps kids to remember the verse. You can add yet another game by breaking into teams and having kids repeat the Bible verse with motions as a team and having judges score them on their accuracy. Kids love team competitions!

Small Groups

After the large group time, kids then move into their small groups. Small group is the time for kids to connect with one another, as well as to build relationships with their adult leaders. It is also time to reinforce the lesson presented during large group time.

Keep Them Small

Small groups should be kept small. We strive to keep our small groups with 6 to 10 kids per group, depending upon the grade. The younger the children, the smaller your group should be. By keeping your groups small, it allows time for kids to share their thoughts and feelings relating to the lesson. It also allows for a deeper connection among the kids and the adult leaders. Ideally, you would have the same group of kids with the same small group leader each week.

> Ideally, you would have the same group of kids with the same small group leader each week.

Consider Crafts

Offering a craft or other small group activity is a great way for the small groups to work together as they build on the Bible lesson. Be sure that each child is able to be involved in whatever activity is chosen. Consider crafts where the small groups work together to create something to be displayed in their classroom or somewhere in the church. This is a great way for kids to learn to work together and to build friendships.

Discuss

During small group time, you will also want to incorporate time for discussing the Bible story, as well as offering some discussion questions for the adult leader to go over with the kids. Allow plenty of time for the Holy Spirit to move among the group. This is how relationships are built!

Commitment Ideas

Have the group talk about ways that they can go home and live out the lesson learned that day. Offer commitment ideas for the kids to choose from to do throughout the upcoming week. Have them report back the following Sunday on how they did with their commitment and what happened as a result of following through with that commitment.

In our church, we recently did a lesson on serving others and offered the kids an opportunity to collect change for orphanages in Africa, India, and Haiti. A little girl who was in kindergarten came up to tell me that she had a lemonade stand to raise money. Her mom then told me that she asked only for donations and that people were very generous. This little girl understood her commitment and followed through in a *big* way, all because of the time her small group leader took to reinforce what it meant to help others!

Repeat the Bible Verse

Allow time to go over the Bible verse. Offer ways for your leaders to help kids memorize their Bible verse, whether it is by repetition, a game, or with the motions learned in large group.

Be sure to have everyone end their time together sharing their joys and concerns for the week and then coming together in prayer.

Adapt Curriculum

So, do you have to find a Large Group/Small Group curriculum or write your own in order to use this model for Sunday school? No! Just about any curriculum can be tailored to work as a Large Group/Small Group model. Yes, it will

take a bit more work than just purchasing a curriculum and using it as is, but the end result is well worth the extra effort!

Utilize the drama, music, and teaching times for your large group time. Maybe add a puppet or two as a recurring character to introduce your lesson. At my previous church, which was a church with about 75 elementary kids, we used the dog puppet from our vacation Bible school curriculum and had a naming contest for him. The kids voted on their favorite name and "Wesley," as he came to be known, was used each week during the large group time.

You will want to work with your large group team to incorporate some of your own creative ideas to enhance the large group lesson. You can then utilize the craft, discussion/questions, and prayer times from your curriculum for use during your small group time.

An Opportunity to Serve

The Large Group/Small Group model offers such a great serving opportunity for the many people in your church who may have never served in children's ministry before. They will be able to find a better fit for their particular gifts, without feeling overwhelmed at having to do it all. We know that when people have a passion for something, they *want* to share it with others.

Large Group/Small Group is also a model that offers kids a wide variety of learning experiences which will equip them to better go out into the world and live as disciples of Christ. My prayer is that by using the Large Group/Small Group model, you will be able to create a dynamic, spirit-filled children's program that brings everyone, both adult leaders and kids, closer to God!

Lisa Hiteshaw has worked with children all her adult life. She was a pediatric registered nurse for eight years and has been working in children's ministry for ten years. Lisa currently serves as the Elementary Program Director at the United Methodist Church of the Resurrection in Leawood, Kansas, where she develops and writes the small group curriculum and ministers to 750 children each week. Lisa is married twenty years to husband Mike, and they have three children.

Notes

Personal Growth

I treasure your word in my heart.

Psalm 119:11

Shepherd or Sheepherder

by Karl Bastian

Remember? Remember when you first got into children's ministry? Remember the calling God gave you? The burden you had for children? The awesome responsibility you accepted? The urgency you felt? Back when it was about reaching lost kids and discipling those who had accepted Christ? Remember when the stories were about changed lives and your conversations were mostly about the kids rather than the problems? Remember when you spent a ridiculous amount of time on some minor but fun aspect of the ministry, just so you could see the faces of the kids light up when they arrived? Remember when you didn't even notice how exhausted you were?

What changed?

You went into children's ministry because you wanted to be a shepherd of children — and all too soon you became more sheepherder than shepherd. Just getting the kids where they needed to be and hoping to have a reasonable adult-to-child ratio became a weekly battle. Managing volunteers, appeasing parents, buying supplies, keeping the senior pastor — as well as the janitor — happy, answering voice mail, e-mail, and snail mail, and going to countless meetings gradually took over. Before you knew it, being a minister gave way to being an administrator. And somewhere the kids got lost in the shuffle. Oh, the kids are fine. Yet you are beginning to feel your heart for ministry fading and you secretly miss when you were just a volunteer and not in charge of the whole operation.

It doesn't have to be that way!

Children's ministry has gone nuts. Seriously. It's less than a hundred years old and yet we've made it into an empire more daunting and menacing than the Galactic Empire! How did the church survive for so many generations and produce such godly saints without all the trappings of our modern ministry? Perhaps all our advances are a part of the problem. Could it be that all we have created to help us has in part become a hindrance? An entire industry of resources and programs (and websites!) has exploded and what do we have to show for it? Just statistics that seem to suggest that kids are worse off spiritually than ever before. How can this be?! Where have we gone wrong?

We forgot our calling to be shepherds.

> "Keep watch over yourselves and all the flock of which the Holy Spirit has made you overseers. Be shepherds of the church of God, which he bought with his own blood." (Acts 20:28, NIV)

I have always loved the title "children's pastor" because it means that you are a shepherd of children. In my first ministry, I was offered the job "coordinator of children's ministry." Fresh out of Bible college, I didn't want to be too presumptuous, but I gently asked that since they had a "pastor" for every other people group in the church, from youth to singles to adults to seniors to missions and even for the music, would they consider allowing me to be a *pastor* for the children instead of a "coordinator." I had no interest in coordinating, but pastoring kids? I was all over that! Granted, there was a lot of coordinating to do, but it's the difference between the end and the means. If you are coordinating in order to shepherd, that's fine. But when you find yourself primarily administrating, the joy gradually, but steadily, evaporates.

Choose to be a shepherd first and foremost!

Whether your "official" title is children's pastor or not — that is what you are. The point is, if you are in a leadership role over children, God has called you to be a shepherd.

> "Be shepherds of God's flock that is under your care, serving as overseers — not because you must, but because you are willing, as God wants you to be . . . eager to serve" (1 Peter 5:2, NIV).

But how do you get *shepherding* back to front and center in your ministry when you are responsible for so much administratively? As with any key change in life or ministry, it starts by asking the right questions. Let me challenge you with some questions that could change your ministry and impact the lives of the children, parents, and volunteers with whom you work. I'm not going to give you "answers," as the answers will vary from person to person and church to church. But I will offer some suggestions that are well worth considering and that can help move your ministry back toward being more focused on shepherding and less on administrating. Let me challenge you to print this article out, and with a fresh pad of paper or journal go to a place where you can think, reflect, and pray without distraction.

What do you think it means to be a shepherd? Don't bother trying to come up with a perfect definition, just describe it — use specific examples or ideas of what you think it looks like to be a shepherd or to experience shepherding from the recipient's perspective.

What aspects of your ministry can be described as shepherding? This is just between you and God, so you can be brutally honest. When do your children, volunteers, or families feel shepherded in your ministry? (Or do they?)

What are your programs actually successful at? List all your programs or activities, then state what the purpose of each is, and describe how well each is fulfilling that purpose. What does success look like? How do you measure success?

What consumes your time? How effective is it? What are the tangible results that

you can point to that merit the time invested? (Example: if you spend ten hours a week on a family newsletter, is that more effective than, say, spending ten hours visiting families in their homes to talk and pray with them? Perhaps the newsletter, as great as it is, needs to go!)

If you discontinued a project, would anyone notice? What do you do "just because"? If you listed everything you do in order of priority, what would be on the bottom half of the list? What if you discontinued that bottom half?

What project would you start that would surprise and delight people? Pretend you had someone to do *all t*he administrative stuff for you, but you still had to work — what would you do to fill your time? Could those things actually be more effective in the long run?

My guess is that when you get to this line, you'll have only read the questions above — not taken the time to answer them. That's okay, but don't neglect to take the time to thoughtfully reflect on them and *write* your answers. There is power in what you commit to paper rather than just allowing your reactions to be passing thoughts. Lee Iacocca said, "The discipline of writing something down is the first step toward making it happen."

After you have taken some time to gather your thoughts on the questions above and whatever other ideas are stimulated, you are ready to start taking some serious and strategic steps toward becoming more of a shepherd and less of a sheepherder. Let me suggest **five steps** you need to walk yourself through. (No one else will do this for you!)

1. Identify What You Would Like to Be Doing

You have more control over your life than you'd like to believe. It is time to stop making excuses and start *doing* what *you* determine is most important. The most important things in life never happen by chance — they must be scheduled.

2. Evaluate What You Are Doing

Take a hard, honest look at how you spend your time. How do you waste time? What is optional? What pays the least dividends while costing the most time? Be ruthless at eliminating the time-killers in your life.

3. Make a List of Priorities

It can be the most powerful thing you do! Make a list of what is most important to you, and then put them in your schedule. Do this as early in the day as possible. If you can't do it, it's okay. At least you will see what didn't get done and be able to reschedule it. But good intentions that are not scheduled will never happen. You will never get everything done, but you can choose what gets left undone. Make sure it isn't the most important that gets left behind!

4. Choose the Best

There is no end of good opportunities that confront you every day. Learn to say *no* to the good for the sake of the great. Look at your priorities every week at the least, (every day is ideal) and determine, "*Today* I will get this done." Discard all your past excuses; there is never anyone to blame but yourself. Own it and live it.

5. Delegate the Rest

Believe it or not, God has wired other people to love doing what you hate doing. I used to feel bad to ask others to do what I didn't enjoy. I thought I was being cruel, until I finally learned there are people who enjoy what I hate, and are better at it! A principle I try to live by in my ministry is "only do what only I can do" and have others do the rest.

> "The hired hand is not the shepherd who owns the sheep. So when he sees the wolf coming, he abandons the sheep and runs away. Then the wolf attacks the flock and scatters it."
> (John 10:12, NIV)

First Peter 5:8 urges us to be "self-controlled and alert" because our enemy, the devil, prowls around like a roaring lion seeking whom he can devour. Our children are his primary targets. You are not a hired hand, you are a shepherd! Determine to be both alert to what our kids truly need and then self-controlled in order to take back your ministry and make it one that shepherds, not just herds.

With God's help and some hard, determined work *you can* do it. What are you waiting for?

_____

*Karl Bastian has over fifteen years of experience as a full-time children's pastor in large, small, and mobile churches. He is also the founder of **Kidology.org**, one of the leading Internet destinations for those who minister to children. He has a Bible theology degree and a master's in children's ministry.*

> You will never get everything done, but you can choose what gets left undone. Make sure it isn't the most important that gets left behind!

Networking

by Beth Morrison

Networking is a supportive system of sharing information and services among individuals and groups having a common interest. Networking involves individuals forming mutually supportive relationships. It is, according to the Merriam-Webster dictionary, "the exchange of information or services among individuals, groups or institutions, specifically: the cultivation of productive relationships for employment or business." It is adding value to peoples' lives. People within our frame of reference have skills and competencies that we don't have, so we are able to help each other.

Today, many social networking sites are available, as well as those dedicated to children's ministry. These are important, even if one does not participate in the forums, to learn from and to ask questions of veterans in ministry. Other options include the ability to post available items that you no longer need. Many ministries with smaller resources have been tremendously blessed by this option.

However, it is also important to network within a smaller, face-to-face framework. Children's ministry is a relational business. Networking among individuals in children's ministry in our own community is especially crucial. God did not intend for us to minister alone. We are connected as the body of Christ. Networking is a valuable way to make those connections, to share information, and to learn from each other. It is the place to mentor those new to the ministry, to welcome those new to the community.

What would cause you to leave an already-too-busy work schedule to attend a monthly meeting? Often fellow church-staff members do not understand the isolation children's leaders feel. The strong bond and camaraderie that we gain from networking is formed among those of us with like minds and ministries. The support from those walking the same journey, understanding the same joys and sorrows and recruitment and security issues, is invaluable. It becomes a genuine give-and-take relationship with each church ministry as we learn from the other. You can gather best practices and lessons learned, and build a ministry family outside your own church, as well as keep abreast of new trends, what's worked and what hasn't, open positions, and more.

Our network meets monthly throughout the school year for lunch, prayer, and a program. Time is valuable, so it is critical to make the time together worthwhile. As we have gotten to know each other, we can better encourage and pray for our various ministries. If an individual has a question about a method or process, they can contact one of our members for assistance. Hands-on networking has also proven worthwhile. This gives them the opportunity to observe different aspects of a different ministry. Cold calls work, but having a face to go with that call provides an open avenue for all of us.

Our network also prays about how we can serve each other by loaning equipment, sharing curriculum and stage sets, and so forth. Why re-invent the wheel? We can use and learn from each other to make our ministries better for the kingdom of God and use our resources wisely.

Our current meeting format was established two years ago. Working from a small list of churches provided by a former networking group, we simply e-mailed the children's ministry directors or pastors to determine the best day to meet. This was and has been our largest obstacle. We ultimately took a consensus vote and chose a day, knowing that it would not work for everyone.

The next step was choosing the place(s) to meet. Our church had hosted it in the past and others asked if we would continue to do that. Two other ministries have hosted; it was a benefit to see other environments.

Hosting the meeting is relatively simple. An e-mail is sent two weeks prior to our meeting requesting an RSVP; this helps us know how much food to order. We charge a minimal amount per person; my church underwrites the rest. Prior to the meeting, we have determined who the speaker will be with suggestions from either the group members or from an outside source. Two of our best meetings happened when testimonies were shared by our members. It was a precious time and a wonderful way to enter into a deeper lever with each other.

Our network is primarily made up of children's pastors and directors, but also includes several Christian businesses that are also looking for ways to network. A group of ladies from a publishing company that works specifically with churches led one meeting, asking us questions and opinions on various aspects of children's ministry and curriculum. This greatly benefited them in ways they could take back and develop. Another time we invited several businesses to attend—a small ministry expo of sorts. This was a great way for contacts to be made for both groups.

The most important thing we expressed to our group initially was that our network did not belong to my church just because it was initiated and meets there. Our network is made up of all of us with equal input. We made it clear to each other that we were not in competition, but that we were all serving Christ and striving to bring children and families to him. I believe this set the tone and has allowed us to be real with each other, sharing our hurts as well as our praises, all for the glory of the Lord.

While many secular networks are focused on employment, we have not crossed that bridge. If a church has an opening, they are welcome to announce it, but our network meeting has not been set up as the place or time for individuals to see new positions. Of course, as relationships are built, this may come about naturally, but it is not currently the focus of our group.

Prayer is such an important part of our lives that we attempt to incorporate it at each meeting. We pray as a group and at our tables—for each other when someone is hurting and for our various ministries. Prayer requests are sent out to our members on weeks when we are not meeting and throughout the summer months. This enables us to keep in touch on an ongoing basis and continue the relationships we have formed.

> Prayer is such an important part of our lives that we attempt to incorporate it at each meeting.

We can survive and function without networking, but does that suffice? Does it become all about "us" and "our" ministry or is it kingdom work? Are we F.A.T. — Faithful, Approachable, and Teachable? Our desire is to hear, "Well done, good and faithful servant" in all aspects of our ministries, including our relationships with those we serve alongside. May the Lord bless you as you reach out to learn from and bless others.

Beth Morrison is currently the Director of Children's Ministries at Woodmen Valley Chapel in Colorado Springs, CO. Prior to that she served as Early Childhood Director at Donelson Fellowship in Nashville, TN. For several years she was the Event Planner for the International Network of Children's Ministry. She is grandmother to four precious grandchildren (with another on the way!). Her passion is to partner with parents and work with them to learn how to be the spiritual heads of their homes.

Unlocking Your Leadership Potential

by Craig Jutila

Leadership and Locks

Do you remember the beloved combination lock? I do. Oh, the horror of remembering the combination. I would rather use a lock with a key. You only need to remember the key! How hard is that? Put the lock where you need it. Put the key on your key chain. Insert the key. Unlock!

The combination lock is a different story. Left to this, right to that, or was it right to this and left to that? I see people at the gym looking at the combination on a piece of paper or the palm of their hand. Heaven forbid you lock that piece of paper with your combination in the locker!

So you're saying, "Craig, who cares about locks and lockers, keys or combinations?" The answer is, we all should. I believe leadership has more to do with remembering a combination of things instead of one key that unlocks everything. With a leadership key you just insert and voila — a leader. I wish it were that easy. Leadership is a combination of what needs to be turned "right" and what needs to be "left." Leadership is a series of numbers dialed in the correct order. When this happens, you will unlock leadership power and potential within yourself and others.

Turn Right to Balance

First turn right to 46, Ecclesiastes 4:6 to be exact. It says, "One handful of peace and quiet is better than two handfuls of hard work and of trying to catch the wind" (GOD'S WORD). Healthy life balance is important. Most leaders miss this. I did. It took me about twenty years to understand the importance of living a life of balance, margin, and healthy pace. When I looked at people who had peace and pace in their life, I usually characterized them as, well, lazy, while I was running around like a chicken with my head cut off, with no balance and margin in my life. My staff named me "Taz" after the Warner Brothers' Tasmanian Devil. "Taz" spins like an out-of-control vortex with no purpose other than knocking stuff over and tearing things up. That was me. I chalked it up to my personality type — type "A" — or my only-child-driven-ness or something arrogant like, "I just have a better work ethic than those 'other' people." The older I get, the more ridiculous this sounds. Most books I have read in the last few years point to a "driven" personality as unhealthy! I was living under the presumption that it was my job to change the world; "be a world-changer" was my mantra. But there was only one person that came to change the world and I just work for him. Take a look at the following verse:

"There are people who are all alone. They have no children or other family members. So there is no end to all the hard work they have to do. Their eyes are never satisfied with riches. But [they never ask themselves] why they are working so hard and depriving themselves of good things. Even this is pointless and a terrible tragedy" (Ecclesiastes 4:8, GOD'S WORD).

When you are in a hurry, you are more inflexible, impatient, and irritable. Each of those words begin with "I" — there may be a lesson in there. The hurried lifestyle can be physically detrimental and can shorten your life span. This driven personality type is a concern in Japan. The Japanese use the word karoshi, meaning death from overwork.

Our problem is that we are "in ministry." We are doing "good stuff." It's difficult to say, "Hey, you baptized fifteen kids last weekend, you need to stop that" or "You had three meetings last week helping volunteer leaders reach their potential, you need to stop that behavior." The things we do at church are good things. They are hard to say no to. Satan is shrewd. One of his tactics is to take up your time, even if it's with good stuff. "Keep them busy"— that's the enemy's motto. The more time you spend "doing," the less time you spend being — being a good spouse, a good parent, a good worshiper of Christ. We weren't created to get stuff done, we were created to love God and others.

"The thief comes only to steal and kill and destroy; I came that they may have life, and have it abundantly" (John 10:10, NASB). Jesus came to give us a full life — a saved life, a redeemed life, and a balanced and abundant life. You cannot have an abundant life when you are moving fast. If you want to unlock your God-given leadership potential then turn right to Ecclesiastes 4:6 . . . turn right to Life Balance.

Turn Left to Pride

Next on the combination is left. Left to 46. James 4:6 says, "God resists the proud, but gives grace to the humble" (NASB). This is the only time in the New Testament when it says God is in opposition to us.

Ever had anyone resist you? If you have children, enough said. My best illustration is my dog, Holiday. She is a golden retriever, the best dog on the planet. She is sitting at my feet right now. If I move, she moves. If I leave, she walks me to the door. If I sit down, she is right there next to me. I don't mean "across the room" next to me, I mean right up against me. When I come home she passes Mary, Cameron, Alec, and Karimy and waits for me. I am her favorite. (Was that arrogant?) She is a great dog and will follow me anywhere, until I try and give her a bath. Remember, she is a retriever — she likes the water. She jumps in the pool and goes for a dip all by herself. Pull out the hose, bring out the shampoo, and Holiday freezes. You can call her and coax her, but eventually you have to carry her to where she will be for the bath. Her resistance is a passive resistance. She doesn't growl or show her teeth. She shows her resistance by lying down. Bath equals resistance for Holiday.

Can you imagine God in full resistance mode? You think bathing a sixty-five-pound golden retriever is tough, try arrogance and pride with your maker. I hope you get the point. Arrogance and pride have no place in a leader's life.

Unfortunately, arrogance will raise its ugly head, usually when you get a compliment or do something extraordinary. That little voice says, "Wow! That was a pretty cool thing you did. How awesome are you!" It's not the voice that makes you arrogant. It's when you start believing it. Attacks from the enemy are rarely head-on. They are subtle temptations that over time wear you down. Then the enemy has you where he wants you. When those thoughts pop into your head, pray out loud, "God, my desire is to be your humble servant. I do not want to be an arrogant person. I am a child of God who, through the power of the Holy Spirit, was used to make a difference in somebody's life today. I renounce, in the name of Jesus, the thoughts in my mind that are causing me to focus on myself."

The root of sin is arrogance, so is it a no-win battle? Of course not. It's part of the combination, though. It needs to be "left" out of our lives. Arrogance isn't thinking about yourself less, it's thinking about others more.

Not being arrogant isn't the end of the journey. It's a start, but according to James 4:6 we are supposed to be humble. First Peter 5:5 (NASB) says, "Clothe yourselves with humility toward one another." This verse says we need to dress ourselves. Well, some of us are poor dressers. Some of us may have a bad wardrobe, but there is hope for those of us who don't have a good eye for spiritual fashion.

Have you watched the show *What Not To Wear* on TLC? People who are not at the top of their fashion game are confronted about their wardrobe and offered $5,000 for a new wardrobe. There is a catch. The fashion criminal must learn to "dress" using the cohosts' guidelines. They must surrender their entire wardrobe to the fashion police to be locked up for life. Once the candidates agree, they are off to New York for a wardrobe makeover. My wife and I sometimes watch the show and say, "Do these people really think they look good in that?" I mean seriously, lose the spandex and flip-flops and get on with life. I'm not the fashion police, far from it, but a simple look at the color wheel will point most people in the right direction.

The show is always the same. The fashion criminals surrender their "old" clothes, go through an emotional crisis, and then "put on" the new clothes they purchased with the help of the cohosts. They then return home for an unveiling party. Side-by-side pictures of the before-and-after wardrobes reveal a remarkable difference.

What Not To Wear could be the title of a show using 1 Peter 5:5. Could you imagine someone secretly videotaping us walking around town clothed in our arrogant outbursts and selfish ambitions? That could bring us to a humble reality. Scripture reminds us to clothe ourselves in humility. Try it on for size. According to my wife, you can wear this all year round.

Turn Right to Courage

After we turn "right" to Balance, and "left" to Pride, we must make one final turn to the right to unlock our leadership potential. Let's turn right to 2 Chronicles 15:7, "But you, be strong and do not lose courage, for there is reward for your work" (NASB). So, turn right to courage!

There are so many situations where courage can be applied. When faced with difficulties or overwhelming odds, or when being bullied, beaten, or berated, we are to have courage. Entire books, websites, and movies have been dedicated to the word. We admire it, preach it, teach it, and hopefully try to apply it to our lives and model it to our kids. Most of us know "What" courage is and "When" to apply it and even "Why" we need to use it, but the "Where" do we find it and "How" do you apply it seem elusive.

"Take courage," "Gather up your courage," or "Muster up the courage." The language implies that courage is in us and we simply have to take it, find it, gather it, or muster it in order to use it. You may hear people say, "I have lost my courage." We talk about courage like it's the key to our car. We usually have it with us but occasionally misplace, lose, or leave it somewhere and can't remember where. Remember the lion in *The Wizard of Oz*? Courage was part of who he was, part of his character! As you know, he just needed a reminder, and so do we. Take a look at our combination verse. Second Chronicles 15:7 says, "Do not lose courage" (NASB). In other words, we had it, but somehow lost it.

Have Courage to Connect

Yes, it does take courage to connect. But just because you live in a fishbowl and get along with everyone doesn't mean you connect on a deeper level.

How does the devil attack you? By isolating you! When the Bible talks about the devil roaming around like a roaring lion looking for someone to devour, it is like a documentary on animals in Africa. Take a herd of wild antelope trying to cross a river. The entire herd is swimming to get across the current. Once they are across and tired, the lion looks for the weakest one of the herd. The lion waits for one to be isolated from the rest—the one who is most tired, most defenseless. Lions aren't just brawn, they are brains too. They don't attack the strongest in the middle of the herd. They attack the one that will put up the least resistance or doesn't even see it coming. They are ruthless and aggressive. There is no chance for this isolated member of the herd. There is a reason "all the believers met together constantly and shared everything they had" (Acts 2:44, NLT). There is safety in numbers!

What does this all mean to us as leaders? It means you need to stop cutting service because something in ministry needs to get done. It means getting into a small group where authenticity and accountability can be actionable items. Just because you are visible doesn't mean you are accountable. Take a risk this week and find the courage to connect with one another on a deeper level where life change can truly take place.

Unlocking your leadership potential doesn't come easy. I wish I had a dollar for every time I hurried to my locker to open the combination, but in my haste missed a number and then had to start all over. Unlocking your leadership potential doesn't come quickly or easily, but through steady and persistent work.

Craig Jutila is founder and president of Empowering Kids, Inc. and Orphan Impact International. He has authored and contributed to more than twelve books, thirty curriculums and various articles championing leadership, children's ministry, and strength and priorities within the family.

Keeping Life Simple

by Jim Wideman

Life can get wild and ministry can get crazy. When you don't think things can get any busier, they can and they do. In my life I've learned *busy* is a relative term. What one person calls busy is not busy to another. The fact is, no matter how you define *busy*, it causes you to deal with pressure. Pressure can create growth or it can also expose weakness in your abilities. Either way, pressure is your friend. People are paid by how much pressure they can handle and deal with.

Jesus is our help and peace in stressful times. He is our help when life gets complicated, but it's up to us to call on that help. He's given us his word that he will help us. Here are just a few of the Scriptures I stand on when life gets crazy for me.

- Psalm 46:1 says, "God is our refuge and strength, an ever-present help in trouble" (NIV).

- John 14:27 tells us, "Peace I leave with you; my peace I give you. I do not give to you as the world gives. Do not let your hearts be troubled and do not be afraid" (NIV).

- John 14:16 promises: "And I will pray to the Father, and He will give you another Helper, that He may abide with you forever" (NKJ). That other helper is also referred to as another comforter.

Jesus never leads you into something that will harm you. He is a safe guide; his Word always works. Jesus is the master of simplifying life. The laws of the Old Testament were many and complex, yet Jesus made it easy to follow them.

Let's take a look at Matthew 22:36-40 (NKJV):

36 "Teacher, which is the great commandment in the law?"

37 Jesus said to him, "'You shall love the Lord your God with all your heart, with all your soul, and with all your mind.'

38 This is the first and great commandment.

39 And the second is like it: 'You shall love your neighbor as yourself.'

40 On these two commandments hang all the Law and the Prophets."

Jesus' answers concerning life are always simple, even though they may not always be easy to carry out. These verses simplified the law but they are a full-time job for each of us.

> Jesus is the master of simplifying life.

Paul had a heart for following the Lord's example. You can tell he patterned his life after the example of Jesus by writing in 2 Corinthians 1:12, "For our rejoicing is this, the testimony of our conscience, that in simplicity and godly sincerity, not with fleshly wisdom, but by the grace of God, we have had our conversation in the world, and more abundantly to you" (KJV).

The devil always tries to complicate life, just like he complicated God's simple instructions to Adam and Eve. He loves to complicate our lives by injecting wrong thoughts into our minds.

Second Corinthians 11:3 tells us: "But I fear, lest by any means, as the serpent beguiled Eve through his subtlety, so your minds should be corrupted from the simplicity that is in Christ" (KJV).

We must choose to keep life simple! Sometimes our responsibilities and the pressures of life affect us in a negative way. We have to choose simplicity.

In Luke 10:38-42 we find the story of two sisters, sisters who made two very different choices in how they reacted to Jesus coming to their home. The Scriptures tell us, "As Jesus and his disciples were on their way, he came to a village where a woman named Martha opened her home to him. She had a sister called Mary, who sat at the Lord's feet listening to what he said. But Martha was distracted by all the preparations that had to be made. She came to him and asked, 'Lord, don't you care that my sister has left me to do the work by myself? Tell her to help me!' 'Martha, Martha,' the Lord answered, 'you are worried and upset about many things, but only one thing is needed. Mary has chosen what is better, and it will not be taken away from her'" (NIV).

The key to simplifying life for me is to be a student of learning better personal and time management. Here are eighteen steps to keeping life simple.

1. Set your priorities.
This is something you have to get in the habit of doing daily. You can't keep priorities if you don't have priorities! Arrange your events, tasks, and duties by priorities!

2. Keep your priorities in order.
This is job one! The fact is, priorities change. The order of your priorities may be different at different times. One of my favorite Scriptures is Proverbs 28:2: "When a country is rebellious, it has many rulers, but a man of understanding and knowledge maintains order" (NIV). This is your responsibility!

3. Delegate to others those things that they can do for you, even if it's short-term.
When you're out of time the only way to get more is to use someone else's. Make a list of everything you are doing that someone else could do and allow them to do it! Use checklists and job descriptions to get others to do the same.

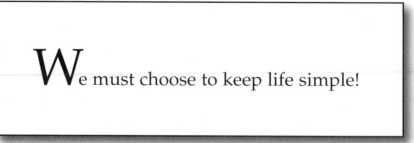

W e must choose to keep life simple!

4. Use time-saving tools.
Some of the tools I use are my iPhone®, a timer, Jott.com, an electronic calendar, voice mail, e-mail, and a laptop computer. But these tools can become time-wasters if you use them wrongly. Know when to talk, not type, and keep your e-mail off when you are working on other things. Add a worker website or let blogging replace worker meetings.

5. Do more than one thing at a time.
Take advantage of commute and wait times to study, have meetings, return messages, and make assignments to others by phone. Use meals to develop people. Ride together and set up what the meeting is about. I pay for these meals, so we'll talk about what I want to cover, and on the way back we wrap up and make assignments on what needs to be carried out. Take reading with you wherever you go, as well as other work. (Here's another reason I love my iPhone®!)

6. Decide what can be postponed or eliminated.
This goes back to your priorities. Keep those activities and events that are urgent or important on top. Don't just look at the task, look at the time it takes to pull it off also. Learn to say *no*! Learning to say *no* also means saying *yes* to right things. To say *yes* to urgent and important matters means you say *no* to less urgent or important things. When time is short, look to focus on now and don't look too far ahead.

7. **Get creative with your family time.**
Take them with you whenever you can and combine family time with business and leisure activities. Call them and let them know you are thinking of them.

8. **Schedule a break, even if it's only for a few hours.**
(Even convicts get time off for good behavior.) Some of my getaway activities are playing guitar or going to the music store, Starbucks®, the bicycle store, and Best Buy®.

9. **Be open to change in your lifestyle.**
(Different results require different actions.) Don't despise change. It's all right to do things differently. Guard your thoughts and your tongue.

10. **Do your homework and see what others do in hectic times.** Check up on busy people — see what they are doing on Facebook or Twitter. Network at conferences, as well as at sites like **cmconnect.org**.

11. **Stop and listen to Jesus.**
Make time for the Word. It is your responsibility to stay refreshed spiritually. Feed your spirit daily as you would feed you belly daily. If you can't go to church, listen to the Bible on CD. But it will really help you to go to church.

12. **When you are tired and busy, don't think.**
Rely on a checklist. Paper is for remembering; your brain is for thinking and

dreaming. Have the information you need with you when you go to meetings, including flowcharts and other reports.

13. **Don't quit or make big decisions during busy and stressful times.**

14. **Don't make people decisions when time is limited.**
Slow down and think it through.

15. **Develop a plan to make next year better the minute an event or activity is over.**
Learn from your experiences and the best time to do this is while it's fresh on your mind.

16. **Get feedback from others.**
A smart person makes time to listen and learn.

17. **When it's over, crash.**
Get some rest. Always schedule a break between big pushes. Watch out for too many irons in the fire.

18. **Do more by doing less.**
Focus on the main thing!

To keep life simple, you must evaluate constantly. Measure your progress, including your fruit, gains, losses, and efficiency. Listen to your spouse on what should you discontinue, change, and/or add. Things naturally get complex on their own. You have to be intentional to keep life simple.

_____

*Jim Wideman is the Associate Pastor/Next Generation at World Outreach Church in Murfreesboro, TN. He also is a children's ministry consultant and leadership coach. For more information, check out **www.jimwideman.com**.*

© 2009 Jim Wideman Ministries, Inc. used by permission

The key to simplifying life for me is to be a student of learning better personal and time management.

Notes

Preteens

B ut the Lord said to me, "Do not say that you are too young, but go to the people I send you to, and tell them everything I command you to say."

(Jeremiah 1:7, GNT)

Who Are They?
A Look Into the Life
of Preteens

by Kim Vaught

Here they come. But the problem is that we are often not ready for them. They're either too old for Children's Ministry or too young for Student Ministry. Ask a preteen, and he or she will tell you that they are not children. Ask the Student Ministry leader, and he or she will likely tell you that preteens should stay in Children's Ministry. So the question is, Who are preteens—children, or students? The answer is both and neither. Have I confused you yet? Preteen years are transitional. The situation begs an answer to these questions. How, as a church, are we addressing their needs? How are we ministering to them? Are they getting lost in the crowd? Do they feel like we care? Are they connected to our ministry?

> So the question is, Who are preteens—children, or students? The answer is both and neither.

Understand the age group.

First, as ministry leaders, we need to make sure that we understand this demographic. Reading about the age group and observing their activities can provide insight. Each year I interview six or seven preteens and videotape their responses to my questions. Each year, it is amazing how these interviews enlighten and entertain. There seems to be a common thread woven through these conversations.

Here are some of the questions I ask the kids:

- What do you miss most about Children's Ministry?
- What do you like most or think about our Preteen Ministry?
- What do you like about coming to church?
- What do you not like about coming to church?
- Would you invite your friends to church?
- What would you like to do to serve God?
- What is your favorite TV program?
- What kind of music do you like?

Preteens are recognized in society as music consumers. They affect over $500 billion a year in music sales. Last year, I asked one fifth grader who his favorite artist was. He answered, "Johnny Cash." Then he proceeded to sing part of "Ring of Fire." It was great!

The common theme these interviews reveal is that kids in this age group are learning how to get along with family, peers, and the adults in their world while they strive for independence.

Here are some characteristics I have discovered in my years of working with preteens:

- They need to talk.
- They want to feel connected to peers.
- They need routine and clear limits.
- They can have dramatic mood swings.
- They desire independence from their parents but like to connect with other adults who are like their parents, possibly college-age adults.

- They move in and out of maturity levels; they're still kids but want to be teens.

- They shift between parent-given faith and personal faith.

- They often create an imaginary audience, assuming that everyone is focused on them.

- They are extremely self-conscious but want your full attention.

Provide a space.

Second, if church is the setting where we have the most interaction with preteens, have we provided them with a space that is relevant? Warehouse 56 is what we call our ministry for fifth and sixth graders. We have designated an area of the building for this age group and decorated accordingly. Your preteen area should communicate that preteens are important...that church is the place to be! You don't have to have a huge budget to create a cool space. You might have to beg and plead for a room, but letting preteens know that you value them by giving them a room that they can call their own is important. Make it a place where they want to invite friends.

How are we doing?

Use these six benchmarks to measure the effectiveness of your ministry:

1. **Are these kids responding spiritually?**
   Are they talking about the Lord? Are they engaged in worship?

2. **Do I have a balanced program that includes worship, biblical literacy, fellowship, and opportunities to serve?**

3. **Does our programming profile more than one kind of student?**
   Are we gender friendly?

4. **Are we culturally relevant?**
   Does the ministry fit the culture of our community?

5. **What are our transition percentages from Children's Ministry to Preteen then Preteen to Middle School?**

6. **How does our Preteen Ministry support the overall church's mission?**

This receptive age group goes through many ups and downs, but they need to know that we value them, want to help them find their identity, empower them as children of God.

Kim Vaught currently serves as the Children's Pastor for Montgomery Community Church in Cincinnati, Ohio, with an average weekly attendance of over 2,300. Kim has over seventeen years in full-time ministry experience with a B.A. and M.A. in Religion. Her easy-going style, wacky sense of humor, and deep love for children enable her to effectively minister to kids. E-mail her at **kvaught@mcc.us***; visit her website at* **www.crosstownkids.us.**

> This receptive age group goes through many ups and downs, but they need to know that we value them, want to help them find their identity, and empower them as children of God.

Reaching Tweens With the Gospel

by Chad Miller

So, how do you reach tweens with the gospel?

In addition to the tens of things on your to-do list, the neverending quest for balance between your ministry and personal life, the mounting list of e-mails that have gone unanswered, and voice mails that you've saved for the last possible time, you face the question, How evangelistic is the tween ministry in your church? Is your ministry not only committed to meeting the spiritual needs of Christian tweens but also driven by the passion to see lost middle schoolers come to know the Lord Jesus Christ?

The Great Commission from Matthew states what I believe to be the heavenly mandate and hovering measure of our ministry: Go and make disciples. I am increasingly convinced that this is the real eternal fruit of the work of our hands as ministers.

We will not be asked about how many flat-screen TVs we installed in our youth center, nor how many articles or books we authored and published. We will not impress heaven, nor insulate ourselves from the purifying fire of judgement, by having the biggest church babysitting children's ministry in town. Nay, we are to make disciples, teaching them to observe all things that Jesus taught.

Making disciples involves two key aspects of ministry to others: evangelism and discipleship. Consider these Scripture passages:

> But how can they call on [God] to save them unless they believe in him? And how can they believe in him if they have never heard about him? And how can they hear about him unless someone tells them?
>
> Romans 10:14 (NLT)

> You have heard me teach things that have been confirmed by many reliable witnesses. Now teach these truths to other trustworthy people who will be able to pass them on to others.
>
> 2 Timothy 2:2 (NLT)

In my dealings with ministry staff across the country, the consistent theme of evangelism still conjures up an event-driven model of outreach. What does it bring to mind when I ask the question, "How are you going to reach the non-believing tweens in your community?" The initial thoughts that student-ministry leaders include:

- What was the best outreach event that I've ever attended?
- How many kids were there?
- Who were the bands?
- What was the draw?
- I wonder how much they spent on marketing.... Wait, all my budget's gone. How did I even hear about it?
- I really liked the speaker. Would my tweens like the speaker?
- How will I get my tweens there? Wait.... Is this for my tweens, or for the ones that aren't going to church?
- I don't know these kids. What do they like? Whom do they listen to?

And on and on those questions can go. They're all valid questions that deserve serious reflection and even a focus group of unreached kids to bounce it off of. There's a lot to consider when it comes to event evangelism. Whether it's outreach based or an "attraction" model, it's still a ton to wade through as you traverse the waters of modern-day proclamation evangelism event planning.

Is your ministry not only committed to meeting the spiritual needs of Christian tweens but also driven by the passion to see lost middle schoolers come to know the Lord Jesus Christ?

But I would love to see another thought pattern emerge in the coming months and years of student ministry. First, let's review a few eye-opening stats and double-click them to see what opens up to us. Forgive me for bludgeoning the dead horse of some of these stats, but they frame the context of a premise for a new approach to engaging lost tweens and middle schoolers with the gospel of Jesus Christ for the hopes of making disciples.

1. Our church kids are in trouble.

Percentages ranging from sixty-seven percent to eighty-two percent of our youth are leaving the church as soon as they get the chance. We know that there's a chasm, generally speaking, between our young people and God.

2. Kids are still very tender for the gospel.

In fact, children between the ages of 5 to 13 are five times more likely to come to Christ than at any other time in their lives. Is there any doubt that reaching kids in this age is some of the most important work we can do as ministers of the gospel?

3. Kids have tremendous influence on other kids.

In fact, no one has the ear of a tween like another tween.

Take a moment and guess where I'm going.

4. A majority of our Christian students don't know how to share the gospel.

Isn't that staggering? These are Jesus-loving, born-again, want-to-change-the-world students who are faithful to our Bible classes. And they're not equipped to share the gospel with their friends and family! So, what exactly are we teaching them, I wonder?

If students reach students better than adults, it sounds like at least one aspect of our evangelistic efforts should include equipping our Christian tweens to reach their friends with the gospel.

At the Billy Graham Evangelistic Association, one of the verses we emphasize with the *Dare to Be a Daniel* youth evangelism project is 1 Peter 3:15 (NIV): "But in your hearts, set apart Christ as Lord. Always be prepared to give an answer to everyone who asks you to give the reason for the hope that you have. But do this with gentleness and respect."

As believers, we're called to put Christ first. Without him as the foundation of our ministry, no amount of entertaining kids will draw them into a loving relationship with the Father. But when we share our faith, we must do so in a way that shows we value the other person and understand where the person is coming from. When it comes to reaching young people, in my experience, nobody can do so as well as another young person—if that person is given the tools to do so.

My advice is to find a Christ-centered, Scripture-driven resource that can equip your youth to share their faith boldly and yet with sensitivity. You can check out *BillyGraham.org* to find out more about how *Dare to Be a Daniel* may be useful to your youth.

If we want to reach a generation that is increasingly uninterested in the gospel, we need to help our young people do the work of evangelism and discipleship. Remember: We're called to make disciples. If we really are making disciples out of our kids, they in turn will be making disciples of others.

*Chad and his wife Ashlie live in Kannapolis, North Carolina, with their two sons. Ordained in 2000 as a nondenominational preacher, Chad is serving as Director of Dare to be a Daniel, a Youth Evangelism Training Project of the Billy Graham Evangelistic Association (**www.billygraham.org**). You can reach him at **cmiller@bgea.org**.*

Spiritual Growth for Tweens in Transition

by Dr. Rob Rienow

We have a new group of people in the church today. They have always been with us, but now we have a name for them: tweens. These young people are somewhere between fourth and seventh grade. They often find themselves awkwardly caught between the world of childhood and the coming pressures of teen culture. These are years of intense spiritual battle and significant spiritual opportunity. Are these boys and girls children, teens, or in a category all to themselves? How the church views them, responds to them, and seeks to nurture faith in "tweens" is of the utmost importance.

What can church leaders do to point these children, who are on the brink of becoming young adults, toward a lifelong faith in Jesus Christ? We can be thankful that God has given us the answers in the Scriptures. In the Bible, we have everything important about everything important and everything that matters about everything that matters. Does the evangelism and discipleship of the next generation matter? It is of supreme importance in the eyes of God, and He has not left us without a strategy and method for how He wants His people, and His church to impress the hearts of children with a love for Christ.

Let's say we locked ourselves in a room with the Bible and asked, "Lord, as I search your Word, will you please show me your plan for reaching "tweens" with the gospel and helping them grow in Christ?" What do you think we would find? This is the essential question church leaders must ask in every area of ministry strategy. What has God said about this ministry issue in His Word? Let's consider how God speaks to the issue of ministry to "tweens".

First, and not surprisingly, the word *tween* is not in the Bible. More importantly, this life stage is not specifically mentioned either. Being a "tweenager" is a new idea, which has been born out of our secular culture. This new stage is little more than an extension of another recent cultural invention: adolescence. Because of this newly invented life stage, we know people between the ages of 12 to 22 to be irresponsible, disrespectful, disconnected, and controlled by hormones. Young people tend to live up to the expectations we have of them, and many of our teens today are doing exactly that. In some senses, the creation of the new tween category is an extension of the false construct of adolescence.

Through the 4,200 combined years of Jewish and Christian history, God's people have seen only two life stages in the Scriptures: childhood and adulthood. The bar or bat mitzvah in the Jewish tradition is held at age thirteen or twelve to transition the young person from childhood into adulthood.

The same principle held true in the Christian world for the first 1,900 years of the church. Children were viewed as children until their transition into adulthood (not necessarily at age thirteen).

Church leaders need to decide whether they will allow God's Word or the culture to determine our labels and categories. Will we mirror what the culture gives us, or will we let the Bible shape our thinking? If we follow the pattern of the Scriptures, we will view "tweens" as children and understand that their next step is to enter the world of young adulthood.

If God views people in this age group as children, our next question is, Lord, what have you said in your Word about how you want children to come to Christ and grow in Him? Tragically, I spent my first ten years in youth ministry without asking this question. I used whatever creative methods that I thought would work. From the perspective of outsiders, I was wildly successful. We would see 500 high school and junior high students participating in our programs each month. I now deal with the harsh reality that the majority of those students who were seemingly on track spiritually as high school students are now, as adults in their twenties, no longer following the Lord.

So, what method does God want us to use in order to lead children toward lifelong faith? This is the million-dollar question for everything we do in Children's Ministry, and there are two essential answers in God's Word that should drive our strategy.

> If we follow the pattern of the Scriptures, we will view tweens as children and understand that their next step is to enter the world of young adulthood.

Mission #1

Equip parents to disciple their children at home, and encourage children to give their hearts to their parents.

In Deuteronomy 6:5-7, we find the Great Commandment and the first action step for a faith community that seeks to love God. "Love the Lord your God with all your heart and with all your soul and with all your strength. These commandments that I give to you today are to be upon your hearts. Impress them on your children. Talk about them when you sit at home" (NIV).

Mothers and fathers are given the primary responsibility to lead their children to Christ, teach them the Scriptures, and equip them to make a difference in the world for the glory of God. Parents are to engage with their children spiritually in the home.

The first practical action step following the Great Commandment is to "talk about [the Word of God] when you sit at home." For centuries, this has been referred to as family worship. At this time, parents, ideally led by the father, gather the family together for prayer, Bible reading, sharing their hearts with one another, and even singing.

The most powerful spiritual event in the life of a child is authentic family worship in the home. Many Scriptures affirm the call on parents to intentionally disciple their children at home. When fathers are present, they bear primary responsibility to lead the family and children in faith. Ephesians 6:4 says, "Fathers, do not exasperate your children; instead, bring them up in the training and instruction of the Lord" (NIV).

Because this is God's primary plan, it is Satan's primary attack point. First, he tempts the parents to keep their hearts at their jobs, with their friends, or in their hobbies. He lures parents with the lie, "It is your job to make sure that your kids are in church and that they have good friends." The enemy also attacks the hearts and minds of children. "Don't give your heart to your parents. It's OK if you want to talk with your friends about things, or even your small group leader; but not mom, not dad."

Another huge barrier we have in regard to family worship is that roughly eighty-five percent of the adults in our churches today did not grow up in a home where family worship was practiced. It will take a long-term strategy of encouragement to renew family worship in our churches. This has been a deep, personal journey for me, as well. For the first five years of my parenting, I had no plan to pass my faith on to my own children. I was giving everything I had to disciple everyone else's children! But I'm thankful that it was not too late for me to repent and turn my heart to the number-one reason why God created me: to do all in my power to impress the hearts of my five children with a love for God and help them get safely home to heaven. I now view my role in leading family worship in our home as my most important ministry responsibility.

So, what can we do as church leaders to move this first part of the mission forward? First, understand that the most important role your staff and volunteers have in your children's ministry is to equip and inspire parents to take the spiritual lead with their kids. Do you have a great idea how to teach the Scriptures to a child? Get that idea into the hands of the parents.

Second, strategize how you can make "family worship" the most important program in your children's ministry. If your team will talk about "family worship" (which happens privately in the homes in the families of your church) as a program that you want to see grow, improve, and succeed, how could you make that happen? Consider sending home "take the lead" sheets with parents. Rather than saying, "Here is what we learned today, and you can keep the conversation going," Have the take-home designed to say, "Take the lead! Next week, we will be talking about prayer. Please take the lead with your son or daughter; and during this week ahead, read these Scriptures, talk about these questions together as a family...."

If church leaders want to follow the biblical model for evangelizing and discipling children to follow Christ, we must begin by doing all that's in our power to equip and inspire parents and grandparents to turn their hearts to their children, encourage children to give their hearts to their parents, and build a church culture where family worship in the home is our most vital discipleship program.

> Mothers and fathers are given the primary responsibility to lead their children to Christ, teach them the Scriptures, and equip them to make a difference in the world for the glory of God. Parents are to engage with their children spiritually in the home.

Mission #2

Welcome and integrate children into the full life of the church, beginning with the weekly worship service.

In the Scriptures, we find a second method that God has prescribed for the discipleship of children. In both the Old and New Testaments, we find children fully integrated into the life of the faith community, in particular in the corporate worship service.

Those of us in the children's and youth ministry world frequently talk about the question, Do kids belong in church? I recently read a six-page article on the subject, with both sides of the issue represented—those who thought that kids should not be in the service with their parents, and those who thought they should. The article was interesting, and many good points were made. There was one thing missing: Not a single Scripture was mentioned. Everyone's case was made based on their opinion, experience, and what they thought would work best. I understand why the article was done this way. Ten years ago, I didn't think that the Bible had anything to say on the subject. I thought that this was one of those ministry issues that we had to figure out for ourselves. That all changed when my senior pastor asked me to do a research project on this question. I was blown away. I found explicit Scriptures throughout the Old and New Testaments which demonstrated that children were intentionally included in the regular worship gathering of God's people! I knew then that this issue was not up for grabs. Either we would follow the model of our culture, which seeks to segregate children from adults at every opportunity, or we would seek to build a Christian, Bible-driven culture where children would be integrated into our worship services.

The question is fundamentally theological. It is rooted in our conviction about the nature of the corporate worship service. What do we believe, at its nature, the weekly worship service truly is? Do we believe it is an adult-education hour? If so, then get the kids out, because they are distracting and the message is not tailored for them. Or, do we believe it is a gathering of the faith community in the presence of God and under the authority of the Word? If that is what we believe the worship service is, then do we consider our children a part of the faith community? If so, then that is where they belong.

Or consider this question: If Jesus himself were going to be the guest preacher this weekend at your church, where would you put the children? I have a hunch that you would have them in the sanctuary that day. The point here is not to puff up your pastor but rather to make sure that your children are hearing the Word of God. Our pastors have been called by God to preach the truth of the Scriptures to the church, not just to the adults.

One of the biggest mistakes I made in youth ministry is that I sought to win the hearts of the teens to the youth group. I wanted them to find their community and their spiritual home there … and I succeeded. I didn't realize that when they graduated, they lost their "home" and many then lost their faith. I should have made it my mission to first help them connect spiritually with their parents and then to connect with the full faith community.

If you want to follow the biblical pattern on this issue and intentionally seek to welcome and integrate children into the worship service, you will be a countercultural church. There will be resistance from those who have become accustomed to the church structuring itself after the patterns of the world. Have you allowed the culture to drive this decision in your church, or have you sought God's direction in the Scriptures?

Some churches seek to address this need with periodic "children/youth Sundays." I think that these special Sundays where children or youth are invited send the wrong message: "This is a service for the adults; but from time to time, you are welcome to come." Is that the pattern we find in the Bible?

Rather than set aside special Sundays to welcome children into the church, include them in regular and natural ways every week. Invite them to help with the ushering. Invite children

to participate in the choir or worship team. Encourage your pastor to occasionally make specific application of the Scripture for that day to children who may be present.

You will likely need to share with your church the biblical basis for why children are invited and included during your worship services. It may take a long time to build a Bible-driven, pro-child atmosphere in your church; but their souls are worth it.

So what do "tweens" need most for their spiritual growth? God has not left us to figure it out on our own. Most importantly, they need a spiritual connection with their parents——beginning with family worship in the home. Secondly, they need to be connected into the church—beginning with weekly worship with the church family.

You have a great opportunity to provide these vital spiritual growth experiences for the children in your church. And when the children in the church begin to receive their primary discipleship at home and through the church service, your children's ministry will be increasingly freed up to pursue ministry with children who do not know Christ and who do not have Christian parents.

Imagine the amazing things God could do through your ministry if your staff and volunteers dedicated themselves to praying, "God, please show us how we can do all in our power to equip parents to disciple their children at home through family worship. Now we can welcome, involve, and integrate children into the full life of our church!"

Rob Rienow has been married to Amy for fifteen years, and they have been blessed with five children. Rob's first ministry is to love his wife and to lead his children to know and love God. Rob has served on the pastoral staff at Wheaton Bible Church in Wheaton, Illinois, for seventeen years, first as Youth Pastor and now as Family Pastor. He is the author of God's Grand Vision for the Home *and* Visionary Parenting. *Rob founded the ministry of Visionary Parenting (***www.visionary parenting.com***) to equip parents to disciple their children and help churches build Bible-driven family ministries.*

Tweens and Service

by Marcia Joslin Stoner

Spirituality is about our whole being, our whole lives. One of the greatest ways for tweens to grow spiritually is through service and outreach. Tweens naturally love doing service, especially if they can interact with the people they are serving, and nothing connects spirituality to life like serving real people in a real way.

Take Inventory

Every Christian is blessed with a variety of gifts to use for ministry in the church. Before you start a service project, complete a ministry inventory with your tweens to discover their gifts and their interests.

Write out the list below on a large sheet of paper or a dry erase board. Ask your tweens to write their names under those things that they are good at and like to do. Add anything to the list that is appropriate for your group and area.

As a group think of the different areas in your church and community where you can use your gifts. Use this list for helping to decide in what service projects your group can participate.

Gifts and Interest List
- art: drawing
- art: painting
- art: other—————————
- cleaning and organizing cabinets
- cooking/baking
- greeter: Sunday morning worship
- greeter: Sunday school class
- helping with activities for younger children
- helping in the office
- computer
- library work
- lighting the altar candles/acolyte
- mowing lawns
- music: singing
- music: playing an instrument
- photography
- praying for others
- reading Scripture in the worship service
- recycling
- talking on the phone
- ushering
- writing

Places to Serve

Tweens are naturally into service, but at times we all need ideas where to serve. Check with your pastor, your mission committee, local agencies, and your national church organization. Listed below are some worthy organizations.

- **New Churches**—When a new church begins it often doesn't have enough money to pay a pastor, build a building, and buy curriculum and toys for the nursery. Find a new church in your area. Do your tweens have books or old toys (in good condition) that they can donate? Raise money to help the church purchase Bibles for the church's Sunday school classrooms.

- **Missionary Support**—Missionaries are a long way from home, and they need help to do their work. Often they work in countries that have very little. But one of the biggest ways to help support missionaries is through letters! They enjoy getting letters from their home country, and the missionaries can help educate your tweens as to the people and conditions in the country they are serving. Pick a missionary and let your group become pen pals with a missionary.

- **America's Second Harvest**—This national network of more than two hundred food banks distributes donated food to hungry Americans. Have a food collection drive and then as a group take the canned food and help sort for an afternoon. Your help will be appreciated. You will need to make an appointment with the food bank first. This is a project tweens really get into because they can actively participate in it.

- **Heifer International**—An international organization attempting to end hunger around the world by helping grass-roots community groups who determine their own needs. They distribute livestock, helping people grow their own herds and become responsible for their own livelihood. Your group may want to raise money for a chicken, a goat, or a cow. Check it out on the Internet at **www.heifer.org**.

- **Bethlehem Centers, Salvation Army, Goodwill Industries**—These organizations all collect donations of old items to help those who are less fortunate. Recycle some of those old clothes and toys in your tweens' closets. As a class have a drive and see how much just your tweens can bring. Then you might want to expand this activity to the whole church. Let your tween class be the sponsor, do the advertising, and put collection containers around the church.

With any of the above service projects, spend some time helping your tweens learn more about the organization they are going to help. For local organizations, plan a group visit, and/or bring someone in from the organization to speak to your class. Often with national organizations there will be a branch in your city or a location nearby. Invite someone in, or ask them to send you more information. Search the Internet for more information; just be sure that you find a legitimate organization and not a group using a variation of the name of a legitimate organization. Connect all service projects to Bible study and worship time.

Be a Servant

The story of Jesus washing the feet of the disciples in John 13:1–20 demonstrates the prefect example of servanthood. Reading this story or other stories of servanthood provide a time for practicing servanthood.

The following is a list of some ways for your tweens to practice servanthood.

- **Servant to Your Community**—Lead a brainstorming session about things that need to be done in your community; or ask your tweens to find out what opportunities for service are available from the newspaper, Internet, or by talking to people. Some possibilities are raking leaves for the elderly, cleaning up a section of a public park, or washing windows at the local school.

- **Servant to Your Church**—Go on a "servanthood treasure hunt." Have your tweens talk with the pastor, the church secretary, the custodian (if present in the building), leaders of other classes, and so forth, and discoveer what are some of the things that need to be done around the church.

Bring the group back together and have them use the "treasure" of ideas they have gathered to decide upon one area in which to be a "servant group" this month. Some possible projects include cleaning a room, videotaping a worship service for a church member who is homebound or hospitalized, helping the secretary fold bulletins for the worship service, washing the toys in the nursery, and so forth.

- **Servant to Your Family**—This is the most difficult place for a tween to be a servant. They often already feel (rightly or wrongly) like a servant in their own homes. The point is for them to be a servant from their hearts without it being asked or expected of them.

Ask the group to brainstorm ways to be a servant at hone. Then challenge them to pick one way and do it. For accountability, they are to report back to the class what they did during the week and how it was received. Some ideas for at-home service are to set the dinner table without being asked and make it especially beautiful or interesting, make place cards with a personal note of appreciation for each member of the family, do a chore that is normally done by a sibling, sweep or vacuum the home, or feed the pets every day before being asked to do so.

From *Tween Spirituality* © 2003 Abingdon Press

Marcia Stoner is editor of Rock Solid: Tweens in Transition *and other tween resources. Marcia earned a M.A. in Christian Education from Scarritt College, and has taught tweens for many years. Marcia is the author of several books including,* Symbols of Faith *and* Bible People of Faith.

Safety

You will be protected and
will rest in safety.

Job 11:18b

Volunteer Background Checks

by Brad Snellings

Background checks alone cannot eliminate the risk of liability and child abuse; we live in a world full of risk. However, a screening program can reduce the chances of ministry and volunteer liability to an acceptable level, when part of a total risk management program, and help reduce the chances of child abuse. This article focuses on how to utilize screening programs and implement background check techniques related to screening volunteers.

It may help you understand what a screening program can do for you by examining a specific situation with a volunteer accused of child sexual abuse:

One of your volunteers is accused of sexual misconduct and has been arrested and charged with child sexual abuse. Now several parents are threatening to sue you and the organization. Are you liable?

With a risk management and screening program in place — no problem. You have several "layers" of protection. Here's how and why.

- Because your organization instituted a program of reasonable screening for children's ministry volunteers, which included a requirement that they complete forms providing information about their backgrounds and experiences and consent for a criminal background checks, and you conduct background checks on volunteers working with children, your directors and leaders are not likely to be personally liable for negligently selecting the volunteer, who lied on his or her application. However, your organization may still be exposed to vicarious liability for the volunteer's sexual misconduct.

- In addition, your program had an ongoing system for training volunteers on child abuse prevention and reviewed and evaluated volunteers, including a background check every two years.

- Finally, since you knew there was a risk of this kind of claim, you made certain that your liability insurance included coverage for this kind of risk. You purchased an endorsement to the standard general liability policy for this specific kind of claim.

Without risk management and a screening program in place — bad news. You never imagined it could happen in your ministry.

- Because it is so difficult to find reliable volunteers, you accept everyone who signs up, with no questions asked.

- Because you took no preventative measures and because some people now are saying that unmistakable signs of the coach's misconduct were overlooked or ignored, your directors and leaders are exposed to personal liability and gross negligence.

- Worse, you are dismayed that the organization's liability insurance explicitly excluded coverage for that kind of claim.

If risk management principles, including the core elements pertaining to a screening program:

1) policies and procedures,
2) education and training,
3) and background checks,

are applied in your ministry, your parents, members, and everyone should be made aware of these elements.

Your organization should develop your own policies and procedures and decide how to best apply them to your ministry, e.g. the two-person-rule, the six-month-rule. Determine if screening will be mandatory for everyone working with children, no matter how long they've been in your church. Every church and ministry is different, so consult with your attorney and utilize the resources available to you as you develop your policies and procedures. *Protect My Ministry* provides sample policies and complete starter kits to help ministries get started toward customizing their own policies and procedures.

Education and training for volunteers on child abuse is essential and just as important as background checks to the screening process. *Protect My Ministry* offers a full DVD and workbook training program to help you implement the training necessary to protect your ministry.

In your child protection policy you should outline your volunteer positions with job descriptions and which positions require background checks and what types of background checks will be conducted.

The volunteer should be required to fill out the ministry application and background check consent forms and review the position descriptions. Once your volunteers fill out the forms, you need to be careful to store their forms in a secure, protected place, along with a background check report.

The process of collecting forms from volunteers can be time consuming and a labor-intensive process. To help streamline this process, *Protect My Ministry* has developed a fully web-based ministry application system that you can use for the online collection and storage of applications, background check consent forms, and background check reports — called *Ministry Mobilizer*.

If your organization provides day care and child care services or performs other services that bring its employees and volunteers into regular contact with minors, you may be subject to state or federal mandatory screening procedures. Check with your local law makers to determine if your day care facility meets their requirements for mandatory screening. Registered day care facilities and programs that receive federal funds

are often required to run criminal background checks on employees and volunteers.

If your organization is not required by law to conduct criminal background checks you should still conduct background checks on volunteers just like you would for an employee. A volunteer is a worker serving the organization, and the organization should put substantially the same amount of work into locating qualified volunteers and placing volunteers according to their skills, talents, and gifts. Volunteers frequently have a highly public role on behalf of the ministry; they are the persons that parents and individuals dealing with your ministry will see first and most often. Whenever possible, use position descriptions for volunteers, analogous to job descriptions for employees.

It may help to define the types of background check services available. The following services are most common to ministries:

- **National Criminal Database Search** — There are various vendors for this service that are all similar in their scope. The data is sourced from various state and local court records. This search is primarily used to screen for convicted felons and those who have served time in a prison for more than one year. This database search is more effective in some states than others. Some states provide very little data, while other states include all felony and misdemeanor data for arrests and convictions. *Protect My Ministry* offers an online consultation, which keeps you up to date on the changes in the national database and helps you determine if this search is sufficient for your state.

- **National Sex Offender Registry Search** — All fifty states' sex offender registries are searched at one time. Some states require special search techniques that you should be aware of, including the need to search by first and last name, while omitting the date of birth from the search technique. This is necessary in thirteen states, as of the date of this article. *Protect My Ministry* automatically adjusts their search techniques by state, so that you get a true 50-state sex offender search.

- **County Court Search** — A search of the local county will reveal all arrests and convictions for felony and misdemeanor level crimes. This search is especially important in states where the National Criminal Database Search is not thorough enough.

- **Statewide Search** — A search of the state police records will reveal all arrests and convictions for felony and misdemeanor crimes. This search is especially important in states where the National Criminal Database Search is not thorough enough. Mandatory statewide fees can be expensive; in those cases *Protect My Ministry* may recommend a county search instead.

- **Social Security Verification** — The Social Security Number (SSN) of an applicant is verified through the social security records for validity, date issued, and the name and date of birth attached to the SSN.

- **Address History Trace** — The addresses attached to a person's credit header including the dates lived.

- **Motor Vehicle Records Search** — A state search using the driver's license number will reveal any traffic infractions and violations. This search is typically used for drivers of church vehicles or volunteers responsible for driving children.

- **Credit History Report** — an up-to-date snapshot of one's personal credit history will reveal the financial accounts, balances, and any liens, holds, or judgments against the individual.

A combination of these services will fit most positions in your ministry, including the National Criminal Database Search, National Sex Offender Registry Search, Social Security Verification, and Address History Trace. The price for these services can range from $10 to $25. An online consultation with criminal background check recommendations is available on the *Protect My Ministry* website (**www.protectmyministry.com**).

You have been presented with a potential lawsuit situation involving the sexual misconduct of a volunteer. Let's examine another area of risk that you should consider running background checks for: the auto accident.

Your volunteer offers to drive a group of children to summer camp. The volunteer is involved in an accident, and some of your children are injured. Are you liable for their injuries?

If your organization's insurance covers the volunteer's personal vehicle and the passengers, you know your insurance will cover you. However, what if the volunteer has a driving record and is at fault in the incident and a motor vehicle search would have revealed his or her prior history and could have prevented the incident. Your organization could be sued for gross negligence if you failed to perform due diligence by performing a motor vehicle records search on the volunteer.

The screening program for your ministry will impact the success of your ministry. For some parents it's imperative that your children's ministry take precautions to ensure the safety of their children, beyond the standards of facility safety. The media has exploded over the past several years with stories of abuse, many of which are in the church. A screening program is no longer just an option, but is a requirement for effective ministry.

Protect My Ministry is an employment and volunteer background screening company established to assist faith-based organizations in implementing and maintaining a thorough background screening process.

Brad Snellings is the co-founder of Protect My Ministry. He is married to Lauren Snellings, and they have three children (Elizabeth, Emma Jane, and John). They attend Idlewild Baptist Church in Lutz, FL.

Safety and Security in Children's Ministry

by Loralee Boe

The subject of safety and security in Children's Ministry is one often overlooked or not emphasized enough. Sometimes this is from a lack of knowledge or from a desire not to offend. As those called to teach children the Gospel, we cannot ignore the environment in which we care for them. A child who does not feel safe is rarely reachable, and few parents will entrust you with their most precious treasure if they are not confident in your competence.

The following is a compilation of policies and procedures that I have written, collected, edited, and researched over the past seventeen years. Many other churches and public agencies have contributed to the core of these policies. Please make them personal for your ministry situation. If being proactive and having training and procedures in place prevents or lessens a child's pain, isn't it worth it to spend some administrative time in implementation?

In our litigious society it is wise to have published policies to protect your church from lawsuits. People often have the unfounded view that all churches have deep pockets and are easy to get money from. Most everyone sees the need for a *Playground Policies*. (Samples are available on page 178 and on the CD-Rom.) A preschool girl was playing on the elementary playground while her mother was at a meeting at our church. Note, this was a playground unsuitable for her age and did not have adult supervision. When she fell and required stitches, legally we were protected because the above policies are on signs attached on our playground fence. Parents are given a policy notebook when their children began attending our programs to help prevent problems and confrontations.

A well-stocked and rigorously maintained **First-Aid Kit** in every classroom or other meeting rooms is imperative. At every church event from Sunday service to a youth volleyball game there needs to be some one with first-aid training and CPR certification. I have been certified and recertified for 30 years and only had to use CPR once. The kindergartner I pulled out of the pool at a home school swim party was totally blue and nonresponsive. She made a total recovery after CPR and observation at a children's hospital. Get CPR training!

Copies of *Injury Procedures and Incident Reports* should be readily available. (Samples are available on pages 176–177 and on the CD-Rom.) Follow-up phone calls or even home or hospital visits will go a long way toward maintaining good relationships with families after an injury at the church or during a church event.

Have you thought of a policy concerning your church's response to HIV/AIDS? Your Elders might not see the need for this concern, but even in a small church the odds are you do have a HIV-positive person in attendance. What if a member of your church is taking in high-risk foster children and wants to put a HIV-positive baby in your nursery? Or a young man who is HIV positive wants to be a camp counselor? Your leadership needs to have a discussion about this issue and to formulate a response. There is a *HIV Policy* (Samples are available on page 175 and on the CD-Rom.) you might use as a starting point for that discussion. *The Communicable Disease Policy* (Samples are available on pages 173–174 and on the CD-Rom.) can be helpful in training your team members to deal with the inevitable vomiting, diarrhea, and nose bleed incidents. You haven't fully experienced Children's Ministry till you walk in on a preschooler painting the bathroom walls with her poop. Such a creative child.

The *Wellness Policy* (Samples are available on page 182 and on the CD-Rom.) can be a boon to your teachers with it's definitions of many common childhood illnesses. When posted, it is easier for a team member to refer to it as a dad is trying to check in his child with red eyes and yellow crusted eyelashes. When he says that he thinks it is just allergies, your response should be that you can't be sure unless he brings a doctor's note stating the same. You do not want impetigo, fifth disease, or conjunctivitis running rampant through your ministry. I have been infected so many times that I personally have both the drops and ointment for pink eye in my medicine cabinet at all times.

Another tough subject to deal with is convicted sexual predators. Our policy has grown from one to four pages over the years, both from experience and from the help and advice of those in law enforcement. It is important to check your local sexual offender's registry on a regular basis and update your team members. We have binders in all classrooms for team reference. Of course there are those who haven't registered as required or will come to church from out of the area. When a problem person is suspected or identified to you it is imperative that you have a way to check out the person's past offenses. It helps to have as much accurate information as possible before you have a meeting with the person to discuss his or her attendance at your church.

In the *Response to Convicted Sexual Offenders* (Samples are available on pages 179–181 and on the CD-Rom.) you will find a draft of the way we deal with such individuals. I have been accused of being paranoid or unforgiving by a convicted pedophile who wanted to work at our "Fallapalooza" (Halloween alternative). My response was twofold. First, if you were a recovering alcoholic I don't think it would be wise for you to work in a bar. Second, if I'm being overprotective and you are a changed man, than I'll apologize to you in heaven. I would much rather do that than beg forgiveness from a child who I had not done my best to protect.

On the news recently was the tragic report of a pastor who was killed while preaching from the pulpit on a Sunday morning. His Bible was shattered by bullets as he raised it in defense. Do you have a crisis/emergency plan? Do your

ushers, staff, and pastors have code words for a dangerous situation that they see developing? Our ushers and elders surrounded an inebriated man who walked down our main aisle yelling questions at the pastor. They walked him to the lobby and prayed over him while in the center of the group a retired police officer patted him down for weapons. We care, but we try not to be naive or foolish.

Do your teachers on Sunday, or during the weekly ministries, know how to go to lockdown mode? If you are in lockdown, do you have the green or red signs to put in your windows? This is a universal sign to emergency personnel to stop (if you have an injury) or bypass your room. (If you are going to do training on this subject, warn your teachers first.) My worst professional mistake came when I was asked to train a new staff person in our emergency procedures. Forgetting that weekday preschool was in session, I first announced over the all-church intercom that there was a man with a gun in the parking lot and for all classrooms to go to lockdown. Then a minute later, I demonstrated our announcements for finding a lost child. After I described his age and clothing my poor teachers were frantically trying to figure out who was missing and how do we look for him if we are on lockdown. As the horror then dawned of what must be going on in the preschool, I calmly announced over the loud speakers, "This was just a drill." Then I got busy writing letters of apology and setting up meetings with any parents who needed my personal groveling.

Child Abuse: Reporting and Investigations (for your use on pages 169–171 and the CD-Rom) is just the basics. There are DVDs and books on the subject, which should be used in training all pastors, staff, and volunteers. These are often available from your church's insurance company. Recently, I had to walk a pastor friend of mine through the online reporting to Child Protection for a young man who had been abused at his church. I have had to document and at times photograph children hit in the face with a pot of spaghetti, whipped with the oil dip stick from a car engine, or forced to eat dog food because of misbehavior. Children's Ministry is not for the faint of heart. However, we are not in this alone. Jesus called the little ones to come to him, and he wants us to care for the fatherless and the neglected. The church ought to be a safe, loving place for the abused and a place of healing for the abuser.

I wanted to briefly consider your personal safety. There are some safeguards that should always be in place. For instance, don't meet with members of the opposite sex in private. If this seems to be absolutely necessary, leave the door ajar or have a window installed in your office door. If you are having potentially explosive or contentious meetings, always have a third-party witness. Another option is to record the conversation, with permission of course. It is amazing how people will be careful with their words when they know they can be held accountable for them. I even have witnesses to my side of the phone conversation when I suspect the parent might be unreceptive or belligerent.

When you discipline a child, do it in view of another adult. A "stern talking to" can go home to the parents as "screaming." A hand on the shoulder can be misrepresented as a hit or pinch. Children can sometimes try to deflect the focus from their misbehavior to you. I have been called a "Nazi" for putting a toddler in timeout, shot at with a bow and arrow for taking privileges away from a fifth grader at camp, and threatened to have my head knocked off by a father who we insisted follow proper procedure to pick up his child. Just to name a few.

What should you do when a child is left at a church event and phone calls to all numbers are unsuccessful? Hours go by. There are risks involved in any decision at this point depending on how well you know the family and what the home situation is like. Your choices include calling the police and Child Protection because you have an abandoned child. Or providing care for the child if you are certain that it is just a bizarre communication between parents or child care providers. Whatever you choose should be discussed with a pastor, elder, and so forth so you have coverage if a problem arises. You could be sued for transporting and feeding a child without permission. I always have a car seat in my office for any emergency.

This chapter is not meant to frighten or overwhelm you. On the contrary, if you are prepared, then the darts that the enemy will throw at you will bounce harmlessly off the shield that you have raised.

Loralee Boe, Children's Minister for Crossroads Christian Church of Vacaville, CA, since July 1992, and presenter for ACSI, AWANA, Vacaville Unified School District, and The National Association of Early Childhood Educators. Married since 1986 to a wonderful husband and the mother of two grown children, she graduated from Pacific Christian College/Hope University in 1980 with a degree in Social Science and a Minor in Child Psychology. Loralee's previous experience was in Private/Corporate Child Care, Human Resources. and Business.

Child Abuse: Reporting and Investigations

Child abuse is a serious crime and *(Your Church Name)* intends to prosecute child abuse in any form to the fullest extent of the law. You are under these obligations as a volunteer.

1. Reporting requirements

All volunteers and employees shall immediately report and document any incident of abuse or violation of which they have knowledge or which they have observed. Any person making such a report shall keep the information strictly confidential.

2. Incident of abuse defined

An "incident of abuse" means any occurrence in which any person:

- Has threatened to inflict or has inflicted physical injury upon a child, youth worker, or vulnerable adult, other than by accidental means, or is reasonably suspected to have done so.

- Commits or allows to be committed any sexual offense against a child, youth, or vulnerable adult or is reasonably suspected to have done so.

- With respect to a child, youth, or vulnerable adult, makes any kind of sexual advance, makes a request for sexual favors, or engages in sexually motivated physical contact or is reasonably suspected to have done so.

- Exposes a child, youth, or vulnerable adult to verbal, visual, or physical conduct of a sexual nature or is reasonably suspected to have done so.

3. Imminent threat

In all cases where an imminent threat of continued or actual abuse exists, any witness shall immediately contact any Pastor, Minister, Ministry Coordinator, or Elder to request that immediate steps be taken to ensure the safety of the alleged victim. After the safety of the alleged victim has been secured, the person witnessing or with knowledge of the incident of abuse shall complete a written report of the incident of abuse and submit the report to the Children's Minister (or in his/her absence other appropriate staff or board member).

4. Obligation to report to Law Enforcement

In all cases where any volunteer or staff member has reasonable cause to believe that a child or youth, known to the volunteer or staff member in a professional capacity, has been or may be abused or neglected by either known or unknown persons inside or outside of *(Your Church Name)*, the worker shall make a report to the local law enforcement agency's child abuse investigators. If the volunteer or staff member is in doubt regarding whether a report should be made, he or she shall telephone the agency anonymously and discuss the situation with an investigator to determine whether the report should be made. The volunteer or staff member shall make a written record of the name and the title of the investigator with whom he or she spoke and the recommendation made by the investigator and submit a copy of the written record to the Children's Minister.

5. Internal Reporting Procedure

The person reporting an incident of abuse shall contact the Children's Minister (or in his/her absence, a pastor or any member of the Board of Elders). The reporter shall provide information regarding all relevant facts with respect to the incident of abuse. Upon receiving a report of an incident of abuse, the person receiving the report, together with the reporter, shall complete a written report of the incident and submit a copy of the report to *(Your Church Name)* Insurance Agency. However, in all cases where the alleged wrongdoer is the person to whom a report should be made, he or she shall be considered absent for the purposes of this reporting procedure and the report should be submitted to another appropriate *(Your Church Name)* representative.

6. Responding to the report

When someone receives a report of an incident of abuse, he or she shall immediately take steps to ensure the safety of the alleged victim. After the safety of the alleged victim has been secured, and after the report has been appropriately documented, the person receiving the report shall:

- Immediately contact the Children's Minister or any member of the Board of Elders who will then contact the parents or guardian of the alleged victim to inform each of them of the incident.

- Immediately contact the Children's Minister or any member of the Board of Elders who will contact Church Mutual Insurance. Church Mutual Insurance shall — within 72 hours of the report — conduct an investigation and determine (along with the Children's Minister) whether there is reasonable cause to believe that the abuse may have occurred.

Permission granted to copy for local church use.

- Take all reasonable steps necessary to ensure that the alleged wrongdoer has no contact with the alleged victim pending investigation.

- Take all steps necessary to ensure that the alleged wrongdoer is barred from further work with children, youth, or vulnerable adults pending the investigation.

Conclusion of no abuse

- If *(Your Church Name)* counsel concludes that there is not reasonable cause to believe the abuse may have occurred, *(Your Church Name)* legal counsel shall provide a written report to the Board of Elders documenting the conclusions reached and the basis for those conclusions. The contents of the report presented by legal counsel where no abuse was found shall be confidential unless requested by law enforcement officials.

Conclusion of abuse

- If *(Your Church Name)* legal counsel concludes that there is reasonable cause to believe that abuse may have occurred, legal counsel shall provide a written account to the Board of Elders.

- The written report shall:

  Identify the alleged victim, the alleged wrongdoer, and all witnesses identified and contacted.

  Set forth the allegations and the steps taken to investigate the allegations.

  Set forth the facts revealed by each significant witness.

  Set forth the temporary actions to be taken to the Board of Elders as well as a recommendation of additional actions to be taken by the Board of Elders.

In addition, *(Your Church Name)* legal counsel shall:

- Report the incident to the appropriate local law enforcement agency's child abuse investigators.

- Report the incident of abuse to all other appropriate governmental authorities.

- Conduct all further investigations as directed by the Board of Elders.

Volunteer/Child Protection

(Your Church Name) intends to ensure the health, safety, and well-being of volunteers and children. As a precaution and to ensure strict accountability from one adult to another, follow these rules:

1. Two team members in room

Two should remain together in a classroom at all times. If a volunteer needs to leave a classroom, please ask another adult or teen helper to step in to maintain the two volunteers in a room policy.

2. Restroom Policy

Volunteers should help a child use the restroom only if the child is four years or younger. If a child is four years or younger, the volunteers should leave the outer door of the restroom open. If a child is over the age of four, the volunteer should check the restroom before the child enters it and then wait outside for the child.

3. Appropriate touch

Appropriate touch is part of a healthy ministry. These are the following guidelines for when, where, and how to use appropriate touch. These are also the guidelines for actions you as a volunteer should *never* take.

A. Using good judgment, the following are appropriate ways to touch kids:

- An arm around the shoulder
- Walking hand in hand
- Carrying small children piggy-back
- Short congratulatory or greeting hugs
- A brief, assuring pat on the back or shoulder
- Handshake and high-fives

B. *Never:*

- Never touch a child in anger or disgust
- Never touch a child in any manner that may be construed as sexually suggestive
- Never touch a child between the belly button and the shin (diapering is the obvious exception)
- Never touch a child's private parts (diapering is the obvious exception)

4. Open door policy

Volunteers must keep classroom doors unlocked at all times for safety and accountability measures.

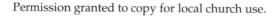

Permission granted to copy for local church use.

Communicable Disease Policy

It is the intent of *(Your Church Name)* to attempt to meet the spiritual needs of each individual who comes to the church honestly seeking worship, fellowship, and spiritual growth. In keeping with such, there will be no exceptions to this policy. This would apply to those with communicable diseases. For those whose diagnosis would require isolation, a proper referral will be made. For those whose diagnosis allows for integration, this will be affected with discretion and sensitivity.

Procedure: Guidelines Relating to Persons with Infectious Diseases.
   a.   workers
   b.   clients i.e., infants, youth

These guidelines apply to infectious diseases transmitted through contact with blood, blood products, excretions, secretions, tissues (including open skin lesions, urine, saliva, vomitus, feces, tears, sweat), drainage from any orifice.

1. **General**
   a. **Careful hand washing before and after contact with all individuals and his/her belongings (i.e., clothing) is the most important personal hygiene practice.** Pay particular attention to around and under fingernails and between the fingers.
   b. **Disposable gloves should be used any time there will be contact with blood or body fluids (i.e., urine, bowel movements, disposable diapers, gauze pads, or dressings).** Gloves need not be worn in ordinary contact.
   c. **Surfaces contaminated with blood or body fluids should be promptly cleaned and disinfected with a solution of household bleach.** The solution should be left on the surface to be disinfected for at least ten minutes before it is rinsed or wiped off. The surface should be wiped with a disposable cloth and then rinsed with another disposable cloth containing warm water.

2. **Personal Contact**
   a. **Affection is an important part of care, especially for children.** Cuddling, hugging, feeding is considered safe.
   b. **Care providers who are accidentally exposed to blood or body fluids (i.e., urine) should wear gloves when removing their soiled clothing and wash with soap and water.** Contaminated garments should be handled as in 4.b "Laundry." When accidental skin exposure occurs, remove blood or body substances by washing exposed areas with soap and water.
   c. **Any biting, i.e. child vs. child, child vs. adult, should be immediately and firmly discouraged.** This activity should then be brought to the attention of the parents by the staff person on duty.

3. Contact with Blood

a. Skin Breaks

Persons providing care should attempt to minimize breaks in their skin. (Chapping of hands can be prevented by the use of hand lotion.) If the ill person has breaks in the skin, the caregiver should use gloves when touching those areas. Good hand washing should be used before and after any direct contact.

b. Bleeding Lesions

Bleeding or oozing cuts or abrasions (either the caregiver or the ill person) should be covered with gauze or adhesive bandages whenever possible. The caregiver's fingernails should be kept trimmed and clean to prevent scratching or cutting the patient.

4. Items that may be contaminated with Secretions and Excretions

a. Food, Dishes, and Utensils

Mouth-to-mouth sharing of food (utensils, spoons, forks, knives) and other objects (i.e., pencils, toys) should be discouraged. Otherwise, special precautions related to food, dishes, and utensils are unnecessary; e.g., separate dishwashing for the dishes and utensils used by the ill person. Dishwashing with soap and hot water is all that is required before use by others.

b. Laundry

(1) Washing with soap and hot water, followed by thorough rinsing, is suggested. If available, a washing machine and dryer should be utilized. In general, separate laundering is not needed for items used by the ill person. (All workers should wear clothing that can be laundered with hot water.)

(2) Before washing, body-fluid-contaminated items only should be stored in plastic bags, and then washed separately in the hottest water setting for at least 25 minutes. A standard laundry soap and ½ cup of bleach should be added per wash load. Gloves should be worn when handling contaminated items.

(3) In order to prevent staining of blood-soiled clothing, laundry may be soaked immediately in one cup of bleach to one-gallon cold water solution for at least ten minutes, then wash as stated above.

c. Disposable Items

(1) Used gloves, gauze pads, disposable diapers, disposable washcloths, or any other disposable materials from the patient should be disposed of and promptly discarded in sealed trash bags or containers.

(2) Do not share toothbrushes, towels, combs, or other personal items. (Disinfect with bleach solution after use.)

5. Disinfectants

a. The most commonly used disinfectant is a solution of household bleach, such as Clorox or Purex. The recommended strength is one cup of bleach per gallon of water. This solution should be prepared fresh daily. Commercially prepared solutions in spray bottles are also acceptable for use.

b. Spilled blood or other body fluids should be disinfected with bleach solution. In order for disinfectants to work, they should be left on areas for at least ten minutes before cleaning with soap and water.

Permission granted to copy for local church use.

A Statement From the Elders on HIV (the AIDS virus) and Our Church's Response to Those Infected

It is the intent of Crossroads Christian Church to encourage practical responsibility and righteousness in the way that we corporately and individually demonstrate the breadth and length and height and depth of Christ's love to all of God's creation (Ephesians 3:14-19). Because of the presence of growing numbers of persons with AIDS in our society and the growing data on HIV, the board of elders of Crossroads Christian Church has adopted the following policy on AIDS to apply to the life of the church.

Christians are called to have compassion on all persons in need. Because we are followers of Jesus Christ, we must follow his example and teaching, as well as those of the Old and New Testament writers in showing comfort and compassion to those who suffer from HIV disease. Just as Jesus showed compassion on those with leprosy (the HIV disease of his day), so must we show concern, compassion, and Christ's love and attempt to comfort those who may have this equally dreaded disease of our day and society. Colossians 3:12 urges us, as God's chosen ones, to be full of compassion, kindness, and gentleness to those afflicted ones among us.

Acquired Immune Deficiency Syndrome (AIDS) is a serious, life-threatening condition. The best scientific evidence indicates that AIDS is caused by a virus known as HIV (human immunodeficiency virus), which is usually transmitted through the exchange of blood or semen by infected sex partners, contaminated hypodermic needles, contaminated donated blood, or infected mothers to their infants.

We acknowledge that there are innocent victims who contract AIDS and other diseases through no fault of their own, such as health care workers, those who contract HIV through blood transfusions and rape, and babies born to HIV-positive mothers. Due to the fact that AIDS has been spread in our nation and world primarily through behavior that is immoral and/or illegal (sexual immorality and drug abuse), we must affirm the biblical teaching that sexual intimacy is to be experienced only in the committed relationship of heterosexual marriage. Other kinds of sexual behavior are dishonoring to God and bear specific consequences of spiritual guilt and physical disease. The abuse of drugs invites a variety of tragic consequences as well, with the possibility of contacting HIV being one of them.

In responding to the knowledge that someone attending CCC can or could possibly be infected with the AIDS virus, the Board of Elders will be guided by current medical knowledge.

An individual who has been diagnosed as being HIV positive or having AIDS would be treated with the same compassion as any other individual attending CCC. In general, CCC intends not to reject or ostracize anyone who is HIV-positive or who has AIDS, as long as that individual presents no real threat to the safety of others in the congregation. The confidentiality of HIV positive individuals will be determined case-by-case based on the risk of potential exposure to others within the church.

In the case of infants or small children who are HIV positive, U.S. Public Health Service guidelines are being followed. (See Communicable Disease Policy handout.) Nursery and children's workers will be trained accordingly.

It is almost certainly true that infection with the HIV virus takes a multiplicity of forms, some disabling and some not, varying not only from individual-to-individual, but also from one phase to another within the same individual. From what is known today, AIDS reduces the body's immune response, leaving the infected person vulnerable to life threatening infection and malignancies. Medical knowledge about AIDS is developing and thus is incomplete. New modes of transmission are discovered as research continues. Therefore to provide the safest possible environment for the congregation of Crossroads Christian Church an HIV-positive individual will participate in a ministry position only with the approval of Elders and Staff.

Permission granted to copy for local church use.

Church_____

Incident Report

Date of Incident: _____ Time of Incident: _____

Location of Incident: _____ Room _____

Incident witnessed by: _____ and _____

Injured Child's name: _____ Age: _____

Child's address: _____

Telephone Numbers_____

Parent's name(s) _____

How and when were parent(s) notified: _____

By whom were parents notified: _____

Are they members of _____? ❏ Yes ❏ No
(Your Church Name)

If not a member, how long have they attended _____? _____
(Your Church Name)

Situation: _____

_____

Did child receive first aid on site? ❏ Yes ❏ No If yes by whom _____

Was an ambulance or paramedic summoned? ❏ Yes ❏ No

Was child transported to a hospital for treatment? ❏ Yes ❏ No

If yes, where was child transported: _____

Status of injured child: _____

_____

Your Name: _____Supervisor's name: _____

_____

For Office Use Only

Minister doing follow up: _____ Date of follow up: _____

Status of follow up: _____

_____

_____Signature: _____

Date resolved: _____

This form is to be filled out in case of accident or injury.

Injury Procedures

Typically an injury can be treated with a little tender loving care, a cool cloth, and a bandage, but we need to be prepared for everything. We keep a well-stocked first-aid kit in each classroom. (Note the cupboard with a Red Cross symbol) Please treat the child and complete an *Incident Report*. Please talk with the parent upon their arrival and let them know what happened. A staff member will follow up with the parent, if necessary, the following week.

Responding to a Minor Injury or Illness

1. Separate the injured or ill student from other children.
2. Isolate the area where any blood or body fluid may have dropped on carpet, toys, chairs, and so forth.
3. Keep other students from having contact with the body fluid.
4. Locate the first-aid kit and put on latex gloves.
5. Attend to the child as needed using *Communicable Disease Policy*.
6. Place all soiled gauze, bandages, and wrappers into the zip-closure bag. Remove latex gloves and place into the bag. Seal and dispose of the bag in a plastic-lined trash container.
7. Wash hands carefully with antibacterial soap.
8. Clean the room following the *Communicable Disease Policy*. This is best accomplished by a custodian.

Keep in mind that we are not authorized to dispense any over-the-counter or prescription medication. In the event that a child needs more attention than we can provide, the parent will be notified.

In the event of an emergency call 911

Responding to a Serious Injury

Serious injuries involving broken bones, convulsions, fainting, unconsciousness, or severe bodily injury should be treated as follows:

1. Keep calm and keep children and injured person as calm as possible. Speak assuringly to the child.
2. Do not move the injured child or leave them alone.
3. Send a leader to find the parent and Children's Minister.
4. The Children's Minister will refer to the parent's details on doctor or hospital preferences.
5. If the child needs to be transported to the hospital immediately and a parent cannot be located in time, the Children's Minister will accompany the child to the hospital.
6. The Children's Minister will follow up with the child as needed.
7. All volunteers and staff members involved in the emergency should write out a report of what happened immediately following the incident.

Playground Policies

1. The playground is designed for ages one through twelve. No one older than sixth grade is allowed on the equipment.

2. The Little Tykes Playground is specifically for ages one through four.

3. The wooden playground is specifically for elementary age children.

4. Please supervise the children at all times and make sure they are on the appropriate play structure. No children should ever be on the playground unsupervised. Two supervisors needed.

5. Gate should be kept latched at all times. Gate should be locked when you leave.

6. It is helpful to take tissues on the playground with you.

7. Please pick up and throw away any dangerous item or trash. Safety should always be on our minds. Any equipment that needs repair should be immediately reported to the Children's Minister.

8. Children needing to go to the restroom should always be accompanied by a team member. (Elementary can go in pairs.) It is helpful to take all children to the bathroom before outside play time.

© 2009 Abingdon Press

> ### Disclaimer
> Before you implement any policy related to this topic, consult with your legal counsel to obtain final approval from your attorney, as these topics are very delicate situations, and to avoid the possibility of violating any person's civil or legal rights.

Safe Church Guidelines Response to Convicted Sexual Offenders

Administration

This policy serves as a guideline to provide a framework that addresses Crossroads Christian Church's response to convicted sexual offenders who visit, attend, become members, or who are already members of Crossroads Christian Church. The Elders of Crossroads Christian Church may modify these guidelines, on a case-by-case basis, to fulfill the intent of these guidelines, based on each unique situation encountered. To this end, enforcement of these guidelines will be at the authority of the Church Elders.

Purpose

Crossroads Christian Church (hereafter, "CCC") is committed to creating and maintaining programs, services, facilities, and a church community in which employees, volunteers, members, attendees, and any other persons served by CCC can worship and work together in a safe atmosphere, free from acts committed by convicted sexual offenders. It is the intention of CCC to take action to prevent and correct behavior that is contrary to these guidelines and, as necessary, to discipline or cause to report and/or arrest those persons who violate these guidelines.

Crossroads Christian Church Role

CCC recognizes that we can play a substantial role in assisting convicted sexual offenders returning to society and rebuilding their lives. As offenders work towards rebuilding their lives, restoring relationships, and overcoming old behaviors, CCC will encourage the offenders' much needed support and assist them with their commitment to faith through a customized approach that addresses individual situations.

CCC is committed to providing a safe and healthy environment in which people of all ages can learn about and experience God's love, as well as a place of healing and change for offenders. If a convicted sexual offender is violating these guidelines and expectations, they may be excluded from attending CCC.

Terminology and Situational Differences

CCC recognizes that the term "sexual offender" covers a wide range of individuals. Therefore, each type of offender presents a different level of risk for committing new offenses, and each situation is unique. Some offenders will be truly repentant, and CCC can play a valuable role in encouraging their faith commitment as they work to conquer old behaviors and urges. Other offenders, unfortunately, may still seek opportunities to approach children or other potentially vulnerable people.

Accountability Procedures

For the protection of employees, volunteers, members, attendees, children, and other potentially vulnerable people, convicted sexual offenders must meet with church staff or CCC Elders before an affiliation with CCC can be established. The purpose of these meetings is for the protection of CCC as well as that of the offenders.

To maximize accountability, CCC may interact with the following agencies, including, but not limited to:

- Parole
- Probation
- Social Workers
- Local Law Enforcement
- Psychologists
- Therapists

Accountability Partnership

In order to shield the offender from temptation and reduce the chances for further offenses while at CCC or church-sponsored events, an Accountability Partner may be assigned to offenders.

Accountability Partners should be trained volunteers who can monitor the offenders while on CCC property or attending CCC-sponsored events. The Accountability Partner may be a CCC staff member, CCC Elder, Law Enforcement (off duty or retired), or other person designated by CCC Elders to act in this role. The Accountability Partner position may be rotated. To avoid miscommunication regarding Accountability Partners' assignments (i.e., "I thought it was Bill's turn this week."), a system should be put in place by the CCC Elders, CCC staff members, or their designee.

The Accountability Partner should have visual awareness of the offender when on CCC property or at church-sponsored events. Accountability Partners should discretely escort offenders away from areas where their access could cause the offender temptation.

Offender Covenant

In order to provide support for offenders' rehabilitation and recovery, yet hold them accountable and aid in the assessment of potential for re-offending, CCC may offer the offender a Covenant. This Covenant is designed to help offenders avoid situations that could provide opportunities to further offend. The Covenant may include, but is not limited to, the following:

- Avoid all contact with children (under 18 years of age), or other vulnerable people, on church property or at church-sponsored events
- Provide copies of offenders' conditions of probation or parole to CCC
- A prohibition to the nursery and children's/youth ministry areas
- Permission to convey information to others about the offenders' conviction, if the church believes it is necessary for protection of children or other vulnerable people
- Permission to contact and collaborate with community agencies and staff such as, but not limited to, probation/parole officers, counselors, psychologists, police officers, and others assigned to work with

rehabilitation for status reports to identify whether or not CCC should allow the offenders to participate, and to what extent
- Agreement to attend ongoing counseling with CCC staff or CCC Elders, and/or outside professional doctors, counselors, or therapists

If an offender fails to comply with the terms of their Covenant, the offender may no longer be permitted to attend CCC. If an offender disagrees with the Covenant terms, the offender can be denied access to CCC and/or church-sponsored activities.

Ongoing Counseling Sessions

If it is necessary, CCC may offer or mandate appropriate ongoing guidance counseling. This counseling may be conducted by pastoral staff or with an outside professional counselor. Ongoing counseling may include, but is not limited to, obtaining updated status of offenders' recovery and assessment of potential risks. Regular written progress reports may be requested by CCC Staff, CCC Elders, or their designee.

Communication with Church Membership

Under the discretion of the CCC Elders and CCC Staff, information related to these Safety Guidelines may be communicated to others. Prior to any disclosure of information regarding specific offenders, the following should consult legal counsel to:
- Ensure that offenders' "rights to privacy" are not violated
- Ensure victims' "rights to privacy" are not violated
- Research legal requirements of California State Law
- Determine who has a "Need to Know / Right to Know" regarding the disclosure of information.
- Pastors, Elders, Youth Ministers, Staff, and others, such as Law Enforcement (off duty or retired), should be made aware that an offender is participating in church activities.
- Disclose that the offender has agreed to a Covenant with CCC that sets limitations on participation, establishes an Accountability Partner for oversight, and precludes any contact with children or other vulnerable people.
- Limit communication to factual statements such as information supported by actual terms of parole or probation.
- Be respectful, considerate, and circumspect
- Avoid slandering or defaming offenders
- Avoid speculation about what might have happened in the past
- Avoid predicting the future
- Be aware that CCC members not originally informed of a specific situation may eventually learn of it.
- Know in advance how to respond.
- Remember "Need to Know / Right to Know."

Resource

The following is a public website for searches regarding convicted sexual offenders: United States Department of Justice — Dru Sjodin National Sex Offender Public Website
http://www.nsopr.gov/

Permission granted to copy for local church use.

Wellness Policy

*To keep our children and team members healthy we ask that parents
not check in children to our ministry with any of the contagious
illness. To help with screening the following list has been prepared.*

To help you recognize common illnesses:

Allergies
(not contagious)

Red, swollen, watery eyes, sneezing, headaches, spasmodic coughing, hives, rash, gas pains, vomiting, diarrhea, eczema, nose rubbing, constant cold.

Chicken Pox
(extremely contagious)

Fever may appear 1 day prior to observance of skin lesions. Lesions are small, clear clusters about the size of a match head. Usually start on face and scalp and move downward. Often behind ears and neck. Blisters easily broken, quickly form itchy crusts or scabs. Contagious until all lesions have crusted over.

Colds
(contagious)

Sneezing, running or stuffy nose, flushed cheeks, dull-looking eyes, little appetite, may have slight fever or cough.

**Conjunctivitis
Pink Eye** *(contagious)*

Sore red eyes, with yellow discharge.

Diaper Rash
(some are contagious)

Small red pimples or patches of rough, shiny, itchy red skin. Pimples may develop white heads or become raw. End of penis may develop rash or ulcerate and bleed (rare). Diapers have an ammonia smell.

Ear Infection
(not contagious)

Infants become irritable, fussy, sleep short intervals, awaken crying, act hungry. May pull at ears.

**Fifth Disease
(Erythema
Infectiosum)**
(mildly contagious)

Fine rash on face, arms, buttocks. Usually occurs between ages four to twelve. Rash comes and goes over period of seven to ten days.

**Hand, Foot and
Mouth Disease**
*(contagious with
close contact)*

Fever, sore throat, blisters develop on hands and feet. Incubation period 3-7 days. Entire illness lasts 5-7 days.)

Impetigo
(extremely contagious)

Starts as small runny blister, often on the face. Sometimes develops into infected sore. Generally staph infection has light tan or honey-colored crust.

© 2009 Abingdon Press

Special Events

This is the day that the LORD has made;
let us rejoice and be glad in it.

(Psalm 118:24)

UGSFAW!
A Unique Way to Build a Vibrant Summer Program

by Kurt Goble

I'm not against VBS. I know that around the world many churches are doing great things through VBS programs. We just aren't one of those churches. VBS became a tedious and exhausting chore for us. Finally, I sat down with my leaders and began the process of wrestling with some tough questions:

1. What are we accomplishing?

2. Why does VBS burn us out?

3. Shouldn't this be fun?

4. Why don't the kids seem to enjoy it?

5. Why do we keep doing it?

6. Are the kids learning anything?

7. Is VBS a viable ministry opportunity, or just "Vacation Baby Sitting"?

8. Is it really possible to reach preschool and elementary students with the same program?

After suffering the collision between our ideals and our reality, we arrived at the following assessment:

- Not one individual or family could be found who had connected to our church because of VBS.

- VBS accounted for 38 percent of our annual children's ministry budget but yielded very few tangible benefits.

- Children were not having fun, connecting with others, or retaining concepts. They were being run through a "rotation mill" that most of them did not enjoy.

- Volunteer numbers were dwindling year after year. Volunteers found the week to be stressful and exhausting.

- We were burning out our volunteers just before September, when we needed them most.

- We were one of 16 churches in our immediate area doing VBS. We were replicating a program that was already saturating our community.

- Almost all of the attendees were already "churched."

- Our primary motivation for doing VBS was because of pressure from those who expected it of us.

- We had no passion for it.

Based on this assessment, I did away with the program, with no plan for replacing it with anything of its kind. People were upset; some even wanted this decision to cost me my job. There was even a group that ran a clandestine little VBS program for their own children. However, this decision ultimately led me to a place where I was free to ask new "what if" questions.

- What if we did something different?

- What if we focused only on elementary students?

- What if we targeted kids who weren't already going to other churches and VBS programs?

- What if a top priority was that volunteers have fun and feel valued?

- What if kids were given choices?

- What if the message was simple, clear, concise, and repeated in creative ways?

- What if we scrapped the traditional format and did something different?

UGSFAW! A Unique Way to Build a Vibrant Summer Program

After struggling with these questions, a vision was born. We called it UGSFAW, which stands for Ultimate, Gnarly, Super-Fantastic, Awesome Week. It is just for kids entering first through fifth grade, and runs Monday through Friday from 9 AM to noon for one week. After six years of UGSFAW, our church has embraced it. Although UGSFAW has many characteristics that differentiate it from VBS, I'd like to tell about a few features that are key elements to success.

We ditched the skits and started making videos.

For us, the cost/benefit ratio for making a good series of videos is comparable to that of putting forth a good drama series. More money is spent on equipment; less is spent on props and sets. More time is spent in preparation and post-production; less time is spent in rehearsals.

The big difference is timing. When you are working with video, by the time your program begins, the work is done. This alleviates an incredible amount of stress. During the busiest week of my year, I don't have to worry about actors showing up on time, people remembering their lines, sets being completed on time, missing props, missed audio and lighting cues—the list goes on.

This has also allowed us to go places that we could never go on our stage. We have interacted with live animals, taken road trips, and shot our own "reality series." A new world of genre and style became available when we moved our action from the stage to the screen.

We ditched our traditional rotation format and created an experience for four large teams.

The impact of this decision became apparent as soon as we began recruiting. Back when we recruited for VBS, we would say things like, "I need to fill a classroom position for elementary. We've made it easy. Each day you come in and do the same lesson and activity five times…." Now my team captains say, "I want you on my team!"

Would you rather be asked to perform a necessary task or asked to join a team? People feel valued and included when team captains invite them to be a part of the action. During the

program, a lighthearted, competitive atmosphere helps create excitement. Our teams always move together. For the sake of safety and accountability, volunteers are in charge of groups within the teams. Sometimes it feels like organized chaos, but we're OK with that. It's one of the things that make us different.

We ditched quantity teaching for quality teaching.

One problem we had at VBS was "information overload." We were delivering so many concepts and ideas during a three-hour period that children were not retaining any of it. So I decided that, each day, we would teach one key concept. Then we would teach it again, and again, and again in different ways so that it is never boring. I'd rather send children home at the end of the week with a few key concepts they will remember for the rest of their lives than with a whole bunch of information that they'll forget by tomorrow.

The first time we teach a concept, it is within the context of a lesson taught in the opening session. The second time the kids hear it is during Competition Prep. Competition Prep is where a team captain reviews the day's lesson and memory verse with the kids, with the purpose of scoring points at the Game Show and winning the Memory Verse Competition. The team captain also has the kids practice team cheers and gets the kids excited about the day. The third time the kids hear the day's concept is during the Game Show, where questions are asked in a buzz-in, get slimed, spin the wheel, make a deal kind of format. It's a big, crazy game show. The fourth time they hear it is during closing session, where we have the Memory Verse Competition and one final team quiz competition.

The retention of concepts is really good. We know of students from our first UGSFAW, six years ago, who are now in junior high and high school and who can recall what they learned at UGSFAW.

We ditched activity and chores for community and choices.

Rotations were the most stressful part of our VBS experience. We had 20 minutes to do a craft. Some compliant students simply went along with it, while some of the girls really got into it and wanted more time. "Sorry, girls. Finish up so that we can keep moving." Then there were the boys who didn't want to do a craft. "Sorry, guys. Just do the craft!"

Snack time presented the same kinds of problems. On the first couple of rotations, many kids weren't hungry when it was their snack time. "Sit down, and eat your snack."

The same problems were prevalent in almost every setting: outdoor games, classrooms, and so forth. There was the boy who didn't want to do a craft because God didn't wire him that way, or the girl who sat there with her arms crossed for 15 minutes because she had just eaten breakfast and wasn't hungry for a snack: These kids were considered behavioral issues. The truth is that these were program issues.

This type of interaction also served to deplete the relationship between child and volunteer. Kids saw their leaders as people who were always hurrying them from place to place and making them do things. Volunteers saw non-compliant children as troublemakers who were making it hard to manage the rest of the group. How are we supposed to befriend these children and mentor them and love them into a relationship with their Creator in this setting? We were setting people up to fail.

At UGSFAW, we don't have these problems. Snack and crafts happen in The Café, along with some other creative and interactive options such as board games and art. Kids have 30 minutes there, and they can choose to do whatever they want. "Don't want to do a craft? That's OK." "Not hungry? You don't have to have a snack."

This place is about building community and relationships. Our volunteers understand this and are trained to keep an eye out for any solo children who might need a friend to play with. It's amazing how many of the older kids choose to just hang out and visit with one another. Sometimes the snacks are creative; usually, they are not. We just give the kids lots of choices. Sometimes the crafts tie in to the lesson; sometimes they don't. Our purpose behind crafts is community and relationship-building. Lesson reinforcement happens in other ways.

The other place where community and interaction happen is the Fun Zone. Each year we set up the best play area we can manage. There are inflatable climbers and bounce houses, videogames, table games, sports, and places to hang out with friends. This is where kids can get their wiggles out, and volunteers can play with them. And kids want to be around adults who will play with them.

In these two areas, we create environments that are semi-structured, where relationships can flourish and spontaneity is allowed.

We ditched volunteer breaks for volunteer care.

At VBS, we used to have a volunteer break room. The schedule was designed so that volunteers would get a break and be able to have a cup of coffee and a snack before returning to their positions. I used to ask myself, "Is this really so bad that we can't ask them to go for three hours without a break?" I wanted my volunteers to have such a good time that they didn't want breaks.

My new volunteer orientation starts like this: "Welcome to UGSFAW. We want you volunteers to have fun. We believe that if you aren't having a great time, then our kids won't have a great time. We want our kids to be surrounded by happy people this week. Volunteer Rule 1 is 'If you aren't having fun, you need to let us know so that we can fix the problem, move you to a position that suits you better, or lovingly excuse you from service.'"

Making it fun for our volunteers requires much. We do some very intentional things to ensure that they are having a good time. My leadership is intentionally top-heavy. Six of us are coordinating volunteers. Four team captains handle the leaders who work with their teams. I coordinate everything production oriented. I have an assistant who handles the Café, the Fun Zone, our volunteer appreciation lunch, and everything else.

We make our volunteers' jobs clear and simple.

Most of our volunteers are group leaders. Team captains lead these groups to their different environments. The captains run the show. We tell our leaders, "It's your job to enjoy and experience UGSFAW with the kids in your group and take care of their immediate needs. Just follow your captain's lead. You worry about the kids; we'll worry about everything else."

We also operate on the principle of open dialogue. We are responsive to our volunteers, and we value their input. We never ask our volunteers to fill out evaluations at the end of the week. Rather, we let them know that, if they have an issue or concern, they need to let us know about it immediately; because at the end of the week, it's too late to fix anything. One year, we had a scheduling problem that came to my attention on Monday. Tuesday morning we handed out new schedules and explained the change.

We make it a priority to take good care of our volunteers. This means donuts, bagels, and coffee before the program every morning at a meeting designed to keep them informed and inspired. This means serving a volunteer appreciation lunch on Wednesday after the program. But most of all, it means being responsive to their needs and input. The volunteers have a blast, and so far nobody has complained about the missing break room.

What we've learned . . .

I don't tell our story to promote a new model for week-long summer programs or to demote the relevance of VBS. We've learned some important lessons in this process, and I think that they will apply to any church program.

- **Evaluation is key**.
  Taking an honest, painful look at our VBS program was a major turning point for us. We needed to be willing to interrogate everything that we do with ruthless integrity. The realities we faced existed long before we recognized their presence. We just had to deal with them.

- **Do what works in your ministry setting.**
  If a more traditional VBS is getting great results at your church, then, by all means, do traditional VBS. It takes all kinds of churches to reach all kinds of people and all kinds of programs to reach all kinds of kids.

I'm not hoping that people follow my model....I'm hoping that people struggle to discover something that is relevant and effective in their unique church settings.

- **Feel free and empowered to shake up your VBS format.**
  Look at your curriculum as a starting point—not a roadmap. This year at UGSFAW, we are using a published curriculum. Of course, by the time we apply it to our format and add our own elements, it will look completely different. As children's pastors, we need to dictate what the final product looks like. Trying to emulate an ideal as described in a book is an impossible task that doesn't take the uniqueness of your people into consideration.

- **Keep it simple, and make it fun**.
  Our devotion to these ideas has made UGSFAW work. I have had plenty of experience struggling to assemble a minimal volunteer force. Last year, we had so many volunteers that we didn't know what to do with all of them. People call months in advance to find out when UGSFAW is scheduled so that they can take off work to help.

Remember that you are doing this for God and for God's kids. It is so easy to get caught up in doing things to impress parents, staff, and volunteers. Whatever you do, remember whom you are doing it for. As long as you are attracting children to God's church and pointing them to their Savior, the expectations and opinions of others aren't as important as we usually make them out to be.

Kurt Goble says that he has made more mistakes than anyone else in the history of children's ministry, but he loves sharing what he's learned from all of those mistakes. For 13 years, Kurt has served as children's pastor at First Christian Church of Huntington Beach, where he uses the technical arts to share God's Word with kids. He is a graduate of Bethel College and a curriculum author. He and his wife, Heidi, are happily married, with two kids.

Why Do VBS? And How Should Churches Plan for It?

by Betsy Nunn Parham and Linda Tozer

Why should churches provide vacation Bible school? Churches should be eager to provide vacation Bible school, since it offers a unique approach to Christian education during the summer months. While at VBS, children are presented stories from the Bible, have time to meet new children, get a chance to spend a good time with friends, and experience new and fun activities. At VBS, children learn Bible verses, sing upbeat music, observe skits, create crafts, participate in recreation, take part in a mission project, and have a snack or a meal.

VBS provides an opportunity to teach children about Jesus so that they can learn ways to be like Christ. "And Jesus increased in wisdom and in years, and in divine and human favor" (Luke 2:52). Children will grow in wisdom as they experience lessons from the Bible, they will grow in divine favor as they learn about God and God's love for them, and they will grow in human favor as they learn life application skills while interacting with others.

Why else should churches offer VBS? VBS offers the church a fun and creative method of teaching Christ-like values and ways to interact with others. VBS also provides a strong biblical foundation for faith development for the children.

VBS is an excellent outreach tool into the community—a way to invite those who do not normally attend church to come into the church, get involved, and build a relationship with others and with Jesus Christ. The entire congregation can get involved in this outreach program, using their God-given talents to share the love of Jesus with their congregation and community. Adults can decorate, teach, shepherd children, prepare food, send invitations, send follow-up cards to visitors, work with publicity, and pray.

How do churches plan for VBS?

- **Begin with prayer.** Pray as a church family for leaders to guide the children. Select a director to administer VBS. Decide on the best date to have VBS at your church, and begin planning 4 to 6 months before that date.

- **Enlist leaders.** Look for leaders who teach Sunday school, and ask parents of the children who will attend. The VBS director and church staff members enlist leaders to guide the children. Secure commitments from your core leaders, such as the Bible storyteller, craft leader, recreations leader, music leader, snack leader, preschool leader, assembly leader, mission leader, and a lead decorator.

- **Evaluate your facility.** Begin to map out the areas for the various rooms that will be needed. Create a map of the church and identify the location of each room and activity area that will be used for VBS.

- **Establish your VBS budget.** Evaluate your children's Sunday school attendance and estimate the prospects that will be invited. Decide on an amount that the church can spend, based on the projected enrollment.

- **Order the curriculum.** Consult the director's book as a guide to planning and preparing for VBS. Watch the preview DVD with the leaders who have already been enlisted.

Three to Four Months Before VBS

- **Schedule leadership training.**

- **Order VBS material.** Have it available for the leaders at this first training session. Let your first training session include the entire VBS leadership team. Take time to share the Bible lessons, verses, and key daily learnings. Display examples of finished crafts. Listen to the VBS music, and teach one of the songs the children will learn. Sample a few snacks.

- **Set up follow-up training sessions.** Provide scheduled opportunities for leaders to plan together in small groups. Provide childcare for the leaders so that effective planning time can be achieved.

- **Request donated craft materials.** Post a list of materials that are needed for crafts.

- **Recruit a publicity team.** Make everyone aware of the upcoming VBS. Make decisions to publicize VBS in your church and in your community. Remember that VBS is an outreach opportunity.

- **Begin VBS preregistration.** Having the numbers in advance will help your church prepare for the children who will attend.

Two Months Before VBS

- **Continue to have planning meetings** with a specific purpose and time for teaching teams to strategize.

- **Review the VBS supply list.** Purchase materials, or ask for donations.

- **Begin your publicity campaign.** Display VBS signs and banners in outdoor and indoor locations.

One Month Before VBS

- **Create a registration area in your church.** Decorate this area so that families and leaders get excited about the upcoming event.

- **Make announcements to create interest in VBS.** Involving a child in a scripted promotion can reinforce the point of the event.

- **Send out invitations through your Sunday school and publicize in your newsletter.**

- **Plan a kickoff event for VBS.**

- **Schedule a decorating day for volunteers to decorate the church.** Use backdrops and designs for doors, hallways, and rooms.

One Week Before VBS

- **Make sure that all leaders have the necessary supplies that were requested.**

- **Determine VBS registration procedures with the leadership.**

- **Put finishing touches on decorating the church facility.**

- **Set up a first-aid checkpoint.**

During VBS

- **Keep records of attendance and offerings;** evaluate supplies and staffing.

- **Conduct brief staff meetings before VBS for times of prayer and devotion.** At the end of the day, meet with staff to evaluate feedback.

- **Make arrangements to send VBS crafts and supplies home.**

Once VBS Is Over

- **Reach out to visitors** by making phone calls or visits to families. Prepare an information packet to invite them to the other services and activities at your church.

- **Thank the leaders and the church family for their support.** Share some of the stories that define the joy of VBS. Give thanks to God for blessing your VBS time.

Betsy Nunn Parham is an associate editor for vacation Bible school at The United Methodist Publishing House. She has 9 years of teaching experience and 14 years of local church experience.

Linda Tozer is the director and senior editor for vacation Bible school at The United Methodist Publishing House.

Sports Camps

by Nick Ransom

It's no secret that youth sports have become very popular in today's world. It's common to meet up with kids that play in multiple sports leagues all at the same time. You often wonder how they keep the schedules they do. Many times the schedules of youth sporting events and your children's programs come into conflict. If your church is anything like mine, sports usually wins the battle. How many times have we wondered what we can do so that our children's ministry program has the same priority as a child's soccer league? I would like to offer one possible answer that involves embracing the idea of a child's (and parents') love for sports and using it to our advantage while, at the same time, reaching our goal of having our kids become committed followers of Jesus. That answer is sports camps.

At our church in Kansas City, we have had 11 years of basketball camp in a church that is less than 20 years old. This camp has grown significantly during these years, from 1 session to 4 sessions and a following that is quite impressive. Our basketball camp has built a great reputation, and that reputation has allowed us to successfully run other sports camps from time to time. Some of the sports camps we've launched and succeeded with are soccer, baseball, cheer, and dance camps.

All of these camps take the respective sport and use it as tool to bring kids to Christ and to help them grow in their faith. The kids get to play their favorite sport, and we get an entire session of camp to help them grow in their faith. We know that parents and kids love sports, and we use this love of sports to our advantage. Here are a few key ingredients for running a terrific sports camp—no matter what sport you choose.

Great leaders are a must. Not only am I talking about a good administrative person to organize the camp, but I'm also talking about the face of your camp: the sport expert, the up-front person for your camp. I can't emphasize enough the importance of having the right leader in the most visible position of your camp. Whether your camp succeeds in the long haul is directly related to who leads your camp.

Here are a few character traits to look for in a camp leader. First, this person must be an expert in whatever sport this camp is focusing on. This will give instant credibility for parents who are sending their child for the sole purpose of improving their skills in the particular sport. This leader might also have a recognizable name in the community, but that is not necessary.

Second, this person must be strong in his or her personal walk with the Lord. The spiritual component of your leader is huge. The leader must be able to convey the message that your campers' relationship with Jesus Christ is more important than how well they play soccer, basketball, and so forth. This must be done not only by your leader's word but by his or her actions.

Third, your camp leader needs to relate well to kids and run a good camp that moves quickly and keeps the kids interested. Sometimes you may find a great high school basketball coach who is strong in his or her faith, loves basketball, but can relate only to teenagers. Your camp leader needs to be able to relate well with the kids.

Keep the appeal of camp wide open. By this, I mean that your camp needs to be a place where the hard-core athlete can come, have a good time, and improve his or her skills. The camp also needs to be a place for the average kid, who kicks the soccer ball around in the neighborhood a few times a month, to come have a good time and just play soccer. When you keep the appeal of camp broad, you open up the camp to a larger range of kids who will be interested in coming to camp. One of the practical ways to do this is to keep a balance of drills and games close to half and half, with a slight slant to more games. The competitive camper and the camper who is just there to have fun will both enjoy the games, and both will be interested in coming back.

Relationships are key. A few

paragraphs ago, I mentioned the importance of having a great up-front leader; but the camp must be supported by excellent volunteers as well. In our sports camps, we call these key volunteers assistant coaches. These assistant coaches are generally high school- and college-age kids who enjoy sports and enjoy working with kids. They do not have to play sports well, because their main job is to make sure that their 8 to 10 kids are having a great time at camp. One of the factors that make sport camps so successful in our ministry are these assistant coaches hanging around with the kids all week long and building relationships with them. The campers already see these assistant coaches as "cool" because of their age; but once they see that these high school- and college-age coaches are taking an interest in them, the kids feel special and want to be at camp every day.

Rules are necessary. Our camps have 4

main rules that we ask the kids to follow every day, and the kids are constantly reminded of these rules. They have proven successful in keeping the camp running smoothly. Here are the 4 rules we campers to follow at sports camp: 1) Pay attention; it pays off. 2) Have fun! 3) Don't mess with anyone else's fun. 4) Never say, "I can't." Always say, "I'll try."

These rules are basic, but they work well. They are most effective when the camp leader is constantly emphasizing them every day to the entire group. These rules are also very helpful when a camper attends who just wants to sit around all day. Reminding him or her of the rules usually gets the camper back into the group, giving the drill or game a chance.

The camp schedule and timing is important to the success of camp. The camp cannot drag on for the kids or even the coaches, or no one will have fun. When providing a camp for Kindergarten–fifth graders, a 3- hour camp that goes for 5 days is usually the max for this age

group. Most of the time, campers have had just the right amount of that particular sport and are ready to move on; but they still wish that there were just a little more camp left. Below is a sample 3-hour camp schedule.

8:55–9:05	Free Play
9:05–9:15	Welcome, Prayer, Camp Rules
9:15–9:25	Stretching
9:25–9:35	Warm-up Drills
9:35–10:15	Instruction Time (*drills to improve everyone's ability in the sport*)
10:15–10:30	Camp-Wide Contest (*Free-Throw Contest, Shootout, and so forth*)
10:30–10:50	Half-time Devotion and Snack
10:50–11:00	Free Play
11:00–11:45	Fun Games and Contests
11:45–12:00	Wrap-up, Prayer, and Announcements

Now you are ready to start a sports camp. Here's how you get started. First, decide on what sport your camp will focus. Next, find your up-front person, your head coach, and your sports expert. Third, locate a venue for your camp and decide dates and times. Fourth, advertise, advertise, advertise. Get the word out. Fifth, recruit assistant coaches. Finally, begin putting together all of the details of camp—from what the devotions will be to whether you'll have camp t-shirts, what age groups may attend camp, how many kids can you have at one time, and so forth—all that good stuff that makes the camp run smoothly.

However you decide to do sports camp with the kids in your ministry, make it exciting and meaningful. Most important, make it your own. You know your kids, and you know what they need. I hope that these ideas are a springboard to help you reach everyone's goal of bringing the kids in our ministry to a deeper relationship with Jesus Christ. Finally, remember to pray and ask God to use sports as a way to bring kids to Christ and to deepen their spiritual walk.

Nick Ransom is the Director of Children's Ministries at The United Methodist Church of the Resurrection, in Kansas City. He has been on staff at the church for 4 years and involved in children's ministry for more than 7 years. He has been married for almost 7 years and has 2- year-old triplet sons.

Successful Seasonal Events

by Sharon Stratmoen

You're already doing amazing things to reach kids. Have you ever thought about super-sizing your children's ministry? I'm not just talking about adding to the number of kids. I'm talking about super-sizing it with sensational seasonal events for major impact! Read on to discover how to super-size your ministry to affect kids in God-size ways.

Deuteronomy 11:18-20 (NLT) says, "So commit yourselves wholeheartedly to these words of mine. Tie them to your hands and wear them on your forehead as reminders. Teach them to your children. Talk about them when you are at home and when you are on the road, when you are going to bed and when you are getting up."

The action words in this passage are **commit, tie, teach, talk**. What do these action words tell us that parents are to do with their children?

"These words of mine" are so important that we need to teach our children at all times, in all places—whether we're sitting, walking, lying down, or getting up—every moment of every day. For our ministry to be effective in helping kids grow in their faith, we have to partner with families. That is the single best way to super-size your ministry. So you already have the secret ingredient to powerfully affect your ministry: families. Are you using it as a tool?

Children's Ministry in the 21st Century states: "Family ministry is a challenge and an opportunity for churches today. Trends and research detail the need for ministry in this area....Parents who value family time are making every effort to make it a

priority." Survey results in the *2009 State of Family Ministry*, by Christine Yount Jones, states: "Parents across the country are saying the most helpful tool for them to take faith home is through family events." So what are we waiting for?

Let me show you how easy it can be to set up sensational seasonal family ministry events that are successful. Our church has discovered that there are 5 key ingredients to a successful seasonal event.

5 Key Ingredients

1. **Be strategic.** Begin by planning unique, strategic events that have an emphasis on outreach. Families today are busier than ever. Less is more. Take advantage of the seasons, and plan your events accordingly. Fall Harvest/Halloween, Christmas, and Easter are three times of the year when families are looking for something special to do with their kids. We have discovered that these types of events are a secret strategy for attracting kids who are often unchurched. If you want proof, drive around your city in early October and count the many Halloween alternative, pumpkin patch, or fall festival signs you see.

> **W**e have discovered that these types of events are a secret strategy for attracting kids who are often unchurched.

If churches are growing in your community, they likely have church-sponsored Easter egg hunts, celebrations with Christ-centered crafts, booths, or games at local festivals or holidays.

Part of your strategy is to determine when to hold these events. We value our kids and parents and don't want our parents to serve on the actual days of Christmas and Easter. So our advice to you is not to plan your seasonal events on the High Holy Days. Choose days before the actual holidays. Keep a pulse on what's going on in your community so that you're not conflicting with another big event.

2. **Invite the entire family.** Current research begs us to extend the invitation to the entire family. Gone are the days of fall festivals, egg hunts, and the like just for kids. We intentionally plan seasonal events that allow kids and parents to be together, which helps build that relationship of parents as the primary faith developer and reduces the number of volunteers you need. Some great resources are available. Our church has had super success using Group Publishing's *A Night in Bethlehem* and *All Around Easter* for curriculum. Both include faith discovery stations for kids and their families. (Look for more details on our events at the end of this article.)

3. **Make it fun.** Effective children's and family ministry outreaches strive to make the church-based events, like a fall festival with jump castles loaded with candy, more attractive than an established alternative, such as trick-or-treating. When your families come to an event like this, you're communicating that Jesus is an absolute blast. I live by Jim Rayburn's principle: "It's a sin to bore a kid with the Gospel." And our custodian can tell you, my motto is, "The bigger the mess, the more fun we had."

4. **Offer spiritual content.** Since we're the church, we get to talk about Jesus. Tie in to seasonal events a gospel message, biblical

craft or keepsake, a lesson on virtues or character traits. Families can then use the event to talk about powerful lessons from Scripture. During an Easter egg hunt, families can discuss why they're running around looking for eggs. Is there a connection between eggs and the meaning of Easter? Challenge the family to come up with one. Send them home with something that can continue the conversation after families have left your event. Consider including a high-value craft that is worthy of keeping. The Bible verses on their keepsakes will remind them for years to come what they have learned.

5. **Make it relevant to kids**. Churches that reach out to your community know that, without relevance, they have no chance to reach unchurched kids. Who had even heard of a church-sponsored sports camp 10 years ago? Many outreach-focused churches understand that kids like sports. Rather than trying to pull kids into unfamiliar events and uncharted territory, churches are using kids' existing interests to help them grow in their faith. SportsLife Camp has become a summertime favorite for kids at our church, and it's an easy way to bring into your ministry new kids who don't know about Jesus. They come for coaching and skills technique and leave with Jesus.

When you combine these 5 key ingredients, your once-seasonal event will be super-sized into a fantastic, faith-filled family event. Families in your church can have powerful and unforgettable, family-centered faith experiences that promote effective family faith-growth. Ready to super-size your ministry to affect kids in God-size ways? Here are some practical tips and 2 ideas to get you started:

> Families in your church can have powerful and unforgettable family-centered faith experiences that promote effective family faith-growth.

Practical Tips & Ministry Ideas

Practical Tips

- Before you begin planning your first event, decide when to have it and how long the event will last. We have found in our community that a 2-hour time frame works for seasonal events and that Sundays between 4:00–6:00 PM are good for families. But each community is different, so invest a little time to discover the best option for most families and your volunteers.

- Gather an event team.

- Set a budget. Decide whether you will charge a fee. If so, how much?

- Delegate responsibilities (publicity, registration, set-up, take-down, volunteer recruitment, program/curriculum development, station leaders, food, and so forth). Break down jobs to manageable tasks so that no single person will be over burdened.

- Consider offering nursery for event volunteers.

- Reserve building space and check in with your custodian for any special help necessary during set-up.

- Have stick-on nametags available for participants and volunteers during the event so that you can build relationships by calling people by name.

- Send your volunteers a thank-you e-mail or a handwritten note.

- Take notes on what went well and what you'd tweak the next time around.

Christmas Event Idea

We have used *Bethlehem Village* and *A Night in Bethlehem* for an incredible Christmas hands-on Holy Land experience. The event draws children and their families. They're surrounded by images of Bethlehem, Jesus, and the manger. The Christmas story really comes to life in a meaningful way as families step back in time and visit the Marketplace shops and meet Bible-time characters who were on the scene when Jesus was born. We even added one of our own shops, The Greenery, where families could use fresh greens to make an advent wreath to take home, complete with a devotion book.

And this event attracts families from the community—a great outreach. People can't wait to see, taste, touch, and feel what is was like in Bethlehem when Jesus was born. Something unique with these events has been that most of our volunteers are not our typical children's ministry people. Retired persons have served as our shopkeepers, so another outcome of an event such as this is that it can broaden your volunteer base.

Easter Event Idea

We created an easy, pizzazz-y Easter family event using *All Around Easter*. Create a path of faith discovery for kids and families with this life-changing Easter walk. You'll transport your families to Jesus' last week on earth so that they can walk in his footsteps. There are 6 easy-to-do discovery stations to help families experience the first Palm Sunday, Good Friday, Easter morning, and more. This event was better than any Easter egg hunt our church could sponsor, and we did it in only 2 hours.

Sharon Stratmoen has made children and family ministry her passion and focus for more than 20 years. She is the director in a church that serves 600 kids, engages more than 100 volunteers weekly, and partners in running a licensed weekday preschool.
sharon@oslcstillwater.org
www.oslcstillwater.org

Going Green = God's Plan?

by Dienna Gotscha

It was a beautiful Minnesota day—green leaves, blue sky, cool breeze, warm sun—a day Minnesotans dream of. We headed to the local arboretum, my three boys and I. After parking, I unloaded the stroller and put the baby in, gave instructions to my 5 year old and 3 year old not to wander far, and we started off on our hike. Not far down the path, we encountered a baby frog and gathered around to admire it.

Capturing a teachable moment, I started into a lesson on the life cycle of a frog. When suddenly, out of seemingly nowhere, a foot descended on the frog crushing the life out of him. My 5 year old and I gasped. Attached to the foot was the leg of my 3 year old. I stuttered, "Why did you do that?" He stared at me blankly.

Deflated, we all trudged back to the car and headed home. No one said a word. No one mentioned the frog again until that night at dinner. After my husband said the blessing, my 5 year old started wailing, "I loved that frog. I really, really loved that frog." My husband looked at me incredibly confused. After I explained the travesty of the day, he looked at the 3 year old and uttered words I have never forgotten: "Don't you ever hurt one of God's creatures. That frog didn't do anything to you. You had no right to hurt it."

Often we encounter our environment like a 3 year old, ready to squash it if we feel like it, without any regard for what our actions may do to others. We take the Genesis 1 words of "subduing, ruling, or dominion" to mean that we have free reign to do whatever we want with the earth. In general, Christians have not taken up the cause of the environment within the church because they do not see it as a spiritual issue.

However, if we are to truly do as Jesus taught, to love God and to love others, care of God's creation must be embraced. This is not just an issue for the "world," it is an issue for the church.

Every kid can tell you ways that we are destroying the environment. Every kid can list for you ways that we can save our environment. They know where the recycling bins are and how long it takes for a plastic bag to break down in the landfill. They know words such as *global warming* and *solar energy*.

> When we take care of the earth, we show our gratitude to God for making a beautiful and creative place for us to live.

But can every kid tell you what God says about taking care of the environment? Do kids understand why this is important to God?

At the very foundation of creation care are the principles of relationship, obedience, gratitude, respect, and justice. We find a concern for the environment through our relationship with Jesus, through whom we learn to love God and love others. Our love for God leads to obedience of God's Word, which directs us toward taking care of God's creation. When we take care of the earth, we show our gratitude to God for making a beautiful and creative place for us to live. When we leave the environment better than we found it, we show respect for all God's creatures.

And taking care of our environment is justice. Those who are marginalized in our world suffer most from our abuse. If we truly love others the way Jesus calls us to, we cannot help but be affected by this.

But how do we instill these foundational elements into kids' thinking? How do we let them see that, when we live a life of excess, we are hurting those we may never meet? By intersecting the environmental science that kids are learning in school, on kids television shows, in kids magazines, and perhaps at home with strong spiritual teaching, we can affect their thinking with a concern for creation care and for making a difference in God's green world. An environmental camp or vacation Bible school is just the place for this intersection between science and faith to take place.

An environmental camp includes many of the same elements that a traditional camp or vacation Bible school would have. Such activities as skits, Bible stories, crafts, snacks, games, and Bible memory are a part of each day.

However, the camp also incorporates environmental experiments and projects where kids learn about God's creation and put into practice what it means to make a difference in the world. Not only are children made aware of the biblical foundation, they also come to appreciate the world that God made for them. They are challenged to act on this awareness and appreciation.

The camp (or VBS) starts with large-group time, where the biblical foundation would be laid. Imagine fun characters such as a wacky environmental scientist, the Green Man Group (similar to the popular Blue Man Group), or a game-show host introducing kids to the concepts of obedience, respect, gratitude, and justice.

> The goal of the camp should be awareness of the environment, appreciation for all God created and action to make a difference.

The main spiritual teaching takes place during a Bible story, ending with a prayer and a challenge to consider what changes the child should consider in his or her life. Application of the teaching takes place during an object lesson using a recycled item pulled from the recycling bin or a lab demonstration of an environmental experiment performed by the wacky scientist Dr. Lime Green.

After the large-group time, the kids break into small groups and travel to different areas in a rotational system. They create crafts from recycled objects, put together fun snacks, test an environmental science experiment, learn Bible memory verses, participate in active games, and dive into the Bible during small group discussion.

All of these activities reinforce the biblical point made during the large-group time. And incorporated into the day are environmental projects such as testing water for pH levels or making a solar oven. Creation scavenger hunts and nature hikes are an integral part of the week, as are local projects to clean up a specific area. World-wide projects such as raising money for **bloodwatermission.org** or other organizations that help those affected by the misuse of the environment give kids a tangible way to make a difference.

During the week-long camp or VBS, kids are challenged to look at their world in a different way. They are challenged to think about the effect their actions have on the environment. They are challenged to look at how their actions reflect their love for God and others. And finally, they are challenged to take steps of action to make changes in their lives.

Including families in an environmental event, whether for one night of the camp or for the entire camp, creates a sense of mission within the entire family and shows them how they can make a difference. The long-term retention and ripple effects of the camp are enhanced when family members all have the same information and challenges. As families talk at home about the event, lasting changes are made—not only in attitude but also in how they choose to live out their lives. Parents will have the tools they need to model creation care for their children.

The goal of the camp should be awareness of the environment, appreciation for all that God has created, and action to make a difference. Although it would be tempting to put personal political views into this type of camp, it is important to allow God to work on the conscience of each family. The camp's focus should not be on pushing convictions on people but rather on building strong biblical foundation. It should not tell families how to take care of the environment so much as to tell them why they should. What they do with the information becomes a continuous journey that they will take throughout life.

> Let's be passionate about kids learning at a young age that their attitudes and actions can truly make a difference in the world.

God has given us a beautiful, creative, life-filled world. Let's teach kids to obey God by taking care of it, showing our gratitude for it, showing respect for others by not destroying it, and providing justice by not allowing misuse to hurt those less fortunate. Let's be passionate about teaching kids how to better love God and how to put into action loving others. Let's be passionate about kids learning at a young age that their attitudes and actions can truly make a difference in the world.

Imagine what you can do by bringing the issue of the environment into the church and equipping kids and their families to make a difference in God's green world.

_____

Dienna Gotscha has led children's ministry for more than 20 years and is co-founder of River's Edge Curriculum (**www.riversedgecurriculum.com**), *where she created the* iGo Green Kid's Camp *curriculum. She serves as Pastor of Families and Children at Real Life Community Church in Minnesota. You can reach her at* **Dienna.goscha@gmail.com**.

Special Needs

Encourage anyone who feels left out, help all who are weak, and be patient with everyone.

1 Thessalonians 5:14, CEV

IT WORKED FOR US

A Mother's Heart to Impact Special Needs

by Mary Ann McPherson

Ten years ago, I heard God's prompting to volunteer as a Sunday school teacher's aide for a child with a disability. It should have been an easy task, as my youngest daughter was born with Down syndrome and I had a degree in Child Development. However, I soon found myself overwhelmed with the challenge of meeting the needs of a child who had significant special needs within a classroom of typically developing children.

This little boy responded very differently than the other children. He spent a lot of time wandering around the classroom and occasionally had a temper tantrum, particularly when the class was noisy. Building relationships was difficult, because he was indifferent to all children and adults. His limited social skills impacted his ability to participate in both large- and small-group settings. In fact, his preference was to be in the quiet, dark classroom next door.

His disability also impacted his cognitive and fine motor development. That made crafts a painful experience. Really, his best time in the classroom was during snack. Even though I cared deeply and prayed often, I knew that what had worked in the past with other children, even other children with disabilities, didn't work with this child. I felt ineffective and frustrated.

You may be in a similar place in your ministry to young children. Unfortunately, a quick trip to the Web page of the Autism Society of America may only increase your anxiety. Statistics taken in 2006 report one child in every 150 births was diagnosed somewhere on the autism spectrum.

Autism is reported to be the fastest-growing developmental disability in America. Also, autism is a "spectrum disorder," so two children with the identical diagnosis can have totally different skills and may act completely different from one another.

My discouragement ultimately led to a time away from the Sunday school classroom. However, I was still serving as a preschool teacher/administrator for our local school district during the week. To meet the requirements of professional development in that setting, I began working on an Early Intervention License. Then two years ago I co-taught a small special education preschool classroom with a teacher who had many years experience working with children who had developmental disabilities. I wondered what would happen if I took the structure of that secular environment and transferred it to a week of vacation Bible school. I was amazed with the results! With a few adaptations, the interventions I used at school were successful in a church setting.

> **W**ith a few adaptations, the interventions I used at school were successful in a church setting.

The first step was to design a classroom routine that never changes. This is as rigid as it sounds, but I have found that children with special needs thrive on routine. The morning begins with quiet center activities, such as blocks, play dough, books, the sensory table, and some kind of a simple art activity that involves coloring, stickers, watercolors, or stringing. A few of the children benefit from having an adult aide, who helps them make and follow a visual picture schedule. That adult is also present to facilitate interactions between children or to give simple directions during play. "Keep sand in the table" instead of "Don't throw the sand on the floor."

I warn the children verbally and with a visual timer five minutes before I begin our "group time." The structure of group time never varies, and a picture schedule shows the children what will happen:

1. A welcome song, where every child's name is sung

2. The Bible verse

3. A Bible story that uses props that the children can see and touch

4. A time for songs that the children choose

5. Prayer time

6. A closing song that never changes

I use the same Scripture verse and Bible story for two to three weeks. During group time some children need to hold Theraputty™ or squishy balls to increase attention. Others need to sit on therapy balls instead of in chairs. Still others benefit from holding the story props.

A structured routine and adaptive equipment may seem very foreign and uncomfortable to you at first. That feeling will change when your children with disabilities learn about God's love for them. Their peers become more accepting of differences and some will become miniature helpers.

I don't need statistics to know that there is an increase of children with developmental disabilities, because they now arrive at my classroom door each year. As I have learned to make adaptations in my curriculum and classroom structure, my concern has shifted away from how to handle challenging behavior.

Now, I wonder how many families in our community are staying home from church because they know that volunteers are not equipped to meet the needs of their child. How many of those children will never know that Jesus loves them and knows their name? Let us strive to be more like Jesus: "Let the little children come to me" (Matthew 19:14).

Adaptive equipment can be found at **BeyondPlay.com** or **Abilitations.com**.

_____

Mary Ann McPherson lives in Cincinnati, Ohio, with her husband, David, and two teenage daughters, Kate and Sarah. She is a Preschool Director and an Early Intervention Specialist for the Madeira City School District. At Montgomery Community Church, she is a teacher for the Special Hope classroom with Crosstown Children's Ministry. Mary Ann also helped write a chapter in the book Special Needs Special Ministry *by Group Publishing. You can contact Mary Ann at* **mamcp@current.net**.

Let us strive to be more like Jesus: "Let the little children come to me" (Matthew 19:14).

Understand the Diagnosis, Understand the Individual

by Amy Fenton Lee

Many churches lack formal programs reaching or intentionally including children with special needs. However, the vast majority of children's ministries, often unknowingly, have participating children with disabilities or developmental delays.

Understanding the traits, symptoms, and characteristics of common special needs diagnoses is imperative for any children's ministry team. Not only will church staff and volunteers grow comfortable accepting children with disclosed diagnoses, they'll also become astute in handling behavior challenges and employing effective teaching methods that can apply in every early childhood education setting.

The Value of a Manual

In 1999, Tonya Langdon was a parent and children's Sunday school volunteer in Skyline Wesleyan Church of Rancho San Diego, California. Langdon began to notice her elementary school age son was struggling in his weekly Sunday morning classroom and frustrating the volunteer teachers along the way. Langdon's son had recently been diagnosed with Attention Deficit Hyperactivity Disorder, Tourette's syndrome, and Oppositional Defiance Disorder.

Realizing that the majority of the church's Sunday school teachers were parents of typical children, she knew the average Sunday school teacher was out of his or her element as soon as her child entered the room. "My son was the square peg, trying to fit in the round hole during the Sunday school hour in our church," explains Langdon.

Langdon knew that, with a little understanding for her son's diagnoses and unique traits, he could thrive in the church's programming. Once her son's teachers became educated on his trigger points and learning style, the Sunday school hour was successful for everyone involved.

Soon after Langdon embarked on her own journey as a parent of a child with multiple diagnoses, she began recognizing different issues with similar solutions inside Skyline's children's ministry. "As I was pondering my own child's situation, I discovered that we had a number of children in our midst who weren't typical. Our church volunteers didn't know what to do with the student who refused to sit down during story time or exhibited a strong aversion to sound, let alone the child who continuously flapped their hands."

> Understanding the traits, symptoms, and characteristics of common special needs diagnoses is imperative for any children's ministry team.

In response to the increase in "unique" situations, Langdon developed a manual of common diagnoses the children's ministry could expect to encounter, or was already experiencing. Ten years after the manual's development, *Skyline Wesleyan Church's Teacher's Manual for Children With Special Needs* is still handed out and covered in every volunteer teacher training session.

Langdon notes, "The manual was the marking of a big culture shift in our church children's ministry. No longer was the question 'Will we admit this child?' into Sunday school or vacation Bible school, but it became 'How can we make the church experience successful for both the child and the volunteer?'"

Today, Skyline Wesleyan Church serves approximately thirty-five children with various known diagnoses and in different areas of their church's children's ministry.

Jackie Mills-Fernald, Director of McLean Bible Church's Access Ministry (McLean, Virginia), echoes a similar perspective and church story: "On any given Sunday, you'll find a copy of the *Access Ministry Differently Abled Diagnoses Manual* in the hands of a ministry volunteer." The volunteers have come to rely on the manual for understanding common characteristics, causes for peculiar or challenging behaviors, and techniques for successful engagement with the students. Volunteers also appreciate having the manual when a parent uses special needs acronyms or lingo while informing the child's teacher of pertinent information.

> A statement that starts with "All children with X diagnosis do this" is never true.

"We can't always spend adequate time equipping lay servants in a formal training setting, due to their time restraints. But we've found that our volunteers take advantage of the manual, reviewing it, and educating themselves, especially as they encounter a child with certain symptoms or a specific diagnosis," explains Mills-Fernald. McLean Bible Church's Access Ministry hosts an estimated 500 families and children as part of their special needs programming.

One Size Doesn't Fit All

The same diagnosis may affect two children in drastically different ways. "It is important to remember that each person is uniquely made, and the emphasis on 'unique' is even more important in the special needs community," McLean Bible Church's Jackie Mills-Fernald reminds her volunteer team.

A statement that starts with "All children with X diagnosis do this" is never true. This is especially important for volunteers to recognize, because a child with a given diagnosis may actually have more in common with a typically-developing peer than with another child with the same diagnosis.

Responding appropriately to a child's needs hinges more on the individual's traits than on the diagnosis. While one child diagnosed with Down syndrome may have limited verbal communication capabilities and struggle in social settings, others may thrive and even grow spiritually during their time in church programming.

Special education teacher Sara Cloud of Newark, Delaware, proudly shares stories of her twenty-two year old brother, Greg. Greg was diagnosed with Down syndrome shortly after birth. Today, Greg is a black-belt in tae kwon do and runs the snack bar and cash register for a local athletic club. Is Greg capable of developing social relationships and understanding Bible teaching? You bet!

Autism is probably the diagnosis with the greatest variance. Allen Meisler, founder of Mitchell's Place, a Birmingham, Alabama based autism intervention center, explains a common misperception is all children with autism have the same behavior nuances and incapability.

"So often when people hear the word 'autistic' as a diagnosis associated with a child, an immediate picture of Rain Man comes to mind." Meisler chuckles as he refers to the popular 1988 film, featuring the unforgettable autistic character Dustin Hoffman portrayed. Indeed, many children with autism spectrum disorder do exhibit similar traits; however, the degree to which a child is affected and the behaviors shaped by the disorder may be radically different between two children with the same diagnosis.

A tremendous number of children who fall on the autism spectrum are "high functioning and capable of thriving in a setting among typically developing children," observes Meisler. While a child with autism generally requires more assistance in reaching his or her full potential than does a typically developing child, many are capable of mastering skills and absorbing information being taught.

In a church setting this may translate to a lower child-to-teacher ratio and/or offering additional teaching techniques for different learning styles. Relatively minor adjustments to church programming may yield great benefits for the child diagnosed with a mild form of autism spectrum disorder, pervasive developmental disorder, or Asperger's syndrome.

Understand the Individual

Grasping a full understanding for the individual child is far more important than becoming an expert in any area of physical, emotional, or intellectual disability. In addition to placing the child in the appropriate setting, successfully handling a single idiosyncrasy for a child may be the difference between a positive and negative experience inside a church's children's programming.

Up-front conversations with parents to learn about a child's nuances are imperative. Meltdowns over any number of changes (snack, routine, color of hand soap, etc.) can all be avoided and/or managed if church staff and volunteers are prepared.

Similarly, when the ministry team is aware of a child's strengths and passions, they can successfully redirect and/or convey the Bible education in a learning style most conducive to that particular child.

When All Else Fails, Love Prevails

Alyssa Barnes, M.Ed, Special Education and PhD student in University of Georgia's Special Education Program with an emphasis on public policy, shares a story from her own church volunteering experience. While serving in the infants' room of First United Methodist Church of Marietta, Georgia, Barnes began caring for a child with profound physical and developmental disabilities. The child was age four, yet functioning on the level of an infant. The longer-serving nursery workers familiar with the little boy quickly explained to Barnes that the child's parents were still pursuing an explanation and diagnosis for the child's condition and that they (the workers) assumed the child had few if any cognitive abilities.

One Sunday, Barnes walked over to the child and told him to touch his nose if he understood what she was saying to him. To every nursery worker's shock, the child touched his nose. Barnes continued with instruction, allowing the child to give nonverbal responses to her simple questions. The child answered each command. As Barnes continued serving in the room, she developed a relationship with the child. Once, when she was holding the little boy, the mother entered the room and noticed the child making a distinct physical gesture. The mother reacted in surprise and delight, explaining that her little boy was trying to tell Barnes he loved her.

Amy Fenton Lee enjoys equipping churches to receive and minister to families of children with special needs. For more on Amy's writing, see **www.amyfentonlee.com**.

Discussion Starters for Children's Ministry & Parents

- My child has received the following diagnosis/diagnoses: _____

_____

- My child has an Individualized Education Plan ☐ **Yes** ☐ **No**

- If answered yes, please describe child's IEP: _____

_____

- My child's main mode of functional communication is: _____

- My child comprehends instruction best in the following form *(circle one)* • **visual** • **auditory**
  • **kinesthetic**

- My child currently receives therapies and instruction in: _____

- The goals I have for my child's development this coming year include (behavioral, social, academic, and so forth): _____

_____

- My child has the following area(s) of interest: _____

- My child can do these things independently: _____

- My child needs assistance with: _____

- My child is uncomfortable with or has an aversion to: _____

- A trigger-point for a meltdown is when: _____

- When/if my child experiences a melt-down he or she calms when we: _____

- Doing/seeing/experiencing this one thing is an important part of my child's routine: _____

_____

- My child *(circle one)* **does / does not** enjoy music.

- My child seems most relaxed in settings of *(circle one)* • **alone,** • **1–3 children,** • **4+ children.**

- My child *(circle one)* **would / would not** enjoy a large-group worship experience.

- My child is really picky about: _____

- My child's behavior may indicate a medical problem requiring immediate attention when:

_____

Placing the Child With Special Needs

by Amy Fenton Lee

Most children's ministers with experience in special needs ministry have at some point felt conflicted in how to best accommodate a specific child with a disability. A child's temperament and learning capacity may vary from one week to another. An occasional parent may push an expectation or agenda not in line with the church's immediate capabilities. And parent-volunteer dilemmas may require the grace and negotiation of a skilled diplomat.

Alyssa Barnes, M.Ed, Special Education and PhD student in University of Georgia's Special Education Program, explains: "The classroom placement of children with special needs is one of the most controversial issues dealt with in the field of special education. As a result, the church should not find it surprising when it, too, struggles to find the perfect fit for a child with a complicated set of needs."

Barnes shares, "In the government funded public school systems, placement decisions involve a team of opinions. The placement process sometimes requires mediation or even due process procedures to settle on a specific child's education path." As a result, churches can expect that it may take time, tenacity, and trial and error before a child with special needs is successfully woven into the church's children's ministry.

Parents and church staff can benefit from the reminder that churches are not tax-funded entities and, when compared with the specially trained educators in the public school system, they utilize big-hearted lay volunteers.

Common Terms
For the purpose of discussing child placement, let's define vocabulary common to the public school system and special needs culture.

Self-Contained Special Education Classroom — Stand-alone classroom setting designed to separate and appropriately accommodate children with a range of identified disabilities. These classes are typically taught by special educators or instructors with experience working in the disability community.

Inclusion — Placing a student with special needs in regular classes and activities for an entire school day. The school system generally provides an aide or special education teacher to accompany and assist the child in the fully inclusive setting.

Reverse Inclusion — Placing a small number of typical students from an age-appropriate class to join the person with special needs in his or her self-contained environment.

Typical — The term used to describe a child-peer without a disability or need for additional assistance.

Individualized Education Plan (IEP) — A formal education plan developed by a team of interested parties (parents, school faculty, medical providers) specifically designed for an individual student with qualifying special needs. An IEP creates goals and the means for their achievement within the public school system.

History and Background
Since 1975 Congress has enacted several significant pieces of legislation shaping the special education environment and other publicly funded programs assisting persons with disabilities. Based on the Individuals with Disabilities Education Act of 1999 and No Child Left Behind Act of 2002, the current trend in public education has moved away from self-contained special education classrooms and

toward full inclusion. Wording such as "least restrictive environment" is common guidance provided by the laws for the schools' placement of children with disabilities. How each local school system interprets and applies the law is different and complicated. Parents' expectations for their church's children's ministries are often shaped by their experiences in the public school systems. And it is for these reasons that it is helpful to become familiar with effective and common practices in both the secular field of special education and established church-based special needs ministries.

One Size Doesn't' Fit All

Churches that simultaneously provide both self-contained classrooms and inclusive environments are best prepared for special needs ministry. One child may thrive in a setting where alternative teaching methods are the primary form of instruction and otherwise distracting noises and body movement are commonplace (self-contained classroom). Conversely, many children are capable and, in fact, thrive as a part of the regular activities and among their typically developing peers (inclusion). And oftentimes, the same child requires both settings during a single day in church programming (sometimes referred to as "partial inclusion").

Volunteer staffing and parent desires can also affect the placement of a child. While a one-to-one ratio and buddy-system is ideal for special needs situations, it isn't always practical or necessary. For example, a child may require a fully devoted caregiver in order to remain participative in the inclusion Sunday school setting, but be able to share a volunteer teacher inside of a self-contained special needs classroom.

Many parents advocate placing their children in a fully inclusive environment. It is my personal belief that creating a welcome environment across all areas of children's ministry is the best way to model Jesus' love and equal value for all developing children. However, inclusion sometimes requires judgment and program modifications.

Churches with preschool and grade school programming incorporating buttoned-up volunteer training and well-executed worship experiences are more likely to have success including children with special needs in their typical settings. Volunteers familiar with behavior modification techniques, redirection, and a sound church policy on handling conduct challenges are less likely to ruffle feathers with the children or their parents.

In the meantime, programs already utilizing music, puppets, skits, and creative movement are more conducive for including participants with a wide range of cognitive abilities and learning styles. When activities are designed to engage all the senses, children with disabilities have a greater chance of constructive participation in the environment. Establishing a sound foundation in the typical children's programming is imperative for successful implementation of an inclusion-friendly special needs culture.

Volunteer Placement

In accommodating children with disabilities, volunteer placement is sometimes more important than child placement. Occasionally, parents resist the idea of a buddy, in their effort to fully integrate their child among their typically developing peers and to provide a "normal church experience." In those instances when reality and parents' wishes don't perfectly align, pad the volunteer team. Discreetly position an additional helper, with the understanding they are tagged to assist the child with a disability. The goal of a buddy should never be to isolate and separate, but to encourage and facilitate full participation to the best of the student's ability.

> When activities are designed to engage all the senses, children with disabilities have a greater chance of constructive participation in the environment.

The Value of the IEP

In cases where the church staff and family struggle to agree on a child's placement inside the church, initiate a discussion regarding the child's Individualized Education Plan. Jackie Mills-Fernald, Director of McLean Bible Church's Access Ministry (McLean, Virginia), explains: "When you know how the public school system is addressing a child's educational, social, and behavioral development, you can glean helpful information on the individual's capabilities and past successes."

Mills-Fernald tells the story of a child who struggled in church programming until Access Ministry staff inquired about the child's IEP. The conversation triggered the parents' disclosure that the child was more likely to maintain controlled behavior as long as his favorite set of books accompanied him in every environment. The revealing discussion helped the Access team determine staffing and logistics for helping the child adjust in the church setting. While the initial conversations were rocky, ultimately the parents were grateful for the church's successful accommodation of their child.

Barnes advises churches to invite the development of a church "IEP." Ask parents to help the church craft and regularly update a strategy, incorporating goals from the school's education plan with personal objectives for their child. Taking a collaborative approach between parents, teachers, and children's ministry staff sets the tone for an atmosphere of partnership and often reveals areas where small adjustments can yield big payoffs. Barnes, a former special education teacher, asked her students' parents to state their aspirations for their child at the beginning of each school year. "By understanding the real drivers for these parents, I could tailor my teaching and make intentional efforts to recognize progress along the way."

Barnes points out that most parents of children with special needs have social objectives equally important to their academic ambitions. She frequently observed parents' stated goals, such as "to have my child invited for a play date," "for my child to be invited to a peer's birthday party," or "for my child to make meaningful friends." Barnes applies this to the church settings: "When the church staff gets to the underlying concerns and addresses the parents' deeper desires, the disagreements over the child's placement may ultimately diminish."

Celebrate the Successes

As parents' goals for their child are implemented into the church setting, be mindful of and recognize even the smallest of achievements. Mills-Fernald of McLean's Access Ministry advises program teachers to regularly celebrate successes with parents: "Point out the fact that the child participated in the typical classroom or group worship for fifteen minutes this Sunday, whereas last week he or she lasted only ten minutes. Relay a sense of victory to the parents." Mills-Fernald explains that these short parting conversations between the child's caregivers and their parents allow parents to leave church on a positive note and with evidence that the ministry team is working with the stated goals in mind.

Similarly, Barnes suggests churches create programming "exit tickets" or "interview sheets" for each child. While a similar exercise is valuable for typically developing children, it can be especially cherished by parents of children with special needs.

"Exit tickets are essentially a personalized recap of what a child learned during a single session of church programming," explains Barnes. Exit tickets convey a child's individual responses to a brief one-on-one interview conducted by a teacher at the end of programming. The child's answer(s) may relay a favorite activity or the subject of the day's lesson. For children who communicate nonverbally, providing visual pictures for the child to place on the day's interview sheet may be equally effective.

As parents observe their child absorbing a basic Bible concept and participating in social interaction, the likelihood for concerns and dissension often disappears.

Amy Fenton Lee enjoys equipping churches to receive and minister to families of children with special needs. For more on Amy's writing, see **www.amyfentonlee.com.**

Special Needs: Your Best Resource May Be Outside the Church

by Amy Fenton Lee

One of the biggest obstacles to starting or growing a special needs program is the intimidation that comes with lack of understanding or knowledge of the world of disability. Writing on this topic has involved learning new lingo and understanding the importance of very particular phrasing.

While I have no background in special education, I've never covered another subject matter where I've discovered as many willing and passionate teachers. At every turn a new person has presented themselves as a resource, giving generously of their own personal time to educate me. This has been true of leaders in established church programs as well as professionals from the secular world of special education, pediatric therapies, and medical providers.

Regardless of their religion or faith, every special needs provider I've encountered has a deep personal interest in helping individuals with disabilities and their families develop support systems.

The Benefits of Networking

The most effective special needs church programs are led by individuals or teams who have built a network of special needs professionals. In 1996, Jackie Mills-Fernald was a secular business woman and Sunday volunteer at McLean Bible Church in McLean, Virginia. She assisted in a Sunday school room with four children diagnosed with autism. Now, thirteen years later, Mills-Fernald is Director of McLean Bible Church's Access Ministry, which is widely recognized as the nation's largest comprehensive church program for the special needs community. Mills-Fernald has no formal training in special education, nor do five of the other six

Access Ministry staff members. But at the top of any Access staff person's resume, you could easily find "master networker and fast learner" as bullet point number one.

The influence of special education teachers; speech pathologists; occupational, physical, and behavioral therapists; pediatric counselors; nutritionists; and other medical providers are noticeable in every area of McLean's special needs programming. Mills-Fernald and other Access team members regularly attend local forums or participate in community committees with special needs interest.

Mills-Fernald explains: "Churches don't have to know all the answers, just where to get them. In the beginning of our ministry, it was especially important that we build our network in the church and community. Over time, our staff has gleaned from the professionals. Thirteen years after the ministry's inception, we require less expert advisement, because we have learned along the way and now we know what to do."

The Access Ministry "Rolodex" of contacts has evolved into an enviable network of essentially free consultants. Rarely are any volunteers or professionals paid. This is a mutually beneficial relationship for most professional contacts. For example, McLean's Access Ministry hosts a monthly special needs lecture series throughout the year. Providers gladly participate as speakers in an effort to build their own private practices. Those same participants and speakers are also the consultants Mills-Fernald calls on to review her training manuals, provide input for space design, or work through issues as they arise in the ministry.

Mills-Fernald shares the story of a behavioral therapist who gladly took her call when a child attending the Access program began expressing tendencies toward violence. While such cases are rare, they do happen. A therapist familiar with common disorders in the special needs population came and observed the child in church care. The provider coached the Access staff and volunteers in minimizing the likelihood for disruptive behavior and advised them in handling delicate conversations with the parents.

At some point, every church has an experience where the information and judgment offered by the parents of a child with special needs doesn't match the observations and opinions of the ministry staff. Relying on a conversation with the trained and qualified specialist is imperative for these infrequent but expected occasions. Mills-Fernald expounds: "Knowing that experts familiar with the law or common practice are only a phone call away gives our team confidence. Utilizing these resources is smart for handling the inevitable challenge as well as keeping any risk to a minimum."

Recruiting Consultants

The most common way churches develop their base of professional contacts is through their participating families. Parents of children with special needs have built their own network of resources out of necessity. These families are often incredibly well-read and familiar with the reliable providers within their own community. Churches may even consider inviting parents who have developed extraordinary interest in the field along with professionals to serve in an advisory roles for the special needs programming.

Developing a working group that meets regularly may also create a committed set of helpmates in the ministry. Professionals serving in an advisory capacity need not necessarily share the same theological background. So long as the ministry leadership and actual Bible teachers (usually church members) are screened for appropriate understanding and application of biblical truths, the nutritionist, psychologist, speech pathologist, and so forth advising the ministry team can come from differing faiths.

The Professional's Role

The regular care-providers, buddies, and teachers in the ministry programs are rarely professionals from the special needs field. Most people employed as pediatric therapists, counselors, and teachers spend every weekday focused on this population. Because engaging individuals with special needs and their families can be emotionally demanding, providers often need a break from intense connection for their own recharge time. The successful and effective church special needs programs respect the limits of their church members who are employed in the special needs field. At the same time, most professionals want to help such a ministry by using their talents and education.

Take the case of Stacie Trottier, who is a pediatric speech pathologist with Children's Healthcare of Atlanta, Georgia. Trottier's training and breadth of experience make her an exceptional resource across the disciplines of speech, occupational, physical, and even behavioral therapies. Hearing of Trottier's talents and knowing of her faith, a local church contacted Trottier in 2008 for advisement in their special needs ministry.

Trottier explains: "I'm passionate about helping children and their families navigate through a disability. It makes sense that I could apply my education and experience somehow in ministry." Trottier welcomes the opportunity to help shape a church's special needs program. Trottier relishes the idea of "interviewing new families and matching children to the appropriate buddy or classroom, training lay volunteer teachers, designing or adjusting Bible curriculum, or creating effective teaching tools for the classroom." Coming from the professional secular world, where both laws and corporate standards demand the highest performance levels, Trottier explains that "skilled and certified individuals are more likely to invest in ministries where the church staff doesn't over-delegate while demonstrating an attitude of excellence for their special needs programs."

Amy Fenton Lee enjoys equipping churches to receive and minister to families of children with special needs. For more on Amy's writing, see **www.amyfentonlee.com**.

Plug in the Professional

- Review existing curriculum and suggest modifications or adaptations for different learners.

- Conduct initial entry meeting between parents and special needs ministry. Ask knowledgeable questions to assist ministry staff in programming placement of the individual.

- Develop manipulative visual and tactile boards for demonstration of Bible lesson.

- Offer appropriate craft ideas suitable for the capability of various ministry participants.

- Recommend helpful equipment and physical aides for classrooms.

- Develop or lead training for lay-person volunteers for both inclusion and stand-alone settings (may be separate set of volunteers and training sessions).

- Create a list of common special needs diagnoses for training manual or ministry handbook.

- Teach volunteers effective methods for redirecting or calming to manage behaviors inside the classroom.

- Speak at a ministry-sponsored function in area of expertise.

- Observe ministry programming occasionally for general or specific advisement.

- Develop any needed legal documents, such as confidentiality statements or waivers of release.

- Advise staff on pertinent and current trends in education and healthcare.

- Conduct ministry risk assessment and advise on risk management.

- Lead music for stand-alone classrooms (may be simple guitar or more involved instruments and individuals).

- Serve as rotating on-call nurse to provide possible medical coverage during on-site activities.

- Develop list of healthy snacks for frequent and approved use in ministry.

- Devise layout of ministry area or classroom.

- Create classroom center stations.

- Design sensory murals and tactile art for ministry area.

- Photograph ministry events for program slide shows or marketing and communication pieces.

- Offer graphic design time for developing ministry literature.

- Assemble craft and/or activity packets for stand-alone classrooms or respite care.

- Offer a special event involving therapy animals.

- Consult with staff on use of nonverbal communication strategies, utilizing picture symbols or sign language.

Amy Fenton Lee

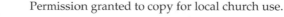

Special Needs:
The Volunteers' Blessings

by Amy Fenton Lee

Thanks to the influence of books such as Rick Warren's *Purpose-Driven Life* and even the push in popular culture to find meaning in everyday living, many churchgoers welcome opportunities for altruistic contribution. Church attendees often are as much in search of significance as they are a community of fellow believers.

Creating a well-coordinated volunteer ministry inside a congregation's special needs program is one way a church may assist its members in finding their own personal ministry.
It's a mission trip without the luggage!

Whereas a short-term mission trip may require raising funds, obtaining vaccinations, and sorting through a host of logistics, special needs service requires none of the above and comparatively minimal training. Volunteering among individuals with disabilities nearly always provides an uncomplicated and satisfying experience for the mission-minded individual.

> Programs that make a point to include their volunteers in the celebration of victories along the way will find loyal helpers, excited to feel a part of a winning ministry.

Darby Gillam, a founding lay leader in Southcliff Baptist Church's JOY special needs ministry (Fort Worth, Texas), says: "When we were first starting up our respite care nights, I would call other area youth groups, college ministry organizations, or graduate schools for occupational, physical, or speech therapy. I would invite their participants to assist during our church-provided respite events. In turn, the volunteer-students' service often fulfilled their need for community service or school credit."

Gillam states: "When speaking with a youth or college minister, my recruiting speech always touched on the idea that this service opportunity would have a similar impact to a mission trip. Volunteers leave our ministry events more grateful and aware of the blessings in their own lives."

Experiencing the Victories Along the Way

The adage "success breeds success" is true. Just as in sports or in the corporate world, everyone wants to be on a winning team. Special needs ministries that are led with tangible goals and effective methods for their achievement keep volunteers purposed. Programs that make a point to include their volunteers in the celebration of victories along the way will find loyal helpers, excited to feel a part of a winning ministry.

Amy Daniels, Senior Coordinator for Special Ministries at Scottsdale Bible Church (Scottsdale, Arizona), says that on any given Monday night, there are as many volunteers as program participants attending the young adult Bible study for individuals with disabilities. She explains: "Our volunteers know that prayer time is the focus of the whole evening. Before a Bible lesson, we open the floor for participants to share and offer prayer requests. The stories that emerge are inspiring and sometimes even comical. But the prayer time is incredibly revealing as to how God is present and active in the lives of these individuals with special needs. I can't tell you how uplifted and encouraged our lay servants feel after they have experienced a window into the souls and God's work in our ministry members."

As with Scottsdale Bible Church, many churches find that volunteers cherish the unique glimpse of God's character that individuals with special needs provide.

Match Individuals' Gifts Appropriately

"Not everyone is wired in a way they can roll with the punches in the way we have to each Sunday," explains Amy Kirby, Director of Shades Mountain Baptist Church's Hand-n-Hand ministry (Birmingham, Alabama). After observing a number of special needs stand-alone classroom settings, including Shades Mountain's, it isn't hard to understand Kirby's statement. At any point in time, a participating child may erupt in boisterous song, leave the craft table early for an unplanned activity, or find a partner to pair up with for unscripted creative movement. Indeed, the type of volunteer who fits well in the special needs stand-alone classroom is someone not easily rattled and who can seamlessly accommodate the children's changing needs.

Kirby acknowledges that not every church member is well suited for this area of service. However, she points out, "What church members often don't realize is that there are numerous other ways to assist a special needs program. One of our ministry's most valuable volunteers is a person gifted in accounting and organization. This lay person is tasked with coordinating the monthly volunteer rotation and handling various administrative needs for our ministry."

Volunteers Find Their Calling

Volunteer stories of lay servants ultimately discovering their personal ministry calling as a result of service in a special needs church program is common. For Amy Daniels, Senior Coordinator for Scottsdale Bible Church's Special Ministries, such is her story. "I'm in my position today one hundred percent because of volunteer service among children with learning disabilities years ago."

After a faith experience and career path Daniels considers anything but coincidence, she is now degreed in special education, has worked in the special needs field for a dozen years, and today leads a special needs ministry hosting nearly fifty participants each week.

_____

Amy Fenton Lee enjoys equipping church staff and lay-leaders for ministry to children and women. Amy, her husband, and preschool-aged son are active in the ministries of Perimeter Church in Atlanta, Georgia.

Indeed, the type of volunteer who fits well in the special needs stand-alone classroom is someone not easily rattled and who can seamlessly accommodate the children's changing needs.

Volunteer Assistance Opportunities

People often say, "I'm not sure I'm suited to teach or care for individuals with special needs. So, how can I help?" Here's how:

- Lead music in stand-alone classroom(s) —- one-person guitar, small praise team, or even expressive singer with CD player.

- Recruit puppeteers from preteen and youth ministries. Present regular puppet shows.

- Coordinate master volunteer schedule of buddies and classroom teachers.

- Prepare art for classroom crafts and activities. (See McLean Bible Church's *Art for the Heart* volunteer crafts ministry: **http://mbcartfromtheheart.blogspot.com**).

- Decorate special needs stand-alone classrooms – updating bulletin boards, seasonal décor, or painting visually stimulating sensory murals.

- Create, maintain, and update a special needs ministry website.

- Produce graphic design for marketing pieces and website.

- Photograph or video program events for website, marketing, and in-church ministry publicity.

- Perform data input of regular updates of computer records for new participants and changes for existing participants (*diagnoses, medications, notes from discussion with family*).

- Provide administrative assistance for volunteer training event preparation.

- Plan, book, and publicize expert guest speaker series.

- Serve as a greeter to outside guests attending special needs lecture series.

- Receive ministry participants immediately before an event, taking note of changes in individuals' medication, schedule, or other areas potentially affecting their time in programming.

- Serve as church care contact (similar to Stephen Ministry) for a family of a member with special needs. Help parents and siblings connect within church and offer physical service, as appropriate.

- Set up and coordinate service activity involving ministry participants (for example, food drive).

- Donate snacks, crafts, classroom equipment, music aides (tambourines and so forth) and other requested items (see **www.mcleanbible.org**, "Access - Disability Ministry," "Ways to Support Access," "Access Wish List").

- Plan and host social or fun activity for ministry participants, families, and/or siblings. Recruit different Sunday school classes or small groups to take on a social or respite care event.

Skit Night or Talent Show

Family Easter Egg Hunt

Bowling Night

Puppets & Popcorn

Movie Night & Crafts

'50s Dress-up & Sock Hop

Museum Tour

Christmas Dance

Friendship Banquet

Picnic at the Park

Dress-up or Character Costume Party

Fall Service Project

Spiritual Formation

I planted, Apollos watered, but God gave the growth.

(1 Corinthians 3:6)

Prayer: Opening the Door

by Karyn Henley

People of most religions pray. For some, prayer takes the form of meditation. Others memorize prescribed prayers and chant them at required times. Many purchase written prayers for specific occasions. All believe that prayer "works," if only to help them focus and gain peace.

Christians expect prayers to be heard and answered by a loving, caring Being as part of a vibrant relationship between creature and Creator. But our view of God dictates our relationship with God and shapes our prayers. If we see God as a tyrant, we relate and pray to God as a fearful slave would. If we see God as a school principal, we relate and pray as a student trying to make the grade or avoid getting caught. If God seems to us like Santa Claus, we relate to God as a dispenser of goodies who makes a list and checks it twice. If God is a polite conversation piece, we relate and pray to God in a distant, uncaring way. So to teach about prayer, we must first teach about God.

Jesus showed us how to relate to God as child to Father. As you teach children about God as Father, it may help to say, "the ideal Father," "the Father you've always wanted," or even "the perfect mentor." Ask children how they would describe a perfect father. Many movies and books have characters who are wise mentors. Ask older children to name some of these. (J.R.R. Tolkien's Gandalf comes to mind.) The type of person you wish you'd had as guide and encourager is real. He is God—Father, Son, and Holy Spirit. So when we talk about prayer, we are talking about relationship.

Author Hope MacDonald calls prayer "a conversation between two friends who love and understand each other. Prayer is the key that opens the door to a whole new world."

When we teach children to pray, we don't just teach a ritual or one of the Christian disciplines.

We actually introduce children to God. "Real prayer comes not from gritting our teeth but from falling in love," says author Richard Foster. Prayer is communication, one of the most important aspects of any relationship. Prayer is one of the most important facets of becoming a life-long Jesus-follower journeying ever deeper into God's life-giving love.

So how do we help children pray?

During their development, children start by imitating us. Next they identify with us. Then they experience God for themselves; after which, by their own choice and in their own way, they personalize their relationship with God. Encourage the youngest children to imitate you, to repeat after you. But don't force a child to pray. Let a child watch and listen until he or she is ready to repeat after you or to voice his or her own prayer.

Next give your child "training wheels" by showing him or her various ways to structure prayer time. You might use the Lord's Prayer. For a visual aid, help your child trace around a hand, fingers together as if in prayer. Then cut out six handprints. On the first, write "Father" and draw a star, representing heaven. On the second, write "kingdom," draw a crown. On the third, write "food," draw a slice of bread. Fourth, write "forgive," draw a cross. Fifth, write "evil," draw a mean face. Sixth, write "glory," and draw a sun. Help your child use his or her own words to follow Jesus' model: Praise God, ask for specifics in spreading the love of God's kingdom, ask for needs to be met, ask for forgiveness and/or forgive others, pray for "evil" situations to be made right, then praise God again.

Another easy method is adapted from the *Children's Ministry Resource Bible*. Hold up one hand, palm out. The thumb is closest to me, so I pray for people close to me (family and friends).

The pointer finger represents people in need I might point at; instead of pointing, I pray for them. The middle finger, "tall man," represents people who watch over me, such as parents, teachers, government leaders. The ring finger is fourth, so the mnemonic is "four," which easily morphs into "foreign" and reminds me to pray for people in other countries. The small finger represents me and my needs.

Older children can keep prayer journals in three sections: "I Prayed," "God Answered," and "God Taught Me." Or they could make it a family prayer journal to use in devotions. Talk about how God answers in a variety of ways. I may hear an inner voice or find the answer in something I read or hear. I may simply sense the wise answer. Answers are not always yes. Sometimes God says no or wait. So the journal's third section is instructive. We sometimes learn more by seeing how God uses no or wait to teach us and draw us closer.

Also discuss how we can tell that what we "hear" is from God and not just our own thoughts. That's not to negate our own thoughts. We often know the answer if we think; and if we're growing in God, we can rely on our wisdom, gained through God. But if your child wants to test an answer, teach the DiTtO test: "Do To Others." Jesus said to treat others the way we want to be treated. So does my answer treat others the way I want to be treated? Or give it the love test. Jesus said that the most important thing is to love God with all your heart, soul, and strength, and love others as yourself. Our job, then, is to learn and practice love. Does the answer help me learn and practice God's life-giving love?

Another set of training wheels is "flash prayer." For example, when you hear an emergency siren, it means that someone is in trouble. Say a quick flash prayer asking God to help him or her. On a beautiful morning, simply "flash" a thank you to God for the beauty around you. As you yourself sincerely model the flash prayer, your child will sense your own growing relationship with a personal God and will see how to relate to God.

There are several ways to encourage children to pray for the needs of people in other nations. One way is to get an inflatable beach ball globe. Toss it to your child. When your child catches it, ask him or her to name the country her right index finger points to. If it's ocean, ask her to look to the nearest finger that is on land. Then quickly pray for that country and its people. For groups, form a circle with the children and have them toss the globe to one another.

Another way is to ask children to find the names of countries or states on labels of items in your pantry and to pray for that country or state. We can also say "news prayers." We often hear distressing news reports. Instead of bemoaning the state of the world, say a flash news prayer for the people involved. Our prayers can reach places we are not physically able to go.

> When we teach children to pray, we don't just teach a ritual or one of the Christian disciplines. We actually introduce children to God.

Or have children turn Bible verses into prayers. For example, Paul writes, "Be alert and self-controlled" (1 Thessalonians 5:6, NIV). To make this a prayer, say, "Dear Lord, help me be alert and self-controlled." Or for Hebrews 13:21, pray, "Dear Lord, equip me with everything good for doing your will, and work in me what is pleasing to you."

The psalms are a natural training ground for prayer. You can teach children to turn many psalms into their own personal communication with God. For example: "I lift up my eyes to the hills—where does my help come from? My help comes from you, Lord. You are the Maker of heaven and earth. You will not let my foot slip. You watch over me, and you will not sleep." (Psalm 121).

Talk with children about why we say, "in Jesus' name, amen." Read aloud Matthew 27:50, 51. A tall curtain in the Temple kept people out of the

Most Holy Place where people thought God's presence came to earth. Only the high priest could enter, and only once a year, to represent the people before God, with sacrifices and prayers. But when Jesus died, the curtain ripped in two from top to bottom, a powerful symbol that meant that everyone now has access to the presence of God. Because Jesus provided the way, and because he, even now, is the human who represents us before the Father, we pray in his name. It's a way to recognize what he has done and to honor him. He is our passport to God, our VIP backstage pass. What does *amen* mean at the end of a prayer? "Let it be." It voices our hope for an answer.

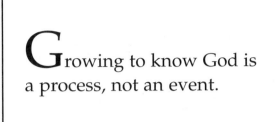

Growing to know God is a process, not an event.

I have a wise friend who says that, to him, all prayer ends in silence. There is a beautiful part of prayer that uses no words but is a time of quiet rest, enjoying God's presence. Ask your child to practice feeling God's presence just for a moment. Still yourself, quiet your mind, see whether you can feel God's nearness, peace, love. It may feel like a gentle hug.

If you yourself have heard God or seen exciting answers to prayer, be careful not to stress your own experience too heavily as though you expect your child to have the same experience. If your child does not feel the same closeness you have with God or does not hear or find answers like you do, your child may feel that he or she is not doing it right or that God does not love him or her as God loves you. God treats us as the individuals God made us to be, and God knows how to speak to each of us. As your child turns to God, God will respond, and they will develop their own relationship.

So encourage your child to choose training wheels or to tell you a method that he or she may already use. Ask him or her to choose a time of day to pray. This planning is important. Theologian John Piper says, "One of the main reasons so many of God's children don't have a significant life of prayer is not so much that we don't want to, but that we don't plan to."

Of course, the whole goal of training wheels is to take them off and ride on your own. After a child is accustomed to communicating with God, he or she can pray any way he or she likes anywhere at any time.

Growing to know God is a process, not an event. Hearing God's voice, recognizing God's nudge comes as we cultivate a life of prayer. It's not a matter of doing it right. Instead, it's about growing to know Love in person, Grace as a Living Being, the One Faithful and True.

In summary, it's up to you to go first and show your children your own growing relationship with God. After that, give your children training wheels and provide the right conditions for them to open the door to a whole new world.

Award-winning author and children's communicator Karyn Henley is best known as the author of the original version of The Beginner's Bible, *which sold more than 5 million copies and was translated into 17 languages. A graduate of Abilene Christian University, Karyn received a Master's of Fine Arts from Vermont College in 2004. She lives in Nashville, Tennessee, where she and her husband, Ralph, homeschooled their 2 now-grown sons and are currently raising two cats—Nip and Tuck. Visit Karyn's website at* **http://www.karynhenley.com**

Who Are We When Nobody Is Looking? Character, Character Education, and Character and Spiritual Formation

by Vernie Schorr

The idea of character education has captured the attention of the White House and Congress, both of which are searching for the appropriate federal role in promoting basic decency. Lawmakers have lent their symbolic support by endorsing "National Character Counts Week." The Department of Education has funded a few character pilot programs. Many states have also created character education requirements. But is that enough? Is that all there is? Does character education alone bring about true and lasting change in the lives of children? What is our responsibility as Christian educators?

What Is Character?

To understand character education, we must first understand what character is and how it is formed. We can then begin to understand the larger concept of character and spiritual formation, which goes far beyond character education.

The word *character* is used in a variety of ways. It is sometimes used to describe a person in a book or play. Sometimes it is used to describe a personality, as in "She's a character," implying a positive or negative attribute of the person. These and other uses of the word *character* may create confusion about its use. For the purposes of this article, when I speak of character, I am speaking of a person's inward nature, what he or she is like when nobody is looking. Its appearance may be constructive or destructive.

Author Dallas Willard defines *character* in this way: "Our character is that internal, overall structure of the self that is revealed by our long-run patterns of behavior and from which our actions more or less automatically arise."

Our character is made of those ideas, principles, and personal qualities that give life direction, meaning, and depth. Character constitutes our inner sense of what is right and wrong, based on who we are, not on external laws or rules of conduct. It is our character that drives our conduct; and it is our character that forms our attitudes, choices, and actions, which demonstrate who we are and who we are becoming.

How Is Character Formed?

Character is formed both intentionally and unintentionally. The intentional positive character formation that once was an intrinsic part of our culture has been replaced with the model of serving self and seeking fame, sexual promiscuity, violence, blame, revenge, and a host of other destructive traits. The result is unintentional formation of these destructive character traits. The outcomes of both the intentional and the unintentional define a person's approach to life and worldview.

The good news is that character can be changed. That is what godly character and spiritual formation is about. That is why we who serve children must be intentional about integrating character and spiritual formation into the Bible stories we tell children, Scripture memorization, Bible learning activities, VBS, and club outreaches.

Dallas Willard says, "The Spirit of God now calls his people to live from an adequate basis for character transformation, resulting in obedience to and abundance in Christ." Our task, as advocates of children, is twofold: to become intentional in our own personal character and spiritual formation toward God and, in turn, to become intentional in our children's character and spiritual formation. In doing so, we reflect God's character and build a conscience that is able to choose right from wrong.

> The good news is that character can be changed. That is what godly character and spiritual formation is about.

can be formed and transformed in the image of God, apart from the work of the Holy Spirit in their lives. Character formation and transformation require an inward working of God's spirit upon a person's spirit. As we guide the formation of God's character in children, we also are guiding the formation of their spiritual lives. This privilege includes introducing them to the person of God, life with God, and an intimate relationship with God through God's Son Jesus with the help and power of the Holy Spirit.

A Popular Misperception

The following appeared in an article on Monday, July 16, 2007, in *Today's Children's Ministry Newsletter*. It begins with a question from someone using a secular character education curriculum.

"Our program and your children's ministry are really trying to do the same thing, right?"

An interesting question, for sure—but a wrong one.

It came from someone who organizes programs for kids to help them develop positive character traits. I'm definitely all in favor of guiding children in character and morality growth. I'm a parent, after all. But I had to disagree with this person. The words of C.S. Lewis, in *Mere Christianity*, explain why:

"We must not suppose that even if we succeeded in making everyone nice we should have saved their souls. A world of nice people, content in their own niceness, looking no further, turned away from God, would be just as desperately in need of salvation as a miserable world—and might even be more difficult to save."

The writer of the above article is pointing out a serious flaw in some character development efforts, which is the idea that children's character

Developing positive character virtues apart from a personal relationship with God is arguably possible to some degree; but living out God's character in relationships, communities, and societies requires the inner presence and power of God's spirit.

Intentional, Godly Character Formation

Everyone receives some type of character formation, just as everyone receives some type of education. The question is what is the standard and model for the character being developed? Is it character traits such as indifference, revenge, or subtle dishonesty (for example, it's OK to tell a white lie)? Or is the standard based on God's character of compassion, forgiveness, and integrity as revealed in God's book, the Bible, and modeled by Christ's life and words?

As a follower of Christ, I work with educators and parents around the country to bring an awareness of the need to change the poverty of character and searing of conscience in our children. I have seen the benefits of intentionally developing character and conscience in children. I have also witnessed character and spiritual transformation in the lives of children whose early character and spiritual formation was less than ideal.

The forming of character is a lifelong process. Character formation begins in infancy, both intentionally and without intention, and extends throughout life.

At the early ages (children ages 2–11), the focus of character and spiritual formation is on the prevention of moral decay. At the middle and upper ages (youth ages 12–18), the focus shifts to intervention in the midst of moral decay. My focus and emphasis is what we can do to help in the forming of character at the early ages to prevent moral decay.

Forming character is more than learning about or changing behavior. Character formation requires the intentional training and developing of spirit, will, and mind toward God. It involves truth-seeking and the discovering of beliefs that transform the spirit. Character formation affects spiritual formation, and spiritual formation affects character formation. Godly character and spiritual formation, therefore, require a commitment of the adults in our society to intentionally reinvest in the lives of individual young people.

Our nation's culture itself is no longer as attentive to the needs of children as it once was. Our task, therefore, is to be intentional about meeting the need for character and spiritual formation in children.

The Adventure Ahead

I am passionate about character and spiritual formation that is the intentional training of spirit and mind toward Christ. It includes identified dos and don'ts of life with others. It involves relationships, rules, and precepts: It is wrong to steal from others, abuse children, kill another person, lie to parents or friends. It is right to return a lost article to its owner, to tell the truth, to help a neighbor, to forgive a wrong.

Character develops and forms through thoughts, words, attitudes, actions, relationships, choices, and conflicts. Godly character formation requires the intentional and personal involvement of others in the process, with example, instruction, and training (practice) in good habits that affect a person's pattern of behavior, personality, and moral strength.

Godly character formation also requires that people assume responsibility within themselves for their thoughts, words, and actions. And it requires that people live out their private, inward transformation. Perhaps most important of all, godly character formation enables the transfer of beliefs, attitudes, and character virtues to others, launching benefit to families, communities, and societies.

The intentional developing of character in the children we serve is more than simply directing them to behave in certain ways. It is more than posting a character-virtue word on a bulletin board. It includes equipping children to think, to discern, to ask questions, and to evaluate answers. It requires creating opportunities for children to actively participate in making choices and decisions and to experience the consequences of their choices and decisions. And it requires practice and habit-forming. Together, these tasks and activities result in character formation in the likeness of Christ and internal character transformation that result in the outward living of God's character.

My challenge is to make you—and all of those others who serve children—acutely aware of the importance of becoming intentional about developing God's character in yourself and in the children you influence.

Are you ready for the adventure?

Vernie Schorr is an author, education consultant, curriculum writer, trainer, and president of Character Choice, a non-profit ministry founded to train and equip teachers and parents to guide character and spiritual formation in children, youth, and adults. She has worked in public and private education in the U.S., Canada, Central America, and Eastern Europe for more than 40 years This article contains excerpts from Vernie's newly released book, Compass: A Guide for Character and Spiritual Formation in Children, _a fresh, relevant, twenty-first century source of information and materials for integrating character and spiritual formation into family, school, sport, and church experiences and curriculum. It is available at the Character Choice ministry website._

To learn more about Character Choice, order a copy of her book, or contact Vernie Schorr, visit **www.characterchoice.org** _and click on "Book."_

Leading a Child to Christ

by Dave Welday

There's a soccer field I pass on the way home. On Saturday mornings, I see throngs of kids all decked out in their bright-colored jerseys, shuffling up and down the field; while passionate parents are screaming a mixture of cheers and instruction from the sidelines. Certainly, the game is played better as children get older and develop their skills and dexterity. But here's something about watching the "little guys" play—the 4, 5 and 6 year olds. "Herd Ball," we called it; because it seems the little tykes who have not yet mastered the concept of playing positions all frantically move toward the soccer ball, wherever on the field it happens to be.

Imagine how silly the game of soccer would be if we were to send kids out on the field with all sorts of instruction about passing, playing position, working on their "touches," without ever making sure that they were clear on the object of the game: to kick the ball into the net of the opposing team more times than the opposing team kicks the ball into yours.

Can you imagine a high school football coach showing his offensive line how to run a set play: "Number 24, you block this guy. Number 32, you sprint off the line 10 yards, cut hard to the right, and look for the ball to be there," without making sure that all of the players understand that the object is to get the pigskin into the opponent's end zone.

Mastering all of the tactics, rules, and plays of the game don't mean much without being certain that everyone on the field knows that the object of the game is to score more points than the opposing team does. Yet, in children's ministry, I see a ton of activity without much attention placed on the goal of the ministry, which is to see children come to faith in Christ. Volunteer teachers prepare their crafts and read through lesson plans. Children's ministry

leaders evaluate the latest curriculum and fret over figuring out how to engage parents and recruit more workers, all without ever leading a child in the prayer of salvation. We do all of our ministry "activity" without making sure that every child has an opportunity to repent of their sins and accept Jesus as their personal savior. Call me old fashioned, but isn't that the goal of our "game"? If all of our activity, fun, Scripture memorization, VBS programs, cool video shorts don't result in children accepting Christ while they are still children, then we're in big trouble.

We're all familiar with the Barna statistics that indicate that the highest likelihood of a person ever coming to faith in Christ occurs before he or she reaches the teen years. The harvest that Jesus talks about in Matthew 9:37 and John 4:35 is filled with children. So how do you lead a child to Christ? Well, the conviction of the Holy Spirit is not a formula, or a pill, or even a program. But I believe that there are some key principles you can use to see more children in your church become converted, committed followers of Jesus while they are under your care. Here are what I refer to as the "three C's" of leading children to Christ: Be committed, clear, and consistent.

Be committed.

As you plan your lessons, make sure that you create opportunities to share the gospel with children on a regular basis. Be intentional about this. On a quarterly or monthly basis or some other frequency that works for you, build in an altar call or opportunity to accept Jesus as Lord and Savior. You may give an invitation to respond to the gospel every week during a certain lesson series. The point is, make sure that the plan of salvation is clearly presented to kids at every age and on multiple occasions throughout the year. Don't wait until a catechism or certain age to allow children the opportunity to respond to Jesus. Throughout the year, you will likely have many teachable moments, when the opportunity to lead children to Christ will flow well with your lesson plans (even if this wasn't even written into the curriculum agenda for that day.)

Don't feel that leading a child to Christ has to always be handled in a group. I hope that you will have the opportunity to connect with children one on one. When you do, use the opportunity to ask the child about his or her walk with the Lord. Take time to personally invite the child to pray to accept Christ. Many children, just like many adults, may not be comfortable making a public confession of faith as part of a group call to action. So look for those teachable moments when you can talk with a child one on one, inviting him or her to accept Jesus Christ as Lord and Savior.

Be clear.

Most of us have become familiar and comfortable with spiritual phrases and concepts such as forgiveness of sin, atonement, the substitutionary work of grace performed on the cross, Jesus' dying for our sins. But we have a hard time explaining those concepts to kids in simpler language. Make sure that you can explain the plan of salvation in very simple terms, without using a lot of religious jargon.

For example, last Sunday I was talking with the kids in my group about what it means to be "born again." I held up two balloons and said, "Both of these balloons look the same, don't they? And yet these balloons aren't working the way they were made to, are they? You see, they were designed to be filled with air. (*I blew up one of the balloons.*) Now this balloon (*pointing to the one filled with air*) can really go places, can't it? (*I let the balloon go, and the air propels it around the room.*) You see, you were designed by God to be filled with God's Spirit. And when you ask Jesus to be the boss or leader of your life, the Bible says that he sends his Holy Spirit to fill you up. You're the same person as you were before, except now you have God filling you on the inside. You can really go places, just like this balloon did. Everyone who accepts Jesus as his or her savior and asks him to be the boss of his or her life becomes a new person on the inside. That person becomes born again, a follower of Christ."

I'm sure you can come up with other, perhaps more effective ways to explain the eternal transformation that occurs when you respond to Christ. But my point is that we have to find creative, clear ways to help children grasp amazing and sometimes deep spiritual concepts.

Be consistent.

I am well aware that preschool children are more concrete thinkers, so analogies and spiritual concepts are somewhat lost on them. Yet the fact that a child may not be able to fully grasp on an intellectual level the significance of what's happening when they surrender their lives to the Lordship of Christ is not a good reason to withhold giving them an opportunity to respond to the Good News. The truth is, if we all had waited until we could fully grasp on an intellectual level, what happens when we call out to a loving God to rescue us from our state of rebellion and separation, we'd never experience redemption. Just because a younger child does not fully grasp the significance of what he or she is praying doesn't mean that we should not give them the opportunity to turn to Christ.

Think about it, the Holy Spirit was working in the life of John the Baptist before he was even born, to the point that he leapt inside Elizabeth's womb when Mary, who was pregnant with Jesus, came into the room. There was no cognitive or intellectual understanding, just spirit responding to spirit. So in your nurseries and preschool and early elementary classes, talk about the importance of following Jesus and inviting him to be your savior.

Will children who make a profession of faith at ages 3, 4, and 5 want to rededicate their lives to Christ when they are older? Perhaps. But there's nothing wrong with that. I made a decision to be committed to my wife for as long as I live, without having much of a clue what all that would entail. God sees and knows our hearts. God's Spirit can woo a young child into the Kingdom, without the trappings of full intellectual understanding of what's going on.

I believe that, as children grow in their intellectual capacity to understand spiritual truth and you repeat the opportunities to respond to the Gospel, when children feel compelled to respond, they will do so with ever-greater reverence, commitment, and assurance.

Once you have these three C's firmly entrenched in your thinking and children's ministry planning, here are a few other ideas that you can add to your salvation strategies:

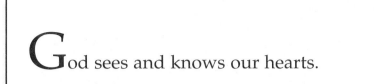

God sees and knows our hearts.

1. **Use some relevant tracts and tools.** *The Billy Graham Evangelistic Association* (**www.bgea.org**) has a wonderful children's discipleship program called "Passageway" (**www.passageway.org**) that features a great little tract called "Your Passageway to God." For the tween ages, that same tract is reformatted to be age appropriate, is called "Steps to Peace With God," and is available through the **daretobeadaniel.com** program.

2. **Feature testimonies**. Have adults, teens, and other children regularly share a testimony about how they came to faith in Christ. Use the show and tell the philosophy. Don't just tell kids that they need to be saved. Show them people who have made that decision. Have others tell their stories of how becoming a follower of Christ changed their lives. Make sure that kids know how you became a Christian and how making that choice changed your life for the better as well as for eternity.

3. **Rely on the Holy Spirit.** It's the role of the Spirit to convict non-believers of sin and righteousness and to draw people to Jesus. So make room in your services for the Holy Spirit to touch young hearts. Also, get kids involved in ministry. Have them pray for people who are serving in the church and their communities. Let them be involved on the worship team or puppet ministry. When kids are involved in doing the works of Jesus and making their faith active and not just something they learn about in class, that sets up an environment where the Holy Spirit can do the work of conviction.

4. **Practice with your leaders.** When was the last time you asked one of your workers to share with you the plan of salvation? Work with your volunteer leaders and require that each one of them share with you his or her testimony of how he or she came to Christ. Devote one of your teacher training sessions to practicing as a team to explain to children the plan of salvation.

Let's not get so wrapped up in our programs and events that we lose sight of the object of our ministry: to see children take the first step into their divine destiny by becoming a child of the living God.

David Welday is president of Next Generation Institute, (NGI) a non-profit organization dedicated to giving parents a Godly game plan for training their sons and daughters in the way God has divinely purposed them to go. He is also president of HigherLife Development Services, Inc., a full-service publishing and publishing consulting company that works with authors and organizations to create innovative books and curriculum with positive, life-changing messages. He is active in local-church ministry and has served as both family ministries director and worship leader. He lives in Oviedo, Florida, and has been married to his wife, Amy, for more than 30 years. They have three wonderful sons, David, Darren, and Jason.

Notes

Technology

See, everything has become new!

2 Corinthians 5:17

If We Do Nothing, Nothing Will Be Done

by Tracy Carpenter

"Never before in the history of telecommunications media in the United States has so much indecent (and obscene) material been so easily accessible by so many minors in so many American homes with so few restrictions." —U.S. Department of Justice

The new millennium was ushered in by a dramatic technological revolution. We now live in an increasingly diverse, globalized, and media-saturated society. At any given moment, kids of all ages are experiencing various aspects of technology and the Internet. Technological advances and the Internet have made computers, phones, and other handheld devices the main sources for gathering information. Kids are connected in every way imaginable, making technology a huge part of their lives.

However, the issue is not so much the use of technology, but the gathering of information and, more importantly, development of relationships. The world is viewed via computing devices. Kids are multitasking like never before: listening to music while surfing the Web, texting friends while playing a video game, and so on. The computer and other technologies represent intellectual appendages to this emergent culture. They are the hands and feet which carry kids of all ages to exciting new experiences.

Today's kids are wired for relationships. Peer groups are extremely important to them. While we adults often see the Internet as an information-gathering tool, teens use it to build a network of friends which often spans the globe. This is what social networking websites are all about. MySpace, Facebook, and Twitter are just a few of the most popular. Unfortunately, there are many dangers which come with the way kids are using these sites and technology in general.

MySpace is a particular danger as it has no filters and no protection for kids. If they are playing, using, surfing, or experiencing MySpace, they are without a doubt experiencing mind-bending images and information. *Dateline* surfed MySpace and found scenes of binge drinking, apparent drug use, teens posing in underwear, members simulating sex and, in some cases, even having it. They also found pages that, though less provocative, were potentially more dangerous. Teens routinely listed not only their names and addresses, but cell phone numbers and after-school schedules. MySpace is not the only threat. Other sites have direct links to pornography in just a click of a button. The Internet is a dangerous place, and it is threatening the purity of thousands of children each day.

Wii® gaming system, iPhone®, and a large percentage of other new mobile phones have Web access. This makes it possible for young people to access content from the Internet from wherever they are, many times without parental or teacher supervision.

So, how do you become an effective pastor to this generation of kids?

First, make a commitment to understand technology and how kids are using it.

Second, talk openly about the many dangers this world brings with it. If we are going to set out to give kids solid information and a proactive approach to staying safe on the Internet. We must comprehend not only how it works but the many dangers which come with it.

If we are going to set out to give kids solid information and a proactive approach to staying safe on the Internet, we must comprehend not only how it works but the many dangers which come with it.

God wants to use His people to prepare, protect, educate, and inform kids today. With pornography, child predators, cyber bullies, unfiltered social networking, and the degree of injustice online being so great, it is sometimes easy to get overwhelmed. What can we do to help kids face the insurmountable pressures of this culture and come out unscathed? The answer … no one knows exactly. But one thing is sure: *if we do nothing, nothing will be done.*

Talk to Your Kids About Internet Dangers——the Do's and Don'ts

DO

- Help kids learn the fundamentals of Christian faith and how to apply them to their culture. Through guided discussions and a biblical worldview, kids can learn to apply their beliefs and moral values to the culture and mass media of entertainment and technology. "Direct my footsteps according to your word …" (Psalm 119:133, NIV).

- Stimulate kids to discover, discern, and reflect on the messages of the media.

- Help kids and parents set guidelines for the Internet and other technology.

- Talk to kids about social issues at a very early age. Do not wait until topics like social networking, cyber bullying, dating, sex, or even pornography become major issues; teach God's guidelines early and articulate them. In fact, the earlier and more often, the better!

- Use role playing. Establishing an open and honest dialogue with kids will create an atmosphere of trust and respect. They need to feel they can come to you with questions. (However, always encourage them to talk to their parents first.) Help kids to visualize and articulate their plans of action. A plan is the before, during, and the after. Give kids tangible ideas of what they can do to be equipped and ready for whatever they may face on the Internet.

- Learn! Understand the basic issues at hand when it comes to pornography, the Internet, the media, and technology and kids' exposure to it. Keep learning and seeking out resources that will help you grow as a child advocate.

- Create innovative programming during high risk hours for kids to engage in. (For example, right after school or during the summer.) We must continuously try to find innovative ways to relate to this explosive, dynamic population of kids.

- Build social networks within your ministry for your kids to participate in. Start looking ahead. Repeatedly ask questions of your team: What is coming? How can we help? How can we educate ourselves and our kids about this culture? How can we give them a solid biblical worldview? How can we better educate our parents to protect and educate their own children? What curriculum is out there to address the needs of our kids?

- Help parents learn how to protect their kids from these dangers. Use handouts that are full of tips and valuable information. This helps them become better equipped at communicating with their kids.

- Get connected in the lives of the kids you minister to. Know what is happening in their lives on a personal basis.

- Increase your computer literacy and encourage your team of leaders to do so as well. (If necessary, sit down at the computer and go right to MySpace, for example. Kids and their parents need to know you know what's up.) Parents will desperately need you to understand when they show up dazed and confused in need of your counsel. Read blogs, text, surf the Web—whatever it takes to know the issues facing kids.

- Help kids and therefore society by providing well-planned online educational experiences—from website development to virtual environments just for kids.

- Provide a safe atmosphere for kids in your ministry to share anything. Offer forms of counseling free of judgment for kids who make mistakes and find themselves in trouble.

- Explain to your kids the truth of what is happening today. (For example, you might say, "Sexual predators live online, and they are out to exploit and harm you."

- Discuss all messages in the media … from Halloween to computers.

DON'T

- Don't overprotect. "But when you are tempted, he will also provide a way out so that you can stand up under it" (1 Corinthians 10:13, NIV).

- Don't fix everything. Encourage parents not to fix everything for them. Instead, allow kids to experience natural consequences and learn the role of discretion in decision making.

- Don't overreact! Stay calm and collected when you are talking about sensitive issues. When overwhelmed with the dangers of technology and media, it's easy to panic! Do not freak out—parents are counting on you!

- Do not avoid tough conversations. "Take no part in the worthless deeds of evil and darkness; instead, rebuke and expose them" (Ephesians 5:11, NLT). We must take a stand for this generation and the generations to come. There is a roaring lion encircling the lives of kids everywhere, and he lives in the computer. If we're not careful the kids of tomorrow won't have a chance.

- Don't be in denial. " 'Everything is permissible for me'—but not everything is beneficial" (1 Corinthians 6:12, NIV). Kids today are intelligent, confident, and getting more independent every day. They will use all types of technology at some point in their lives. Make sure you talk to them before that happens.

This age of information will continue to change not only the way kids view the world, but how they interpret it. Today kids are dealing with divorce, Internet issues, death, illness, obesity, drugs, abuse, poverty, anger, bullies, ADD, witchcraft, and much more. We need to teach a balance of worldview, biblical worldview, worship, prayer, and Old and New Testament. If not, kids could be swallowed up by the enemy, having lots of great knowledge of the Bible in their heads but not in their hearts.

We as pastors must open our eyes to the culture and the world in which the kids we minister to live. It is quite different than the world we as pastors and children's leaders grew up in! If we are truly going to get involved, make a difference, and transform kid's lives, we need to immerse ourselves in their world and show them Christ in ours!

*Tracy Carpenter is currently the Chief Creative Officer for Kidsworld Studios Inc., a missional-minded organization committed to creating spiritually kid-focused projects, programs, support, resources, and ministry. She is the Director of Creative Development for **theporntalk.com**, which talks to kids about pornography and Internet dangers. She has been published multiple times in national magazines and is known as a kids' "futurist." She has dedicated her ministry to the emergent culture and to growing ministries both internally and externally.*

Statistics on Internet Use

- Four million children are posting content to the Web every day. (**www.netlingo.com**)

- Many kids use the Internet at home or school by the time they are 6 years old. (**www.microsoft.com/protect/family/guidelines/faq.mspx**)

- One out of every four 5-year-olds uses the Internet. (**www.redorbit.com**)

- Ninety-three percent of all Americans between ages 12 and 17 use the Internet. (**temptationofageneration.com**)

- Fifteen million youth use instant messaging. (**www.netlingo.com**)

- Seventy-six percent of parents don't have rules about what their kids can do on the computer. (**www.netlingo.com**)

- One out of 17 kids have been harassed, threatened, or bullied online. (**www.netlingo.com**)

- Nine out of 10 parents will never know that any inappropriate contact has occurred online. (**www.netlingo.com**)

- Sixty-one percent of children between the ages of 13 and 17 have a personal profile on a social networking site. (**www.netlingo.com**)

Statistics on Pornography

- Average age of first Internet exposure to pornography is 11 years old. (**internet-filter-review.com**)

- Nine out of 10 children between the ages of 8 and 16 have viewed pornography on the Internet, in most cases unintentionally. (London School of Economics)

- Adult industry says traffic is 20–30% children. (NRC Report 2002, 3.3)

- There are 4.2 million pornographic websites, 420 million pornographic webpages, and 68 million daily pornographic search engine requests. (internet filter review, 2006)

- Twenty-six popular children's characters, such as Pokémon®, My Little Pony, and Action Man, revealed thousands of links to porn sites. Thirty percent were hard-core. (HealthLife24, 2007)

- Pornographers disguise their sites (i.e. "stealth" sites) with common brand names, including Disney, Barbie®, ESPN, etc., to entrap children. (Cyveillance Study, March 1999)

- One in 5 children between the ages of 10 and 17 receives unwanted sexual solicitations online. (Youth Internet Safety Survey, U.S. Department of Justice)

Statistics on Internet Predators

- Federal authorities believe that at least 500,000 to 750,000 predators are online on a daily basis. (Clint Van Zandt, MSNBC analyst and former FBI profiler)

- Two in 5 abductions of children ages 15 to 17 are due to Internet contact. (San Diego Police Dept.)

- Seventy-six percent of victims in Net-initiated sexual exploitation cases were 13 to 15; 75% were girls. "Most cases progressed to sexual encounters," and 93% of the face-to-face meetings involved illegal sex. (*Journal of Adolescent Health*, November 2004).

© 2009 Abingdon Press

Kids and Technology: Rotary Telephones in a Cell-phone World

by Erik K. Jarvis

Our relationship with technology is quite a paradox. After all, who hasn't been thrilled to order something online only to curse the machine for crashing or locking up a moment later, or who doesn't love the express self-checkout lane until the light starts flashing and you have to wait for the attendant to come save you? How about a technology that we become pervasively familiar with only to see something new emerge within a short time that is preferable to what we are using?

I'm sure you have come face to face with these things and have yourself had the love/hate relationship with technology. Some of you reading this will remember the days of the rotary telephone. I'll admit, I had no complaints using one. However, times surely have changed, and today I could hardly live without my cell phone (though sometimes I think I'd like to give it a try), and I have no desire to go back to using a rotary phones; they were slow and subject to misdials from time to time.

At its core, technology is merely how we communicate. That's it. Pick your area; whether it's voice to voice as with phones, film to eyes and ears as with TV and movies, or global positioning systems for our cars to tell us where to turn, it's all about communicating. These devices and media that we've come to rely upon communicate messages to our senses and beings about the world around us. The world we live in has become quite good at it too! Technology changes so quickly it can be hard to keep up with it. Things that were modern a few years ago are so dated and obsolete today.

But what amazes me is how quickly children seem to pick up and master these technologies. Anyone of us can be caught off-guard when it comes to technology. I myself am no slouch when it comes to technological things, but even I'll admit that I've been blindsided a number of times over the past few years. The worst part is who blindsided me—the kids! Just when I think I have something mastered some kid comes along and shows me a shortcut or a more efficient way of using the technology.

When you put that into perspective, our ministries don't necessarily need to be on the leading edge of technology, but we do need to reach an audience that lives there. So here are a few basic things for you to think about when it comes to technology and your children's ministry.

> When you put that into perspective, our ministries don't necessarily need to be on the leading edge of technology, but we do need to reach an audience that lives there.

Time to Update

Like it or not, children love technology. They like to email their friends, they like to surf the web, they love to listen to music and MP3 players, some of them like to text and send messages on their cell phones or communication devices, they have social networking accounts, and almost all of them have access to online games of some sort. They've all seen animated and CGI (Computer Generated Imagery) films as well as TV shows.

The point is, while our kids are running around with cell phones, sometimes our ministries reflect a rotary telephone mentality. Our ministries represent a day gone by that was great but now represents something that is slow and inefficient. This mentality can easily lend itself to boring children or sending them in a direction where they may be disinterested altogether.

Take a hard look at the programming for all of your children's ministries. Does the programming incorporate any technology? Does your church have a website that kids can visit? Does your curriculum incorporate visually stimulating pieces?

So you really only have two options: you can run from it or you can try to tame it and use it to your advantage.

Better yet, answer this question: How does my ministry technology connect with kids where they are today? Have you tried sending web-blasts or posting the "question of the week" on the website? What things help you stay connected to the children to whom you're trying to minister? If we are to be effective ministers to the children God has entrusted to our care, we need to make our best attempt to meet them where they are. So again the question is raised: does my ministry technology connect with kids where they are today? If you can't think of an area, it's time to update!

Incorporate the Masters

Resources, resources, resources — they're everywhere, and sometimes we don't even see them! When it comes to technology some of your greatest assets are right there in your congregation and you've never even thought of them. Most teenagers have previously mastered many of the technology pieces you may want to incorporate. I challenge you to try and send a text message faster than any teen in your congregation. Many of the teens in your church

would probably love to help you set up a Web page, a page on a social networking site, or a weekly e-mail blast to help you stay connected. Some churches have found teens who have a love of video and film and are willing to edit video and create some terrific memories DVDs of VBS, summer camp, or other programming.

Further, many congregations have college students who are home during the summer months and have been taking classes in the latest technologies, and these student would be thrilled to try out some of the new things they have learned. Most of these students will have never thought of helping the children's ministry department at their home church.

How many adults in your congregation have jobs that are in media or technology? You may be surprised at the number of adults who could help your ministry reach the next technological level that would never have thought of helping in children's ministry because they're not gifted teachers or have never considered children's ministry as an area in which they can be useful. These people are tremendous resources who can give your ministry a boost with their technological skills. Even a good photographer with a digital camera can be very helpful to a children's ministry that is constantly creating fresh visual promotions and brochures. Once you're committed to making your children's ministry pop in the technology area, start looking beyond your teachers to get you there. With a little investigation and persuasion you should be able to outfit your ministry with some tremendous talent in a short period of time.

Overcome Your Fear

Okay, so technology is a big snarling animal standing between you and the children to whom you're trying to minister. It's definitely intimidating and perhaps a little overwhelming, but the longer you wait, the bigger the animal grows and the farther behind you fall. So you really have only two options: you can run from it or you can try to tame it and use it to your advantage.

I've always found it encouraging to think about history and remember that somewhere along the way someone thought to record a voice, lay a wire across the Atlantic Ocean floor, put a satellite into space, and all the other things that have helped us communicate better and more efficiently. If any one of those individuals had been polarized by fear of the unknown we wouldn't be where we are today.

The same can be true of your ministry. If you become stoic in your approach to technology you risk missing the best communication you can possible have with a generation of children. We all know that children grow up so quickly, and missing the communication mark with today's kids can have devastating results in the future. Don't be afraid of technology—embrace it and use it to your advantage to reach children for God's kingdom.

Technology Respite

The final piece when it comes to technology is learning when to step away from it. There is something very refreshing about hiking a trail, climbing a mountain, or camping out in an area where you cannot get a cell-phone call, there's no Internet service, and there's no TV. It's in the quiet of these times that the absence of technology becomes the new chic way of communicating. After spending many years in Christian Camping, the beauty of the ministry

was never the tents, the outhouses, or the bugs; it was the quiet times talking about God around a campfire or the long walks through the woods enjoying the nature God created.

Technology, for all its benefits, occasionally benefits us more when it's not around. If your children's ministry is tech-savvy, consider ways to give your kids a break from technology every now and then. Just be sure it's a break and not a total departure. Too many ministries make the mistake of trying to make a departure from all technology. Don't kid yourself; there's a reason we're not using rotary phones today. While it's fun to look back, no one really wants to go there.

Erik Jarvis has a ministry background in Christian Camping, children, youth, and college ministries and currently serves as an Associate Pastor at Fellowship Alliance Chapel in Medford, N.J. Erik has worked on numerous video and media productions and has served annually as the General Session Producer for Children's Pastors' Conference and other conferences throughout the Northeast.

D on't be afraid of technology, embrace it and use it to your advantage to reach children for God's kingdom.

So You Want to Shoot and Edit Video?

by Kurt Goble

The use of in-house video is an increasingly popular trend in children's ministry. But for the person who has no experience shooting and editing, it can be hard to know where to start. Let's take an entry-level look at basic video production for children's ministry.

A set of questions that seems automatically to come to mind when one decides to delve into this medium. What kind of equipment is needed? How much will it cost? How does the process work? What benefits can I expect? How can I make it look and sound good? Let's begin by taking a look at why this trend is becoming so popular.

Videos that are produced by curriculum and publishing companies are a great resource. For example *Kidmo*, *Timbuktoons*, *Live B.I.G.*, and *Elevate* offer us high-quality, well-produced video products that would be far too expensive, time consuming, and technically advanced for most of us to create on our own. These products can work great within their marketed context, or as components of your own program. So why not just stick with these resources? Although you will probably not achieve the same production qualities, in-house videos offer some powerful advantages.

The foremost of these is the fact that you get to decide what the content of the video will be. You get to take that great idea or powerful concept and bring it to life on the screen. You get to create something that works perfectly within the context of your lesson.

Another great advantage is that your kids get to see you and your volunteers onscreen creating a powerful connection and engaging students on a different level. You and your staff or volunteers can get away with being silly, poking fun at yourselves, and employing inside jokes. There's also the fact that you know your kids well enough to know what they will respond to in terms of age-appropriateness, humor, and pop-culture references. It all begins with a solid concept and good content.

Before getting into the specifics of equipment and software, a basic principal of video production should be understood. Good videos begin with good concepts. This is important to remember because a great concept will carry your video much further than fancy camera work or editing. No amount of soundtrack or flash will carry a video that doesn't have a solid working concept. Ninety percent of your success will depend on your concept. In fact, if you make a video with bad lighting, sloppy camera work, compromised sound quality, and rudimentary editing, it will be wildly successful if your concept is great. This is so important because many have a propensity toward spending too much time shooting and editing and not enough time conceptualizing and planning.

So what does a good concept look like? First of all, you have to start with your purpose. Think about what you are teaching and what you want to communicate with your kids. A good example would look like this: "With our preteens, we are studying Judges. We're talking about how Israel had no king and everyone did as they saw fit. They were a nation in anarchy. God wanted to be their king, but they didn't want to follow Him. The story ends in murder, civil war, kidnapping, and all sorts of evil. This speaks to us because it illustrates that life without God's authority is a mess. How can we illustrate this idea for the kids?"

A bad example of conceptualizing would look like this: "With our preteens we are studying Judges. You know what would be funny? Let's be the judges from *American Idol!*" Although there is a semantic connection here, this concept would lock us into a format that doesn't illustrate the main point of our story. That is, when we reach to make a connection, the video gets complicated and looses its effectiveness. A good video will be easy to follow and center on one concept.

Good conceptualizing happens when you thoughtfully consider what you want to communicate before you decide how you want to communicate it. If you will notice, in the "good" example, we decided exactly what we wanted the video to illustrate. This guides and directs our process by defining our task.

"We need to make a video that will illustrate that life without God's authority is a mess." This is where the brainstorming begins. When you brainstorm you come up with ideas that illustrate your point and then run them through the filter of feasibility: "No authority, no king, no God, no rules. What if you had a classroom with no rules? No, that would take a huge cast. No rules? Driving with no rules. What if we drove around and didn't follow the rules of the road? Too dangerous! But I'm liking this "no-rules" thing. No rules in sports."

"Could we do a sport? Something one on one. Tennis? "No-rules" tennis? That's not physical enough. How about basketball? We'll get two guys to agree to play no-rules one-on-one basketball. They can act like they are tripping and tackling each other on the court, and then we can end it with them with bandages and crutches talking about what a bad idea it was to play with no rules."

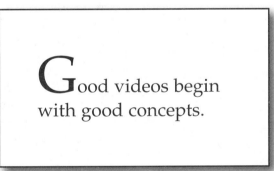

G ood videos begin with good concepts.

After this we have to state the purpose of our video so that we can stick to the concept and make the point as effectively as possible. "I am teaching the kids that life without God's authority is a mess. We are going to illustrate this in a video that shows what a mess a game of basketball would be if you removed the authority of the rules." At this point our task is very clear. We

aren't making a video for the sake of being cool or silly or relevant. We are making a video for a specific purpose, to communicate a specific idea.

Now we can start talking about equipment. Since we are only able to scratch the surface of video production here, I am going to make recommendations based on the following assumptions: (1) You have little or no experience producing videos. (2) You have not yet invested in any equipment. (3) You are going to begin on an entry level in terms of equipment, software and budget.

Camera

My entry-level recommendation for a camera would be a Flip Video® camcorder. This is a small video recorder with a built-in microphone and automatic focus, exposure, and audio compression. It is about the size of a digital point-and-shoot camera and is an amazing value for what it does. Although this camera will not afford you the ability to zoom or perform any advanced techniques like overexposure or artistic focusing, the advantages are abundant for the beginner. The Flip® is simple to use and inexpensive. The cost starts at $150, with the HD version starting at $200. It stores an hour of video on flash memory. Transferring video to your computer is a snap because the camera turns each clip into a file making the process just like transferring pictures from your digital camera. Although Mini DV cameras have their advantages, video must be "captured" from the tape and turned into computer files. This is often a long and tedious process that is bypassed when using a flash-video recorder like the Flip®.

Computer

In terms of system stability, ease of use, render time (how long you have to wait while the computer "thinks"), and final product, Apple® is the better choice for editing video. Apple® computers come loaded with iMovie®, which is a very basic and user-friendly video editing program. When choosing an Apple®, avoid the Mac mini®, which isn't quite powerful enough to edit video quickly and seamlessly. The more memory and processing power you have, the faster and easier your editing will be.

If you are going to edit on a PC, make sure you have at least 2 GB of RAM and a 2Ghz processor. In either case, you will need enough hard drive space to handle your projects. Videos files are typically very large and can fill up your hard drive faster than you would expect. As with an Apple®, more memory and processing power is always better.

Software

Although the Apple® comes loaded with iMovie®, the addition of Final Cut Express® will open up a world of possibilities. This software will take some time to learn, but helpful tutorials are available to get you started. Final Cut Express® has lots of fun effects and transitions built in that allow you to do things like cropping, titles, and adjusting the speed of your video. Final Cut Express® costs $200 and is available through Apple®.

Most likely, a new PC will also come with basic preloaded editing software. But I would recommend that PC users upgrade to Adobe Premier Elements®. This program is comparable to Final Cut Express® in its features and functionality. Premier Elements® costs $150, and is available through Adobe®.

With either program on either computing format, it is going to take time to learn what you are doing. Basic video editing consists of importing your video clips into a bin and then dropping them into a timeline in your desired order. After that there's cutting, volume adjustments, color adjustments, and exporting, just to name a few of the operations you will need to learn. It takes time and patience, but video editing is a worthwhile skill.

Some More Tips

- **Movement is good!**
  While shooting your video you will want to put your camera on a tripod for still shots. But when your camera is handheld, it is impossible to hold it perfectly stable. This makes your video look shaky. If you are

shooting handheld, slowly and steadily move the camera around as you shoot your subject. This makes your movement look intentional and gives the whole video a sense of motion.

- **A different way of looking at things.**
  Use extreme angles. Put the camera right next to the ground and shoot a hard up-angle. Hold it up high and shoot down. This provides variety and makes your video more interesting.

- **Keep it short.**
  While editing, make your video as short as possible. Cut out dead space and awkward transitions. This will make for a more fast-paced and engaging video.

- **Don't get too fancy.**
  Don't go crazy with preloaded transitions and effects. If you start to use too many of these, your video will come across as cheap and amateur. Too much flash can also be distracting. It can take away from the personal and familiar nature of your in-house video. If you try too hard to look professional, your video will probably look like you were trying too hard. Go for a basic, homespun look.

- **Set up concepts.**
  Some of the best videos are ones that communicate a basic concept to set up a lesson. Trying to tell a whole story or teach a lesson via video can be cumbersome.

- **End with a punch line.**
  Try to end your video with a punch line. This can be anything that provokes a thought or gets a laugh. Your transition out of the video and into your lesson or activity will be much smoother if the video doesn't just "trail off" at the end.

Kurt Goble has made more mistakes than anyone in the history of Children's Ministry. But he loves sharing what he's learned from all those mistakes. For thirteen years Kurt has served as children's pastor at First Christian Church of Huntington Beach, where he shares God's Word with kids through the technical arts. He is a graduate of Bethel College and a curriculum author. He and Heidi are happily married with two kids.

Volunteers

For we are God's servants, working together.

1 Corinthians 3:9

The Three *R*'s of Volunteerism

by Kim Vaught

Ask any children's ministry leader, "What is your greatest challenge in ministry today?" One might think that the answer would be to keep children engaged during children's worship or to fill the extra time when "big church" services go over. But for the majority of children's ministries, the greatest challenge is to have enough committed volunteers—the keyword being *committed.*

Today, as well as in past decades, it is not enough to have warm bodies filling the spots of teachers and assistants in our classrooms. As leaders of children's ministries, we have the job of helping people realize the value of serving, see the need, catch the vision, and see the worth of the children they serve.

Many of us grew up with the concept of the Three *R*'s—Reading, Writing, and Arithmetic. We have been told that these *R*'s were the basis, or the most important part, of education (even though we know that only one of them starts with an *R*.) I have chosen to use this format as we talk about motivating people to volunteer in children's ministry and how we keep them engaged as they serve. Read on for some tips on Recruiting, Training, and Retaining.

Recruitment

So how do you recruit? Recruitment must become a part of the DNA of your church's culture. It must be an ongoing process, not just once or twice a year. The staff, including most importantly the senior pastor, must see recruitment as a priority. You must have leadership in place to carry out a successful recruitment plan. So how do you begin? In my ministry experience, I've found that people want to be a part of something that has vision and is going somewhere—something that is fun and exciting but doesn't waste their time.

Step One: Pray for laborers.

Don't begin anything until you have committed it to God and asked for His help and for the right people to come forward. You not only desire a warm body; you also want people who use their gifts and are committed to the Kingdom and having an impact on kids' lives. Consider this model in 1 Peter:

> God's gifts of grace come in many forms. Each of you has received a gift in order to serve others. You should use it faithfully. If you speak, you should do it like one speaking God's very words. If you serve, you should do it with the strength God provides. Then in all things God will be praised through Jesus Christ.
>
> 1 Peter 4:10-11 (NIRV)

Connect with parents.

In your quest for volunteers, one of the biggest assets to your ministry are parents. Our job is to start connecting with parents earlier to clarify their role right from the start. Deuteronomy 6:5-7 states:

> Love the LORD your God with all your heart and with all your soul and with all your strength. These commandments that I give you today are to be upon your hearts. Impress them on your children. Talk about them when you sit at home and when you walk along the road, when you lie down and when you get up.
>
> Deuteronomy 6:5-7 (NIV)

Help parents imagine these verses. Encourage them to focus their priorities on what matters most. Express how the church can partner with them in their role.

After their child is born, recruiting parents to serve in your ministry can be viewed as free training for their role at home. Serving would make it possible for parents to know what was presented on the weekends in children's ministry so that the learning happens all week long.

I love this quotation I heard recently: "Renters don't paint, don't decorate, don't worry about how the carpet looks…but owners do." If parents understand the significance of the weekend experience as they see it first hand, they are going to start acting like owners.

A huge win occurs when parents and the church come together to make a bigger impact. Parents can be convinced of the importance of their role but will feel relieved that they don't have to parent alone.

> A huge win occurs when parents and the church come together to make a bigger impact. Parents can be convinced of the importance of their role but will feel relieved that they don't have to parent alone.

Step Two: Communicate the vision.

Communicate the vision, the mission statement, and the goals that you have for children's ministry. Educate your people on what is happening. Lay out the plan. People need to know what you are all about.

The mission statement at Crosstown Church is, "To impact the lives of kids with the love and message of Jesus Christ in an atmosphere where kids feel a sense of belonging." This statement covers the relational aspects of our ministry, as well as the biblical literacy and relevancy. We want kids to feel as though this is their church too, not just mom and dad's.

If you have other children's ministry staff as part of your leadership team, they need to live, eat, drink, and breathe this vision in all that they do, so as to not send any confusing messages. We are all speaking the same language. We must demonstrate there are no silos or islands when working in ministry. We are a team, we are a community, and eventually we become like family.

Market your vision.

- Put your mission statement on anything and everything you can, so that people are constantly reminded of what your ministry is all about. (Think: bulletins, diaper tags, walls in your area, letterhead, the church's website, and so on.)

- Use public relations in "big church," whether it's a video montage of kids having fun or a children's choir singing. Seize every moment you can to be in front of the congregation.

Step Three: Be specific.

Have a job description for every position, including:

- the age group that needs volunteers;

- which service assistance is needed (if you have more than one service);

- how regularly you need them to serve (once a month or every week);

- whether curriculum is provided;

- the preparation time;

- the skills needed for the particular position (to help volunteers find their sweet spot);

- whom they will report to;

- the benefit they will receive as they give of themselves.

Step Four: Try various channels.

- Your pastor: Talk to your senior pastor about incorporating volunteerism into a sermon series.

- One on one: A current children's ministry volunteer can personally invite a friend or family member. I tell my team they are the best volunteer commercial. They are walking billboards.

- Ministry fairs: Host a booth to highlight the many facets and opportunities in children's ministry.

- Your own personal observations: In a church, you will observe many people and see their potential and gifts. You will see how they might fit into the children's ministry picture.

- Website: List the job descriptions and positions needed on the Web. It's convenient for people to review, especially if they have lost their hard copy.

Training

Now that you have them, what do you do next?

Be prepared in advance.

Before you implement your recruitment process, have your training sessions and times scheduled. When making those plans, be considerate of your laity and their time. They don't want or need another meeting.

At Crosstown Church, we offer training during two of our three service times. We keep the session an hour long and conduct new volunteer training four times a year. Then we provide, many times throughout the year, specific training for our regular volunteers to sharpen their skills and challenge them to expand their involvement. Training may be presented by one of our staff members or someone from outside our church. We've also created an Early Childhood Training DVD for those who may have a conflict with the training times, with specific details on the age level the volunteer will be working with.

On-the-job training is a good way to bring someone alongside you to observe you in action.

> Continuously honor and appreciate your volunteers. Everyone needs encouragement. Everyone desires to know that he or she is important.

Most people learn by doing rather than by lecture.

Give it away.

Encourage your paid staff, or dedicated lay people, to duplicate themselves. Help them to let go of some of their responsibilities. We must be like Jesus and make disciples of people. The ministry is not about us, it's about giving it away to others (and them, in turn, giving it away). The ministry should be able to continue even in our absence.

Encourage Feedback

Also, during this process of equipping and training, you need to create an atmosphere where the volunteer can provide feedback. As you pray for God to send laborers, He may send some who can help you see new ways to do things. Or, they might affirm the way you are doing what you're doing. Volunteers are now a part of the team ,and they need to feel validated by being heard.

Retaining

Most church leaders know that finding volunteers is only half the battle. So how do you keep them? Continuously honor and appreciate your volunteers. Everyone needs encouragement. Everyone desires to know that he or she is important.

Are you blessed with great volunteers? Do you see how you cannot do your job alone, that you need the team? Then always make sure you are showing your appreciation.

Appreciate your volunteers.

- Publically recognize them. On a weekend, have a moment in "big church" where you bring your volunteers up front or have them stand where they are. Have the pastor recognize them, pray for them, and invite the congregation to applaud.

- Cards, notes, phone calls, and e-mails sent frequently by the staff are important.

- Plan banquets or brunches with a special speaker.

- Give gifts or tokens of appreciation (such as a license plate, a pen, or items that reinforce your annual theme.)

- Give weekly affirmations—connect with them each week before they serve. Go to their rooms, giving them a hug or high five. Be specific when asking how they are doing. If you know that they have some physical problems or issues with their kids or work, let them know you are praying for them. If time permits, pause and pray with them.

- When the senior pastor isn't scheduled to preach, invite the pastor to visit the children's area. The pastor will want to tell our volunteers how much they are appreciated for what they do each week.

- Take your volunteers out for coffee or a meal, and build a positive relationship. They need to see that you genuinely care for them as a person, not just as a worker bee.

When you honor your team of volunteers, they will see the connection between appreciation and motivation. They will want others to experience that, and that is how the cycle continues.

Strive for excellence.

Our experience at Crosstown Church has been that as we follow these guidelines, we have volunteers that become "lifers" in Children's Ministry. They are in it for the long haul.

Keep this thought in mind: Always strive for excellence. Settle for nothing less than God's best. Know that as kids lives are affected, families are affected and the Kingdom is affected.

Consider this quotation from George Barna: "The role of the church is to enable people to use their gifts in areas of passion to produce benefits that spill over into the home, the marketplace and the church itself."

> God will not forget your work and the love you have shown him as you have helped his people and continue to help them.
>
> Hebrews 6:10 (NIV)

Kim Vaught currently serves as the Children's Pastor for Montgomery Community Church in Cincinnati, Ohio, with an average weekly attendance of over 2,300. Kim has over seventeen years in full-time ministry experience with a B.A. and M.A. in Religion. Her easy-going style, wacky sense of humor, and deep love for children enable her to effectively minister to kids. E-mail her at **kvaught@mcc.us;** *visit her website at* **www.crosstownkids.us.**

Keep this thought in mind: Always strive for excellence. Settle for nothing less than God's best. Know that as kids' lives are affected, families are affected and the Kingdom is affected.

Training Without the Meeting

by Michelle Romain

Volunteers Are Busy

Anyone who's spent time in children's ministry knows the difficulty of having a well-attended training meeting. My experience is that twenty-five percent of your volunteers show up—the ones who are already doing it right. The other seventy-five percent who need the training do not attend. Now you have to personally contact the absentees or mail your notes to them, hoping they'll actually read them.

In a time when baseball practice, school plays, PTA meetings, basketball games, piano lessons, doctors appointments, maintenance appointments, overtime, church meetings, board meetings, Sunday school preparation, and more are a part of our everyday lives, the last thing volunteers want in their schedule is another training meeting. As children's pastors, we need to show our team that we are considerate of their time.

Alternative Approaches

Communication and training are the keys to successful volunteers. As ministers, we constantly have new ideas, procedures, and visions that our volunteers need to know. So, the question is not *whether* volunteers need to be trained but *how*. The days of scheduling a generic training event and expecting most, or all, of your volunteers to attend is over for most churches.

Therefore, the key to providing effective training to an overbooked volunteer staff is to offer alternative approaches.

Begin to view training as small bites instead of offering a full buffet. In other words, don't plan on having all departments meet each time or attempt to tell your volunteers everything you want them to know at one meeting. Read on for ways to take small bites.

Weekly Newsletters

Weekly newsletters can be sent through mail or e-mail. A written copy serves as a tangible reminder that volunteers can keep in front of them. In keeping with our idea that volunteers are busy, the best part of the newsletter is that it arrives directly to them.

When writing newsletters, be consistent. Send it regularly on the same day each week. This ensures that you write it and that volunteers expect it. Look at a weekly newsletter like a scheduled checkup to keep your team healthy.

Keep your information consistent by making a template, using the same headings each week. Lay out the page clearly and creatively, allowing space between sections and keeping paragraphs short. If you have a long training article, present it in weekly segments.

Include the following in your template for weekly newsletters:

- **Training** — Send the newsletter to individual ministry areas, such as elementary Sunday school teachers. This method allows you to provide customized training. Training articles can be ones that you write yourself or a quotation from a book; or consider adding a link to an article on the Web.

- **Information** — Include information about coming events for the entire children's ministry. This information helps create a bond among your team and enables teachers in one department to "talk up" another area. Consistently remind your volunteers of the children's ministry weekly schedule, highlighting an activity or area.

- **Reminders** — The scientific law of entropy states that anything left to itself will disintegrate until it reaches the most basic form. In other words, if it is not maintained, it will fall apart. As a minister, keep your mission statement and vision in front of your volunteers on a weekly basis. If you have a theme or goals for the year, remind your team of those and how your team can continue to achieve them.

This is also a good place to include reminders that you want to maintain, such as washing preschool toys after each service.

> The key to providing effective training to an overbooked volunteer staff is to offer alternative approaches.

- **Encouragement** — In this section, acknowledge teachers who have shown exceptional service, such as doing something special for a child, visitor, or parent. Give compliments that come to you regarding the ministry.

In the Old Testament, victories were celebrated by building an altar. Doing so testified to God's greatness to all who passed by. It's always a great idea to show ministry victories. Examples include salvation decisions and baptisms, successful events, visitors, testimonies of children's lives, or God's blessings of resources.

- **Challenges** — Challenges are twofold. The first is to challenge teachers to grow through research and study. You might add the question in your newsletter to elementary Sunday school teachers, "If Jesus were your student, how would you have met his learning style?"

The second is simply to encourage volunteers to read the newsletter. Give a trivia question; and when they can answer it, give them a prize. An example question is, "What are three children's ministry events that will happen during the summer?"

Audio/Visual

Audio/visual training is a way volunteers can train during their own time. Some of these methods are limited to your technical ability and resources.

- Have a CD or DVD of a training message. Record it by using your own words, or find a teacher-training resource that you can purchase and distribute to your volunteers.

- Make a video recording of a training subject, and upload your video to YouTube. E-mail the link to your volunteers.

- Podcasts can be recorded and placed on your ministry's website for volunteers to download to their devices.

- Recommend books or online articles for your volunteers to read. Include some study questions that coincide with the reading.

Director Support System

This system simplifies the lines of communication for your ministry. Divide your ministry areas into smaller groups, and establish a director over each group. For example, assign a director for babies through two-year-olds, three-year-olds through pre-K, kindergarten through second grade, and third through fifth grade.

Now when you need to train, you train the directors and they train their groups. Instead of contacting many individual teachers, you now contact only the directors. In our example above, that would be four directors. This system also helps to meet specific needs of volunteers, such as different levels of experience or different learning styles.

Peer-to-Peer Support System

Pair teachers to stay in contact with each other. Establish guidelines to help your teachers keep each other accountable and motivated by contacting each other one time per week, praying for and with each other, discussing the weekly lesson, and so forth.

Personal Greeting

Arrive early enough so that you can give your volunteers a personal greeting and touch base with them on any important issues. Leaders call this MBWA (Ministry by Walking Around). This personal touch allows you to minister directly to those who volunteer.

W hen training, listening is just as important as teaching.

Teacher Resource Room

This room is a great place for teachers to view information, reminders, updates, resources, outreach materials, announcements, birthdays, or new ideas and procedures. To encourage volunteers to visit the room, serve refreshments or offer contests such as door prizes for those who come by your teacher resource room.

Tokens

Repetition is one of the best ways to learn. The best training can go by the wayside if there is no follow-up or consistency. Provide symbolic tokens to teachers who keep your theme, mission statement, vision, and requirements in front of them. Examples include printed bookmarks, pens, buttons, badges, and posters.

Questionnaire

When training, listening is just as important as teaching. Offer questionnaires once a year that give teachers an opportunity to express their thoughts, needs, and ideas for the ministry. The questionnaire can contain questions that lead the teacher to think about their own service more deeply such as, "How many hours a week do you prepare for your lesson?" or "How many students do you contact per week on an average basis?"

Incentives

Incentives are one of the best motivational tools. Make a short list of requirements you would like to see your volunteers accomplish, such as calling their students during the week, visiting your resource room, wearing their nametags, or recruiting other teachers. Give them points to earn rewards for these. (See Home Run Derby on page 251 and the CD-ROM for an example of this incentive.)

The Meeting That Doesn't Feel Like a Meeting

If you must have a training meeting, make it not feel like a meeting. These suggestions will motivate volunteers to set aside the time to attend:

- **Dreaming Session** — Instead of having a "training" meeting, have an enrichment, brainstorming, dreaming, or vision meeting. These sessions give volunteers ownership and value as their input is heard.

- **Preparation** — Do your research, and plan meetings that are creative, motivational, and relative. A great meeting will encourage volunteers to come to the next one. As you speak, be visionary and bigger than life. A technique that salespeople use is to "assume the sale." For a children's pastor, this means to state your goals and assume the accomplishment, using proactive statements, such as, "We will" and "We can." Keep the meetings fresh by planning the unexpected with a surprise speaker or activity.

- **Inspiring of Excellence** — Help volunteers understand the importance of their ministry. It is a life-saving job! Doctors, policemen, and fireman save physical lives; children's workers help save spiritual lives! Understanding this will help volunteers pursue excellence and will challenge them to uphold their commitments. A great tool to inspire excellence is the testimony of other volunteers.

- **Assessing Progress** — Portray a realistic picture of how the ministry or their particular area is doing. Compare this reality to your mission statement, vision, and goals. Give standards that will help volunteers assess this progress, and discuss plans for necessary changes.

- **Making It Accessible** — When the reasons for not attending a meeting are removed, then the turnout will be better. Try these simple ideas to help accommodate volunteers schedules:

  - Offer childcare
  - Plan the meeting during mealtime, and serve a meal.
  - Meet when volunteers are already at church. For example, meet with your Sunday school teachers during the Wednesday night service.
  - Plan only information that applies to everyone.

- **Appreciation** — Show your volunteers you care by taking the extra step to express your appreciation. Give them a hand-written note. It's easy to discuss the changes that need to be done, but remember to also talk about what is going well.

- **Ministering Reminder** — Remind volunteers of the need to serve out of love for God and a desire to bring glory to Him. Challenge them to line up all they do with the Word of God, including their preparation. Encourage them to understand the importance of prayer in their ministry.

Being a children's pastor is a calling to lead children, parents, and volunteers. As you continually grow in learning how to do so, keep Galatians 6:9 before you: "Let us not become weary in doing good, for at the proper time we will reap a harvest if we do not give up" (NIV).

Michelle is a speaker and writer for children's ministry. She is the author and creator of Shapin' Up Fitness Camp, *a Bible-based health and nutrition program for children. As a former children's pastor and with over twenty years of experience in children's ministry, Michelle's passion is for kids to love God with all of their heart, mind, and body. Michelle has three children and lives in Lexington, Kentucky, with her husband, Denny.*

Being a children's pastor is a calling to lead children, parents, and volunteers. As you continually grow in learning how to do so, keep Galatians 6:9 before you: "Let us not become weary in doing good, for at the proper time we will reap a harvest if we do not give up" (NIV).

Home Run Derby

(Your Church Name)
Children's Ministry

(Your Date)

Teachers

Announcing the Children's Ministry Home Run Derby. This is your opportunity to hit a Grand Slam with your class, and we want to reward you.

What: A contest to score home runs by making classroom goals

When: Your Dates

How: Run the bases by scoring points

Bases: Accumulate points to advance bases. As you reach each base, you will be awarded a prize. When you make a home run, in addition to your prize, you will be entered into a drawing for a (name your incentive, e.g. $50 gift certificate to a restaurant). You may make as many home runs as possible in this 4 month period.

1 Base	100 Points
2 Base	200 Points
3 Base	300 Points
Home Run	400 Points

Points:

5	Attending
5	Wearing your name tag
10	Arriving 15 minutes before your class time
10	Reading your lesson on Monday
10	Answering weekly newsletter question
25	Contacting 5 students by phone or card
25	Per visitor in your class
50	Volunteering for a Children's Ministry event
50	Recruiting volunteers for Children's Ministry events
100	Recruiting teachers for Sunday School or VBS

Rules of the Game:

Each week, turn in your stats card to the dugout (e.g. Children's Welcome Center) that lists your stats for the week. The score keeper will tally the scores and move your name around the bases. You can check your standings on the Allstars Scoreboard (your location). As you move to each base, visit the dugout for your prize.

If you have any questions, contact your head coach, (Coach name) at (555-5555) or (email address). Play ball!!!

Permission granted to copy for local church use.

Home Run Derby

Stats Card

(Your Church Name) Children's Ministry
(Your Dates)

Please mark your points and turn card in to the Dugout (your location).

Stat	Points	Your Score
Attending	5	
Wearing Name Tag	5	
Arriving 15 min. before your class time	10	
Reading your lesson on Monday	10	
Answering weekly newsletter question	10	
Contacting 5 students by phone or card	25	
Per visitor in your class	25	_____ (Visitor name)
Volunteering for a Children's event	50	_____ (Event)
Recruiting volunteers for Children's events	50	_____ (Volunteer / Event)
Recruiting teachers for Sunday School or VBS	100	_____ (Volunteer / Area)

Name _____

Date _____

If You Build It...

by Deb Moncauskas

There is a lot of talk about building teams, working with teams, or team leadership. There are books, conferences, and seminars devoted to the subject. Just the other day, I went out to lunch with the pastoral team from my church; and my fortune cookie said, "You would do well to work as a team in the coming week." Yes, we hear "team" language everywhere.

I am certainly an advocate for team leadership and ministry teams. I teach it at Bethel Seminary, and I live and breath "team" in my ministry setting as a children and family pastor. Teams help us accomplish far greater things together than we could have ever accomplished alone. Ken Blanchard says it so clearly: "None of us is as smart as all of us."

Teams are about relationships and people. Successful teams meet the needs of its participants through encouragement, accountability, and affirmation. Teams have more fun. Our youth pastor often says, "It's better together." No matter what we are doing, where we are going, or what we need to accomplish, being together makes it good.

how do we build a successful team that will go the distance, meeting goals and realizing visions?

I have come to understand that team building begins long before you have people in place. Before the team leader asks that first person to join the team, a lot of prayer, self-assessment, thought, planning, and more prayer have taken place. If the team leader does put the work in on the front end, the chances of their team experience being satisfying, rewarding, and successful is greatly increased. I would like to walk through this process of team preparation with you, beginning with the preparation of the team leader and then moving to the groundwork that needs to be done before you call the first member of your team.

When I speak of the team leader, I am speaking of the person responsible for forming the team and the person who will most likely be accountable for the team's success, having responsibility to keep the team aligned with the vision and focused on the goal. I am also speaking specifically to Christian leaders, although most leadership principles are applicable outside the church.

Christ modeled for us servant leadership.

Successful teams bring people together with various gifts, talents, strengths, and abilities, to cooperate, collaborate, and contribute to a common goal or purpose. They bring a uniquely created individual into a unique situation or challenge, at a specific time and place, to work with others toward a compelling vision. There is a common understanding that everyone is unique and each adds value to the team. But

What are the attributes of an effective team leader? What does the leader have to know, do, or be if he or she is to be considered a strong team leader? The first attribute to consider is character and a heart after God. Give thought to your walk with God. Do you live a lifestyle that is consistent with Scripture? Do you spend time daily with God? Is He your source of strength, or do you rely on your own strength? Do you walk the walk and talk the talk? Are you a person of integrity? Can you be trusted? Peter Drucker speaks of "the mirror test." Is the person you see in the mirror each morning the kind of person you want to be, respect, and believe in? Is there an inconsistency between who you are in public and who you are in private? Inconsistency has led to the fall of Christian leaders. An intense self-assessment is vital and necessary before you ask others to join you on the journey.

"It is amazing what can be accomplished when nobody cares about who gets the credit," says football coach Tom Coughlin. A team leader must be willing to share power, credit, and control with others on his or her team. Power and control can be intoxicating, leading to sickness and dysfunction within a team environment. Are you willing to give up total control? Are you willing to recognize, affirm, and celebrate the gifts, strengths and abilities of those around you and allow each to lead from their strengths?

> The first step in team building is to have a God-inspired vision and the ability to articulate it in such a way that others want to join you in making it happen.

Effective teams consist of leaders heading in the same direction. Are you able to lead from your God-given strengths rather than simply your position? Are you able to allow others to do the same? Teamwork, simply stated, is less of me and more of we. "Only when we realize that God has called every single one of us with an equally divine imperative, can the church and its congregants begin to reach their fullest potential," says George Barna in *The Power of Team Leadership*[1] (page 58).

Christ modeled for us servant leadership. He said, "Do not be called leaders; for One is your Leader, that is Christ. But the greatest among you shall be your servant" (Matthew 23:10, NASB). A team leader must be willing to serve others. Servant leadership is at the heart of Christian leadership. How do we do so? We lead by encouraging the people we serve and enabling them to succeed. Whom are you serving? Are you willing to make a difference humbly, without regard for recognition, pride, ego, or self-preservation?

Once team leaders have taken a hard look at themselves and determined whether they are the right person to lead the team, then they need to give thought to some foundational issues and answer some important questions before placing warm bodies in positions. The first step to consider is vision.

Proverbs 29:18 says, "Where there is no vision, the people perish" (KJV). Vision paints a picture of what could be. Leadership is about gathering people and getting them to join you toward a shared vision. Without vision, there is no leadership. There is no reason to go forward. Before you gather a team together, you must have a clear and compelling reason to do so. What is God's vision for the ministry? Grasping, and then casting, God's vision is a central task for the team leader. In *The Power of Team Leadership*, George Barna states, "That if you cannot articulate a clear picture of what you are seeking to achieve, how can you lead people there?"[1] The first step in team building is having a God-inspired vision and the ability to articulate it in such a way that others want to join you in making it happen.

The next step involves mission or purpose. Who are we? What do we do? Why do we do it? How will we get there? Whom do we serve? Think about goals, outcomes and contributions. Why put this team together?

After vision and mission, consider what needs to be done and how you are going to go about doing it. Who is needed to accomplish the goals and realize vision? What are the gifts, strengths, and abilities needed for the tasks at hand? What strengths do you bring to the team, and what strengths do others need to bring? "You don't get harmony when everybody sings the same note," said Doug Floyd. Consider the diversity of gifts needed for the team. Matching the right person to the right task is a key to success.

How will your team work together? Be very clear about expectations you have for team members, should they decide to join. What does it mean to be part of this team? Think about the amount of time expected from each member on a weekly basis and what the long-term commitment might be. Will this team collaborate on tasks? Is risk-taking encouraged? Are questions encouraged? What happens when they fail? How will they know when they succeed? Anyone considering joining your team needs to be able to count the cost.

Consider job or role descriptions so that members will be clear about their specific tasks and can quickly see how their role compliments and supports the team effort. It is important that members understand the roles and responsibilities of the other members as well. How will they work together effectively within their specific roles? What does collaboration look like? Think through relationships between team positions.

Now that you've laid the foundation for the team, you will want to consider whom you might ask to be part of this team adventure. Ah, yes, the fun part! In thinking about individuals for the roles, consider these three things:

- **Competency** — Do they have the necessary competencies to meet the expectations of the role? Being your friend or simply a nice guy is not necessarily what you are looking for in this position. What gifts, talents, strengths, and skills will they bring with them? What do you need?

- **Calling** — Consider their calling. How has God prepared them, and do they have a sense that this area is the right place for them to serve? Would they join you out of obligation, friendship, a need for recognition, or because they are called to serve by God?

- **Character** — Do they live a life of integrity? Are they trustworthy? Will they bring harmony to the team, or divisiveness? Where do you see strength in their character? What are their weaknesses?

If you build your team with prayer, a God-given vision, and a strong foundation, then your team will be one that can go the distance and accomplish great things for the kingdom of God. The process takes time, but it is well worth it!

> None of us, including me, ever do great things. But we can all do small things, with great love, and together we can do something wonderful.
>
> —Mother Teresa

[1]*The Power of Team Leadership,* by George Barna (WaterBrook Press, 2001; ISBN 9781578564248).

Deb Moncauskas serves as the Children & Family Pastor at Faith Community Church in San Diego, California. She has a Masters Degree in Children & Family Ministry from Bethel Seminary and currently teaches in the program. She is working toward her Doctorate in Strengths-Based Congregational Leadership. Deb has been married to Rick for thirty-five years and has two sons, Matt and Jeremy.

> "None of us, including me, never do great things. But we can all do small things, with great love, and together we can do something wonderful."
> —Mother Teresa

Notes

IT WORKED FOR US